DICK KERESEY

BLUEJACKET BOOKS

Naval Institute Press
Annapolis, Maryland

Naval Institute Press
291 Wood Road
Annapolis, MD 21402

First Bluejacket Books printing, 2003
ISBN 1-55750-469-5

The Library of Congress has cataloged the hardcover edition as follows:
Keresey, Dick, 1916–
    PT 105 / Dick Keresey.
    p. cm.
    ISBN 1-55750-460-1
    1. Keresey, Dick, 1916– . 2. World War, 1939–1945—Naval opera-
        tions, American. 3. Torpedo-boats—United States. 4. World War,
        1939–1945—Campaigns—Pacific Area. 5. World War,
        1939–1945—Personal narratives, American. 6. Sailors—United
        States—Biography. 7. United States. Navy—Biography. I. Title.
    D770.K45 1996
    940.54'5973—dc20   96-13062

Printed in the United States of America on acid-free paper ∞
10 09 08 07 06 05 04 03   9 8 7 6 5 4 3 2 1

PT 105

CONTENTS

Contents

PREFACE

I was the captain of PT 105, the greatest wooden boat ever built.

Pound for pound, she and her sisters were the most heavily armed U.S. Navy vessels in World War II.

Ferocious fighters, they prowled at night and attacked anything that moved—mostly the enemy, but not always. They were nearsighted and when hunting in a pack of three if a fourth blob appeared, they opened fire.

Tough fighters, they had a cornered rat's ability to survive.

Versatile fighters, they did more damage as gunboats in close-in fire-fights than they did as torpedo boats.

Superb rescuers, they saved hundreds from death or capture: downed fliers, sunk sailors, trapped Marines, coastwatchers, stranded nuns, and Gen. Douglas MacArthur.

Long ago I stopped talking about her because, when I said that I'd been the captain of PT 105, people asked "Oh, is that so? Did you know Jack Kennedy?" Sure, I knew Jack Kennedy, a nice guy, but I never seemed to get the conversation beyond him. So I thought, why bother, leave her to the historians.

Now I've changed my mind.

I cherish the memory of PT 105. I took her newborn from the builder's yard. I lived aboard her for fifteen months. She slammed and bounced through choppy seas as if it were all a game of break-the-china, and she was racking up extra points for cracking my skull. Her engines ran three lifetimes; and when the need was there, when she ran for her life and mine, she attained speeds well beyond her rated forty-two knots. Her torpedoes ran true and her guns always fired. I hate to see her place in history, however small it was, demeaned by those who write only of John F. Kennedy's performance as skipper of her sister, PT 109.

Take this passage about U.S. Navy PT boats from *A Question of Character* by Thomas C. Reeves (Macmillan, 1991): ". . . militarily ineffective, made of plywood, they carried three thousand gallons of gasoline for their three engines; one well placed bullet could turn a vessel into a firebomb. Their engines often took on water and conked out." The practice of belittling the PT boat goes back a long way. James Michener described them in his early best seller, *Tales of the South Pacific* (1949). "They were rotten, tricky little craft for the immense job they were supposed to do. They were improvised, often unseaworthy, desperate little boats."

Balderdash! The total score of torpedo and gunboat attacks (carried out on an almost nightly basis) in the Solomon Islands, New Guinea, the Mediterranean, and the English Channel, was a good 250,000 tons of enemy shipping. Plywood? The PT hull consisted of two planks of mahogany on an internal framework of spruce and oak. I watched PT 105 take shape in the hands of master boatbuilders whose careful work would have pleased the eye of an eighteenth-century cabinet maker. Plywood was used only in the deckhouses where weight, not strength, was the deciding factor. Improvised? She was created through the combined efforts of the finest speedboat and marine-engine builders in England and the United States.

Probably the reason the Kennedy writers dishonor the boat is because they never saw one. The U.S. Navy PT boat was conceived and created for World War II, was born, lived, and died in little more than those years. They may have known the man but they did not know his boat. That being the case, I propose to tell the story of PT 105 who lived through much the same times as her sister PT 109. Maybe historians will then see JFK somewhat differently, and maybe they won't. I don't care: certainly they will get a better view of a great fighting craft.

ACKNOWL-
EDGMENTS

I got as much joy from the many who helped me as I did from writing *PT 105*. When I faltered, which was often, there was always someone to pick me up—for instance, Joe Medlicot and the students in his writing seminar at Dartmouth, who inspired me to start; Paul Wilderson, the Naval Institute's executive editor, whose rejection of my first submission was so cheerful that I tried again; John Lorelli, whose book *The Battle of the Komandorski Islands* and personal advice restarted me after I had gone back to the gin rummy table; my great-nephew, Mark Lange (I have an extended family with a bewildering assortment of talents), who massaged my ramblings into a semblance of coherence; Kasha Piotrzkowski, my copyeditor, who put some clarity into my murky prose; Barney Martin, a banker with a lifelong love of the Japanese language who translated letters from the Japanese sailors I helped rescue and who taught me enough Japanese to greet Takahashi San in his own language; Doc Phillips, who patiently and wisely advised me on the perils of publishing; Harland Wade, who took the picture on the

x   Acknowledgments

back of the jacket that makes me look like I wish I did; Alyce Mary Guthrie, who provided details of PT operations from the records of PT Boats Inc., our enthusiastic alumni association; and Lou Zotto, Sue Salmon, and Janet Fisher, who helped me stagger through the world of computers without serious injury.

In this love story about a PT boat and its captain there are traces of another love story. The captain almost causes a "disaster in the Titanic class" by racing the 105 down the Hudson River in order to keep a date with a girl in Montclair, New Jersey; and in the perils of the Solomons, her image appears when he hears that forgettable song "I Met a Peach in Orange, New Jersey, in Apple Blossom Time." She is in the next room even as I write. Maybe I should go into more detail— no, it's too late and too imprudent. Instead I dedicate *PT 105* to my wife, Barbara Lindsay Keresey.

PROLOGUE

My own PT experience? I once figured out I'd been shot at, shelled, or bombed on twenty-one different occasions—including once by U.S. Destroyer Division 23, and twice in land combat when I found myself temporarily attached to the 2nd Marine Parachute Battalion. (Jack Searles got shot at or bombed twenty-eight times.) My personal experience is therefore pretty good. I was recommended for a Legion of Merit and a Silver Star, which ended up as a Bronze Star because headquarters said that the first two were for actions that did not do "damage to the enemy." In *Lt. John F. Kennedy, Expendable* (Universal Publishing Co., 1962) Chandler Whipple curiously describes me as "a cool customer in combat."

Rather pompous? How do I deflate this? I was a good several rungs below PT men like Joe Burk, the greatest barge-buster of them all; John Bulkeley, savior of MacArthur and a model of PT aggressiveness; Les Gamble and Jack Searles, who fought through the grim early days of Guadalcanal; Murray Preston, who endured two and a half hours under enemy fire to rescue a downed pilot; Ed DuBose and Stanley

Author Dick Keresey (*left*) with Joe Roberts, PT 105's exec and author of the poem "Gunga Dick." (author's collection)

Barnes, who went up against the German F-lighters in the Mediterranean; and a score of others who were better at it than I was.

Kennedy was sometimes called "Shafty" because, when given some dreary job, he would observe to his friends, "shafted again." Likewise I was sometimes called "Gunga Dick." This distortion of Kipling came from Joe Roberts who served as my boat exec for longer than he thought necessary until he was finally promoted to a boat of his own. Picture the Marlboro man and you have Joe: rugged, handsome, with a big rust-colored mustache, Joe was usually taciturn to match his looks. One idle day near the close of our tour in the Solomons, he appropriated the base typewriter and pecked away at it into the evening. He produced an ode about me that entertained the base for days. Omitting the more scurrilous passages, it goes like this:

Now Gunga Dick—he was no beauty
But his legs would do their duty
Tho to look at them you'd always wonder why.
The uniform he wore
Was damn near always tore
And there most always were no buttons on his fly.

His hair was a tangled mess
That matched the way he'd dress
And his fingernails were gnawed clean to the bone.
All in all he looked like hell
But from long, tall tales he'd tell
You'd think in love and war he stood alone.

I hope to forget the date
Of that farce in Blackett Strait
When the Express was running into PT confusion.
The radio was a screaming fright
And the flares a fearful sight,
So Gunga fired twice to be amusin'.

When he hollers at his next flare
He will take off in the air
And Mephisto will claim his withered soul.
So I'll meet him when I kicks
As I cross the river Styx
Where it's always condition red with no foxholes.

He'll be sprawled in a shambles—
No one listens as he rambles—
And I'll hear a yarn in Hell from Gunga Dick.
But for all his sordid tales
On each venture he never fails—
What a man! What a man! Gunga Dick

So there you have me in the year 1943. If the tone of an old lawyer
occasionally leaks through here, it means that my two lives have
blurred—but only along the edges. For the most part you'll hear the
voice of a tall, skinny, fidgety PT captain with that thousand-yard stare
that comes to those who are close to the edge and the arrogance to hold
him on the near side for a while longer.

PT 105

HOW I GOT
THERE

One night in August 1943, PT 105 was stopped and drifting on station when it occurred to me that we were farther within Japanese-controlled waters than any other U.S. surface craft. I was alone in the dark, wondering what was out there, unsure of where I was, my feet and legs in pain from the hours and hours of standing on a hard, constantly moving, and sometimes bouncing, deck. I was dozing off on my feet when Zichella, the cook, nudged me with a cup of coffee. "How," I asked myself plaintively, "did I get here?" It took many twists and turns.

There have been few big decisions in my life that really mattered—it was the little ones that made the difference. Certainly turning down a career in the diplomatic service was a big decision, and one that did matter. I worried and wrestled with it until it began affecting my law studies. I had entered Columbia Law School as a stopgap while waiting for an appointment to the Foreign Service. A diplomatic career had been my goal in college, and I had spent a year at l'Ecole Libre des Sciences Politiques in Paris. However, it took me a year and a half to pass the foreign service examinations and by then I was doing surprisingly well in law school. I had made closer friends while at Columbia than at any other time in my life. I liked the study of law and beavered away until I made editor of the *Law Review.* The lure of the Foreign Service dimmed after I realized that most of the successful career men I'd met were either born wealthy in their own right or had married money. My father put me through an Ivy League college, a year of study in Paris and three years of law school, but I knew that from that point on I had to make my own living.

In January 1940, when the foreign service appointment came through, I worried and pondered until I knew I had to make a decision or risk flunking the midyear law exams. I put the problem to Professor Julius Goebel, one of the great scholars in the field of legal history. His advice went to the heart of the matter. "Keresey," he said, "Don't be a jackass. You don't want to go into the Foreign Service. If you do, I'll tell you where you'll be two years from now: in some tropical dump like Panama drinking yourself to death." This advice triggered my decision, and I declined the foreign service appointment. Two years later, I was sitting in a bar in Panama, wearing the sweat-stained khakis of a PT captain and working on my third martini. I wrote a postcard to old Julius Goebel.

Goebel could not have foreseen the gross change of circumstance that would occur shortly after our meeting, as the United States began to prepare for war. As a foreign service officer, I would have been exempt from the draft, but as a young lawyer, I was prime material. So when the draft was instituted and I got a low number, I knew that unless I took evasive measures, I was off to Camp Dix and "left foot, right foot." Mission: avoid the draft. One day, after learning that the FBI would have none of me, I stopped off at the naval recruiting office to inquire about the newly instituted midshipman program that produced officers in 120 days.

I struck up a conversation with a friendly recruiting officer, who informed me that I was not qualified because I had no college mathematics. He then suggested that I try the recruiting office in New Rochelle, which had just opened and had no business, because it did not occur to anyone that the Navy would have a recruiting office in such a nice suburb. He knew for a fact that the officer there was desperate to make his quota. I caught his drift, took the train to New Rochelle, and found the office, hidden away on a lovely suburban street.

It had a recruiting officer (who bore a startling resemblance to my advisor in New York and may well have been his brother), an examining physician, a pharmacist's mate, and a yeoman, all with no one to recruit but me. They were delighted. I passed the physical handily and then the recruiting officer examined my college transcript. An inner voice told me to volunteer nothing. "It says here you took a lot of sciences," he said, looking at me eagerly. He pointed to the page listing my courses at l'Ecole Libre des Sciences Politiques—which was entirely in French. The French tend to use the word *science* to describe courses on political history and economic geography. "There must have been a lot of math in them, eh?" he continued. "Yes sir," I lied—and was promptly sworn in.

I returned to school in the fall of 1940, legally an apprentice seaman in the U.S. Naval Reserve. I was to report for duty in September 1941 and thus was safe from the draft. September 1941 was a long way off. I did not think for a moment that the United States would go to war, and even less that I would go to war. I went about my third year in law school as if nothing would interfere with my career. During the summer of 1940 I had clerked for Cravath Swaine and Moore; after graduation and passing the bar exam in June 1941, I went to work for them on a permanent basis, my September date with the U.S. Navy notwithstanding. I still hoped the whole thing would go away, or they would find they already had enough midshipmen, or I would be deferred to a later time, if any.

Does that seem bizarre? Less than six months to Pearl Harbor, war was staring me in the face. How could this be? I, who had been appointed to the Foreign Service, awarded the Colby Prize in political science, *ancien élève* of l'Ecole Libre des Sciences Politiques? Incroyable? Not at all: during my year in Paris I had been taught that the French army was Europe's greatest; that most German tanks we saw parading in films were made of wood; and incredibly, that the Polish cavalry could crush a German attack to the east. By September 1941 all of these theories had been proved untrue, yet I still held to the premise that the war between the European countries was not our business. I was all for aid to embattled Britain, short of going myself.

As for the Japanese, from what I read, we had a weak supposal of their worth. However reprehensible our government found their conduct in China, we were not about to come to blows over it, and I read nothing suggesting that they would attack *us*. So when I reported for duty on the morning of 15 September 1941, my mind-set was that if I could survive midshipman school, the Navy would assign me to some desk job in naval intelligence for a year or so until the whole thing blew over and I could go back to being a lawyer.

I showed up at the downtown New York recruiting office along with a hundred others and was told to report back at 1700. I promptly took off on the subway to Times Square and wandered up and down Broadway. In those years Times Square was one of the most fascinating couple of acres in the world, with luxurious movie palaces, plays, musicals, burlesque shows, and the world's best vaudeville. I knew the area well but had never had the chance to spend a whole day there. I had a splendid time all by myself. I bought a small leather toilet kit just big enough for a toothbrush, razor, comb, toothpaste, and brushless shaving cream. It served me faithfully until I had to leave it behind in the jungles of Choiseul two years later. Unlike most people—including JFK, who brought home a great collection of scrimshaw—I have not one material souvenir from my days in the Pacific. When I left for home I did not need or want any reminders. If I had brought anything back, it would have been that little leather bag, a reminder of my last day as a civilian. I hope it has had another life, maybe as an amulet holder for a Solomons' native; perhaps it still lies among the roots of the banyan tree, awaiting my return.

Having satiated myself with looking, I went to Radio City Music Hall and saw *The Little Foxes* with Bette Davis. I sat through to the end, but this was heavy stuff and a bit too much on the gloom-and-doom side for someone about to become an apprentice seaman in the Navy. My new life started when I rejoined the group downtown. From their disconsolate looks, I deduced that most of them had spent the day there. We loaded aboard a bus, went to Pennsylvania Station and reloaded aboard a train for Chicago. I was pleasantly surprised to see that we had been assigned sleeping berths as well as meal tickets for the dining car. Meals in railroad dining cars were invariably good then; I have never understood why, in the march of progress, dining car fare has deteriorated.

Lying in my berth that night I took stock of my situation. After three years of hard study that saw me admitted to the Bar of the State of New York and employed by one of the most prestigious law firms in the country, I was now an apprentice seaman. I was not even a midshipman. That dubious distinction would take thirty days and might not come at all if I flunked the preliminaries: a distinct possibility, given my underachievement in mathematics. If I did flunk out, I'd become an enlisted man—I couldn't just go home and try some other program.

I awaited the onset of sadness but I was surprised. I was not sad. I did not fear for the future or regret the past. It came to me that for the first time in many years I had spent a day of aimless, contented wandering, without once thinking that I should be doing something useful. I promptly fell asleep and slept like the newborn I was.

Our train was not the Twentieth Century, which left New York at exactly six P.M. and arrived in Chicago at exactly eight A.M. the next morning. Trains did that then, you know. But not ours, which shuffled along all night and well into the afternoon of the next day, often standing abjectly aside for civilian trains. It didn't bother me. I wasn't going anywhere. Besides, opposite me in the Pullman seat was a fellow who looked like Hamlet with a bad hangover. His name was David Payne, and he did have a bad hangover. He was from Yale. This background had left a patina of refinement, reserve, and arrogance—shared only by those from Harvard.

I, on the other hand, was a product of parochial and public schools. The seven years of education at Dartmouth, l'Ecole Libre des Sciences Politiques, and Columbia Law School had produced only a thin veneer of refinement, no reserve to speak of, and had merely abetted an arrogance inherited from my Irish forebears off the Hoboken docks. Even my Hotchkiss- and Harvard-educated law school roommate and lifelong chum, John Bainbridge (class poet at Harvard and descendant of the great Commodore Bainbridge), occasionally lamented what he described as my "lack of couth." Therefore I had no suspicion that the long, lean shape in the rumpled tweed jacket and grey flannels, slouched across the opposite seat—who seemed to be viewing his surroundings, including me, with faint distaste—would become my closest friend in the war.

His hangover reduced Payne's resistance to such a point that the two of us began a conversation that lasted throughout the long and otherwise boring day. We eventually found that, beneath our different patinas, we had much in common.

We were both unashamed intellectuals who from the beginning sought to outdo each other in erudition: he would casually quote Shakespeare while I would expound on the Treaty of Vienna, the relevance of which I have forgotten. When this got out of hand, we would reduce the conversation to moronic gutturals. Dave had a small chess set, and each of us knew the moves but little else. We started playing on that train. Mostly by coincidence in the beginning, and later by mutual contrivance, we went together to torpedo school, torpedo boat school, and Squadron Five. Our boats, the 105 and the 106, moored together and we rode patrols together whenever we could arrange it. We played hundreds of chess games, which he, in the beginning, mostly won. I racked up a long winning streak on the tanker ride across the Pacific because in Panama I had secretly acquired a book called *Twenty Great Chess Moves*. He became incensed when he discovered the book, but regained his composure when I explained that he was so much smarter than I that I needed the book to make the game more interesting.

"We few, we happy few, we band of brothers, for he today that sheds his blood with me shall be my brother." That's Shakespeare's Henry V. Dave was the first of the "happy few." The friendship of those who fight side-by-side creates a bond so strong it transcends fear; a year and a half later, when Dave lay desperately wounded with his boat caught in murderous gunfire, it was the 105, running for its own life, that turned around, came back, and laid a sheltering smoke screen.

Our perceptions of what was to come were happily different as our train slow-poked its way to the midwest. We arrived in Chicago late in the afternoon and were hustled from Union Station to our new home as if the Navy was embarrassed by our unmilitary location. When the Navy opened its four-month-long reserve officers training program, it borrowed Northwestern University's Abbott Hall, a newly built law school fronting Lake Michigan downtown. Our living quarters were in an elderly apartment hotel called Tower Hall, at the intersection of Michigan Avenue and Chicago Avenue. On the back side of Tower Hall was Rush Street, the center of the nightclub district. Across Chicago Avenue in those days was Rickett's, a world-class bar that never closed. When we were in the chow line on the top deck at 0600 we could look down on customers going in and out of Rickett's.

How the Navy selected that site for a midshipman school was a mystery until I got to know Chicago—then the answer was obvious. If Chicago was to host such a wonderful collection of young men preparing to fight for the United States, then let them have some fun! My fellow midshipmen in Tower Hall will agree to a man with my site-selection theory. Chicago was like a big, bosomy woman who showered us with kisses and kindness.

Of course, the night of our arrival we were not aware of all these wonderful things; instead we were herded into a large, high-ceilinged room in Tower Hall that might once have been a dining room or nightclub. Whatever it had been, it was now dark and dreary. We sat on the floor, or, I should say, deck. Everything in this building, which was as unnautical in design as possible, was given its naval term. This seemed ludicrous at first, but turned out to make sense: in the Navy, few gaffes were more humiliating than asking questions like, "Where's the toilet?"

The introduction to our new life was delivered by a stout lieutenant commander wearing a curiously wrinkled and shabby uniform. I do not recall seeing any other officer at the school who matched him in untidiness. He vanished after that first night and I concluded that the commandant had fired him. I think the welcoming speaker modeled his address after those given by marine drill sergeants at Parris Island. He dotted his remarks with a number of "Bring you up sharp!" threats.

None of his cautions and remonstrances took hold; witness when, at the end, he barked, "Any questions?" A hand shot up in the front row. "Is there a store?" Now the fellow asking the question may have thought this important (maybe he had forgotten his toothbrush), but all it elicited from the lieutenant commander was a few seconds of an eye-bulging glare, followed by "No! Where do you think you are? The Waldorf?" Another undaunted hand shot up. "When is liberty?" Good question, I thought, but bad timing. "The way you people are starting out—never! Dismissed!" All in all, a bad start for what turned out to be a most happy experience.

We did get liberty, from 1200 Saturday until 1700 Sunday. What could a young midshipman do in Chicago on a Saturday night? Whatever suited his fancy, and if he had no initiative he could choose from a list of local invitations read off by the company commissioned officer at Thursday night muster. There was one accepted invitation which illustrates how I felt about Chicago.

A midshipman whose name escapes me—we called him Stumpy— had alleged that all he had to do was circle Tower Hall and he had a date. He called this "trawling," and I had considerable doubts about it because I tried it once without getting a bite, and I was more handsome than Stumpy, who was short and squat. At a Thursday night muster about three weeks into the term, Stumpy surprised us all by volunteering for a weekend invitation in Evanston. I don't know what he expected, but what he got were two elderly maiden sisters who wanted to do their bit for the war effort. Stumpy was a natural comic and his account of balancing his big butt on a spindly antique chair while having tea with his hostesses provided the chuckles that Sunday night. I privately wondered who was more surprised when the door opened and the two sides saw what they each had to deal with for the weekend.

Two weeks later, one of his roommates reported that Stumpy had again gone to Evanston and his visits to the sisters became regular, including a stay through Christmas and the New Year—when most of us went home. We surmised that there had to be a young chick—a niece, maybe—somewhere in the picture. The answer to the puzzle of Stumpy and his weekend trips to Evanston came after our graduation ceremony.

We all stood around in the hall saying our good-byes before packing and heading home. I saw Stumpy standing with his two elderly ladies. They were chattering away to him and he was smiling back, but he seemed just a bit forlorn. One of the ladies reached out, touched his forearm, and looked away. Then it all made sense. I knew him well enough to know that he had no family that cared enough to write. Mismatch that it had seemed, he had found his family. That was the Chicago I knew and loved.

"Where is Pearl Harbor?" Art Van Kirk had just yelled from downstairs that the Japanese had attacked Pearl Harbor. Everyone in my generation knows exactly where they were when they first heard the news—but very few knew where Pearl Harbor was. I had spent the weekend with Art, a fraternity brother, at his family's home. At that moment, I was enjoying a luxury, getting up late and taking a leisurely bath. I got out of the tub, took a few swipes with a towel, pulled on pants and a shirt and ran downstairs, where Art and his parents were listening to the radio. The announcer had little information about the attack itself, but said that the Japanese had suffered heavy casualties after inflicting some damage on our ships and shore defenses. The skimpy and wildly optimistic broadcast told me that this was no longer a year or two hiatus, but that my life had been changed. I knew then, standing in the living room with Art and his parents—no one sat that morning—that this was going to be a long war. I took the first train back to Chicago.

When I boarded the train the conductor saluted me. Train conductors were all dignified men, proud of their positions, with a tendency to be grumpy with young midshipmen. The day before his salute might have been intended as some kind of joke. Not on this day, to which nothing else in my life compares. I saluted back, trying to look as military as I could, but feeling that saluting me was a joke. Underneath this military getup there was only a lawyer who would end up behind a desk, doing his bit by handling paperwork.

I spent the next weekend in a Chicago suburb and was touched by one of the thousands of personal tragedies wreaked on American families by the disaster at Pearl Harbor. Neighbors down the block had lost their son on the battleship *Arizona*. He had received his ensign's commission four months before from Tower Hall and had happily departed for a choice assignment. He was now entombed somewhere in the sunken hull of the *Arizona*. I think this was especially tragic because it was so unexpected; his mother and father had not made any inner preparation. One moment their son was alive and smiling in their consciousness, and then there was the officer standing in the doorway.

A few days after Pearl Harbor, I got a brief letter from my mother. She told me that I should not worry about her and that she knew I would do my duty. The letter startled me at first with its assumption that I would fight in the war but then I realized that she was preparing herself. Years later, Mother told me that, after hearing the news, she had a premonition that I would be in "terrible battles." We had always been extremely close and she knew that concern for her would make things more difficult for me. She spent that Sunday alone, thinking about what to say, and that evening she wrote those few lines. They seemed naive when I first read them, but later, when I was indeed confronting all she had foreseen, they were of great comfort.

Curiously, midshipman school programs were not changed after Pearl Harbor. A routine had been established and was followed—as if the greatest event in our lives had not occurred. I expected some sort of lecture on Pearl Harbor, but I learned all I knew about the attack from weekend newsreels and the newspapers. We were given campaign ribbons to wear on our jackets, commemorating what we immediately dubbed "Asleep at the Switch."

Other than learning that Chicago was a great place to fight for; that you should never whistle because it might be confused with a bosun's pipe; that you could only smoke when the smoking lamp was lit (whatever and wherever that was); and that anything hanging over the side when it shouldn't be was called an "Irish pennant," I can't recall learn-

ing much that ultimately proved useful. We had excellent officer instructors who did a good job of teaching us the Navy as they knew it,
which was the peacetime Navy. I applied myself diligently to the task
of learning flag signals, buoys, running lights, and the like. How was I,
or my instructors, to know that almost all the early naval battles in the
Pacific were to be fought at night? There were no buoys and there sure
as hell weren't any ships showing running lights.

When the course in navigation began I feared that I would be un-
masked, since it was assumed that I was on a first-name basis with sines,
cosines, and tangents. But luck intervened. I had five roommates, all of
whom had majored in mathematics, and two had even taught it. After
a few nights of frustrating attempts to teach me theory, they regrouped;
each night, one or two would predict the next day's quiz and help me
learn the answers by rote. This worked remarkably well. Once, when
they missed, the teacher stared at me and said, "This answer is inexplicable." But he went on to something else and my average answers
proved close enough.

Graduation day was 15 January 1942, and was marked by a speech
from the commodore, wherein he revealed the secret of a good naval
officer. "Young gentlemen, I will tell you the secret," he said. I sat forward in my chair, eager to learn the secret. "Posture!" he roared and
threw back his shoulders, stuck out his pot belly, and did a turn on the
stage, gazing at us triumphantly. I had expected something else, something with more of a ring to it, but when I thought more about it, "Posture!" wasn't all bad. There was no way the Navy could turn us into
good officers in four months—so the commodore was telling us to fake
it until time did the job.

About a week before graduation, we had each filled out a long, detailed questionnaire about our educational background, complete with
boxes to check indicating which branch of the Navy we preferred. I of
course marked the several categories for which I was eminently suited,
all of which had to do with naval intelligence. The girl I was pursuing
at the time still alleges, after fifty years of marriage, that I told her I was
going to volunteer for bomb disposal. I may have done so to create the
appropriate atmosphere, but never would I have stepped forward for
anything of the sort.

Assignments in naval intelligence meant postings in Washington,
London, or perhaps a major foreign capital in the free world. I understood my duties would include attending functions such as embassy

cocktail parties. To get off the mark in good order, I went out and bought four white uniforms, a sword, and calling cards. Calling cards were essential to the formal paying of calls. When I opened my orders on graduation day, I stared, astonished, at the words, "report to Torpedo School, Newport, Rhode Island."

Torpedo school? Perhaps these orders were for someone else. My name stared back at me. I thought, this must be a mistake. I went back to my room, where my five roommates were busy packing, and held out my orders for them to see. "Do you think they could have made a mistake?" I asked. Each looked at my orders and each shook his head. "Maybe I should go to the commandant's office and just check," I ventured. They shook their heads again. One of them said, "You go near that office and you could get armed guard on the Murmansk run." Pointing to his orders, another said, "How about a minesweeper?" A third, Chuck White, grinned at me. "I got torpedo school, too. That's a good assignment." If that's a good assignment, I'd better not say anything, I thought. There were moments in the next several months when I regretted not taking a chance and checking with the commandant's office.

PT BOAT
CAPTAIN

After ten days' leave I reported to the torpedo school in Newport, Rhode Island. The summer home of the very wealthy, Newport in January was as dreary a place as I'd ever seen. When it wasn't cold and raining it was cold and threatening to rain. The mansions on the harbor and seaside were empty, and had an air about them that suggested they would always be empty. Newport had not yet recovered from the Depression so a number of these big places were, in fact, uninhabited year round. I lived with five other ensigns in one that had been bought at a sheriff's sale by a local contractor; he rented it to us for a few dollars a week. It looked like a scene from *Wuthering Heights*.

I was truly bumping along the bottom in my naval career. The torpedo school, and I say this with complete assurance, was the worst school in the history of naval education. About sixty of us were led into a room and seated around tables. At the head of each table was a chief torpedoman who had served his time and was waiting it out until his retirement. Each day our instructor would explain, in unintelligible navalese, some part of the torpedo. A torpedo had an astounding number of parts; all of which had to pull together or the torpedo would run amok, sometimes even turning around and blowing up its mother ship. The chief at my table put a permanent lock on my comprehension. I never did understand torpedoes.

After five weeks of torpedo school, I was on my way to an unsatisfactory fitness report when a miracle occurred. In the middle of a dull morning—as if there were any other kind—a Navy lieutenant walked in and stood at the end of the room. "A new school has opened at Melville," a town five miles to the west of Newport, "that needs officer students. It's the torpedo boat training center and we're looking for volunteers for the first class." There was a moment's silence, and then two-thirds of the room jumped to their feet. I jumped the highest. He could have said it was a school for bomb disposal and I would have clamored for the opportunity. I was not alone in my attitude, of course.

If this officer thought he was getting eager recruits, he was deluded. Most of those jumping up were escaping, not volunteering. Let me not, however, disabuse you of the widespread belief that all PT officers were volunteers selected for their physical ruggedness and aggressive spirit. We came in before John Bulkeley returned in glory from the Philippines and took charge of PT recruitment. He was the one who insisted that PT duty required athletes and especially football players. Nevertheless, the group of officers who did attend the first session at Melville tended toward the better all-round performers because the Newport Torpedo School had been allotted a healthy share of the best-performing midshipmen. Even at its most hurried and distracted, as the Navy was in January 1942, the excellent selection process continued to function.

I had already come to terms with the fact that my future in the Navy was sea duty. The four white uniforms, the sword, and the calling cards had already been stashed away. The prospect of a career in torpedo boats was simply better than the thought of slogging it out at torpedo school and the distinct possibility that my natural ineptness would lead not to destroyers, but to something like first officer on a net tender. So when I arrived at Melville, my attitude was that this was better than the alternative.

They took us down to the dock and showed us a seventy-seven foot Elco torpedo boat. She was all menace and power. Slight wave action from the wakes of ships passing in the harbor made the boat pull against the mooring lines as if she were telling us that she wanted to go out and do some damage. When her three 1,250-horsepower engines started up with a whine, a cough, and a low rumble—a sound so unique that I still hear it in memory's ear—I knew I had found my trade.

Since we were the first class I expected that there would be the usual start-up confusion. Fortunately Lieutenant Commander Specht, who ran the school, was a first-rate administrator and the boat captains who taught us knew their trade. They believed that PT officers should be able to perform the work of every rating on the boat. We trained to repair, take apart, and put together everything—except the torpedoes. Our instructors assumed we knew all about torpedoes.

Only once during the war did the lawyer in me surface, and then it was only briefly. In the summer of 1944 I was back in Melville, teaching gunboat and torpedo tactics. One of my former law professors had become head of a Navy law function and had orders cut calling for my transfer to Washington. Commander Walsh, the PT base commander, called me to his office where he confronted the officer who had come up from Washington with the orders. "What's wrong with those IBM machines down there?" he yelled at the startled, confused, and intimidated officer in his blue uniform with two shiny brass stripes. "They've got the wrong man! This here officer," pointing at me, "has been in PT boats for three years. That's all he knows! This is the most dumbass thing!" He looked at me. "You don't know anything about contracts, do you?" The Washington officer and I exchanged looks. He was telling me by his look that it was my call. There had been moments in the Solomons when I had prayed for orders like these and there might be more of those moments ahead. "No, Commander, I don't know anything about contracts," I said. From that first day on the dock in Melville I was hooked.

In June 1942, I was assigned to the newly organized Squadron Five. This squadron was the first to get the eighty-foot Elco and I had the honor of being the boat captain who took the first of this class from the Elco Boat Works in Bayonne, New Jersey. Such an honor you can spare me. I had handled a torpedo boat maybe four or five times for four or five minutes before being shunted aside so some other student could have his turn at the wheel. My experience in docking and undocking consisted of one attempt at each. PT boat designers had clearly thought a lot about the problems involved in moving at high speed but apparently they had not considered the boat's performance at slow speed; the tiny rudders were adequate for high speed turns but had little effect at slow speed.

To maneuver at under ten knots was done mostly by the wing engines with rudders playing a secondary role; for example, starboard engine ahead with port engine astern and rudders hard over to port caused the boat to go to port. It sounds easy but unless you timed it right it could be an awful bollocks. To bring a PT boat into or away from a dock was an acquired art. The man at the wheel developed a sense of timing with the engineer who was shifting the engines into forward or reverse, following the signals on his panel. And the eighty-foot hull of a PT boat was mostly above water, so that in addition to the tidal currents that are the nemesis of any vessel trying to dock or undock at slow speed, the man at the wheel of a PT boat had to contend with the wind, which can propel the hull as if it were a sail.

I got to Bayonne for the Navy acceptance ceremony by subway and bus, an easy trip since I had been there nearly every day, watching the boats being built. When I arrived, I sensed trouble. I had been told that once I got to the boatyard, someone would take me aboard the new boat and teach me how to run her, or at the very least, how to get her out of the little boatyard cove and into the open waters of Newark Bay, where I could maybe run her up and down and practice docking before I brought her to the Brooklyn Navy Yard. The red, white, and blue bunting decorating the yard signaled to me that this was doubtful.

There was a grandstand facing the dock where the PT 103 lay glistening in the sunlight, motionless but ready to go, and dock workers were already standing at the lines ready to cast off. In the grandstand were many important looking civilians and naval officers, including an admiral. I didn't see anyone who looked ready to give me a lesson on how to get that thing away from the dock. Someone told me to stand on the dock, but not to step aboard the boat until she had been officially turned over to the Navy. There were speeches, none of which I listened to, because I was mentally practicing: port ahead a touch to get the stern out, then starboard astern, followed by port astern to move away from the pier; rudders hard over to starboard for a moment to cause the boat to crab sideways; then wind her around to head away from the dock by port astern and starboard ahead—but not too much or the stern will bang into the dock. Suddenly someone tapped me on the shoulder, said something, and led me to the pier and onto the boat. I did note some familiar enlisted men's faces on board and saw one man go down the hatch into the engine room.

The admiral made some final remarks, concluding by trumpeting, "Take her away, Navy!" That meant me. I put what I remembered as the port throttle in the ahead position, but it turned out to be the starboard throttle. (Throttles had been moved from left hand on the training boats to right hand on this new boat.) The stern of the boat promptly nuzzled into the dock and as we moved ahead, I could hear, feel, and see wood splinters peeling off both the boat and the dock. Realizing my mistake, I put the starboard throttle astern and splinters sailed off the bow of the boat, which was now grinding her way backwards down the dock. Deciding to collect my thoughts, I put both engines in neutral. I noted dimly that the band was playing a rousing "Anchors Aweigh" while the admiral was mouthing to a flustered aide, "Get that man's name!" While I was collecting my thoughts, a civilian pilot quickly jumped aboard, shoved me aside, and, with a few deft throttle moves, had the boat heading toward open water. Then he ran back and leaped gracefully onto the dock, the son-of-a-bitch.

Once outside the boatyard, I took the 103 down Newark Bay to the entrance of New York Harbor, stopped, and went into the charthouse to look at the chart. There was no chart. I remembered seeing a list of items to be supplied, including local charts, a handheld pelorus for taking bearings, parallel rulers, dividers, and such. The charthouse was bare. I also remembered that I had hastily signed an inventory paper of some sort while the band played "Anchors Aweigh." I wondered whether the anchor was still aboard. It was thus brought home to me that nautical people tend to be light fingered and like to take home souvenirs. Well, I sure wasn't going back to where that admiral was. For the first of many times to come, my quartermaster Tommy Mechin, who later followed me to the 105, cheered me up: "We pick up the 104 tomorrow, skipper,"—the first time I was called that—"we'll lift an extra set of those things and a few more."

That was my introduction to the art of pilfering, for which PT boat sailors became famous. Lacking the clout to obtain adequate supplies or spare parts, PT sailors would liberate items from warehouses and other ships with awesome dexterity. Once while we were in Norfolk, Miles, my chief engineer, discovered that the auxiliary generator supplied to the 105 was a lemon beyond salvage. He and his two firemen pulled it out and marched down the dock carrying it. Two hours later they marched back carrying another such generator. The defunct piece had taken its place on some unlucky ship where the watch had been cozened into believing that Miles and his helpers were base force mechanics replacing their generator with a better one. Such pilfering was raised to a fine art.

We had a chaplain in the Solomons, a very holy man who had the incongruous nickname of Petit Larceny bestowed upon him after he accompanied our supply chief (naturally called Grand Larceny) to a large warehouse full of badly needed spare parts. Petit Larceny went to the front entrance and introduced himself to the resident chief with the suggestion that the warehouse crew might appreciate a little talk and benediction. The warehouse chief agreed and ordered all his men outside to hear the chaplain, whereupon Grand Larceny and his helpers entered by the back door and carried off the necessaries.

Back in the harbor, I still faced the immediate task of locating the East River, and from there, the Brooklyn Navy Yard. I was thereupon introduced to tugboat captains, the guardian angels of PT boats in New York Harbor. They loved PT boats and the one who stopped a few yards from me was no exception. "How ya doin'?" he hollered down from his pilothouse. "Okay," I hollered back, "But can you give me a course to the East River?" Seeing his puzzled look, I added, "I have no chart of the harbor." I had no charts at all but I kept this to myself. He ducked inside and after a few seconds leaned out, shouting the course and distance to the entrance. With lots of waving we parted company and I came upon the East River just where he said it would be. However, my piloting problems were far from over.

On its eastern bank, the East River was a clutter of piers, cranes, masts, warehouses, docked ships, and other objects—none of which displayed any signs for the Brooklyn Navy Yard. It was now close to 1700 hours. I could wander up and down until dark looking for the right slip. Just then another tugboat came by close aboard, its captain looking down with a big grin. I waved for him to stop, which he did. "Where is the Navy yard, Captain?" He took this in, thought for a moment, and then called down, "Folley me!" So I got astern and folleyed him. A scant quarter mile up he came out of the pilot house and wigwagged to starboard. Sure enough. I remembered that in the slip opposite our supply barge was the light cruiser *Marblehead*, in for repairs after suffering a mauling in the early battles near Java. And there she was, with hundreds of men working away as they did day and night. Finally we've made it, I thought. Not so. I had another lesson to learn. As the 103 nosed into the slip, I had her going ahead at barely three or four knots, which seemed the prudent thing to do considering that my docking skills were on a par with my undocking. When the bow entered the quiet water of the slip, the stern suddenly swiveled to port and the incoming tidal current swung me against the pilings on the port side. The boat stuck there as if glued, occasionally emitting wood shavings as I went forward and then reverse with different wing-engine combinations. For a while it looked like we would spend the war there, but finally one of my combinations worked and the entire boat scraped her way into the quiet water of the slip. It still wasn't over.

The squadron commander had issued instructions that all boats tie up with bows facing out—I guess so we could make a quick getaway if the Brooklyn Navy Yard was attacked. This meant that I had to turn the boat around 180 degrees. There came a time when I could turn the 105, or "wind it" (as in winding a clock), in little more than its own length by using the wing engines, but that day had not yet come. I went forward and astern and forward and astern. Three young crewmen scurried back and forth like base runners caught in a triple run down, trying to place fenders between the stern and the side of the *Marblehead* or between the bow and the barge. Finally the boat came around enough so that the crew managed to toss lines to the barge, and the 103 was hauled in. I signaled the engine room to stop engines and for an instant there was no sound. Then came thunderous cheers from the thousand—or so it seemed—workmen on the superstructure of the *Marblehead*, who had been watching my spectacular entry. They were cheering me as if I'd hit a winning homer in Ebbets Field. I turned toward them, lifted my cap, and bowed. They loved it and cheered louder. All in all, it had been a learning experience.

I read one book on John F. Kennedy where the author notes that Kennedy was dubbed "Crash" after running his boat into a dock, implying that he was a poor boat handler. I was also named "Crash" for a while. Almost all boat captains were called "Crash" at one time or another. In the early days while learning how to operate PT boats, we were like novice wranglers trying to tame wild horses—we all got thrown a couple of times.

During our stay in the Brooklyn Navy Yard, the 105 came perilously close to ending its short life on the slimy bottom of Newtown Creek, which emptied into the East River after winding through the industrial part of Queens. For a mile or two of its length, the river was navigable for tugs and barges. About a mile from its entrance was a fuel depot; shortly after picking up the 105, I got orders to go up there and fill her tanks. As I started up the creek I realized that it was very narrow, and was made even more so by the wide barges docked on either side. If we met a tug towing barges downstream, what would I do? As I thought this over, I noticed a gap between barges docked on my starboard side at a pier that was long enough for a PT boat. Just as I passed this spot, a tug with barges astern came around the bend two hundred yards ahead.

"Aha," I said, "I shall now back down and, with a couple of well-timed aheads and asterns, slide the 105 into that space." I turned to look astern and there was a tug just fifty yards behind me. Now, the rules of the road that I learned in midshipman school stated that a vessel proceeding astern shall give three toots on its horn. I gave three toots on what I thought was the horn button, but was actually the engine room horn button, and three toots on that meant "Stop Engines." There was a sudden silence.

Miles, my new chief engineer, was sitting on deck enjoying the scenery. He didn't ask whether it was my intention to lie in the middle of Newtown Creek and be crushed by the oncoming tug, which, you appreciate, could not have stopped with its stern tow of three huge barges. He leaped to his feet, raced to the stern and dropped down the engine room hatch. I heard the first engine whine, start up, and go astern, followed by the sounds of the second and third. I had agonizing moments with nothing to do so I looked behind at the tug coming upstream. We were now so close that the tug captain could read my thoughts; he leaned out of his pilot house and yelled, "Don't worry about me sonny, worry about that guy ahead." I was doing just that.

The tug was looming over my bow and less than ten feet away when my sternway caught up to his forward way. We were so close that my three young crewmen scampered again to the bow with their fenders, as they had when I made my first docking. Of course, fenders would not have helped. Even if the tug avoided me the barges wouldn't have. The square bow of the barge immediately astern of the tug already loomed over the 105 and would have remorselessly ridden over our bow and down we'd have gone to the bottom of Newtown Creek. Through some trick of the light I didn't see anyone in the tug's pilothouse and

PT 105 at cruising speed. (James C. Fahey Collection, U.S. Naval Institute)

no one was on deck. I thought someone should have come out on deck and at least frantically waved for me to get the hell out of the way. But the tug seemed empty, as if this was merely a bad dream.

With all three engines pulling astern, I backed down to where my stern was abeam the upstream gap between the docked barges on my right. I then put the center engine in neutral, my starboard engine ahead, and left the port engine backing. I should say that I signaled that to Miles, but he was already so attuned to my thinking that it seemed as if I was actually shifting gears myself. The stern of the 105 swung into the gap; I threw the wing engines into neutral and let the boat coast backwards into the gap as the downstream tug moved into the space occupied by the 105 only seconds before. The three fender handlers raced down the side toward the stern in case I hit the dock or a barge. A touch ahead on the port engine and the 105 was sitting in a parking space like a New York taxi waiting for a fare.

Somehow the tug going upstream managed to get by the downstream tow. As I stood in the cockpit letting my nerves settle down, the captain leaned out of his pilot house, waved, and hollered, "Nice going, buddy!" I tried to grin nonchalantly but it felt a bit lopsided. Then it occurred to me that the 105 and I had just completed the course in advanced PT boat handling. From then on we docked and undocked with grace—in fast currents, high winds and alongside ships in rough seas. Once we even nudged carefully against the conning tower of a submarine to effect a transfer and the 105 never so much as bumped. The three young sailors continued running back and forth with their fenders, just in case.

Having successfully passed advanced boat handling in Newtown Creek, I began unconsciously acquiring an arrogant bravado. It was the same kind of mind-set that causes newly graduated fighter pilots to fly under bridges. Close to the end of our stay in Brooklyn I nearly became the perpetrator of a naval disaster of the *Titanic* class. One July morning in 1942 I was dispatched to a munitions plant up the Hudson to pick up some depth charges. It took most of the day to reach the depot and load up, and by the time I got back to the George Washington Bridge it was close to 1700. A PT boat threw a tremendous wake at cruising speed which could easily break tow lines between tugs and barges, so we were under strict instructions to run at idling speed when tugs were in the area. The river all the way down to the Battery was full of them. This presented a serious problem.

I had a date with a luscious girl in Montclair, New Jersey that night and if I traveled at idling speed, I would miss the train out of Hoboken and she might despair and go out with one of the little twerps who hung around her all the time. As the 105 passed slowly under the bridge, the solution came to me. The gravamen of the prohibition against running at cruising speed was the wake. But I knew there were two speeds where there was no wake: idling and full speed. At her forty-two knot full speed, the PT boat skimmed across the top of the water and threw no more wake than at idling speed, something to do with the hull pushing the water that caused big waves. At any rate it was a fact. At forty-two knots, catching the train out of Hoboken was a sure thing. So up went the throttles and PT 105 roared down the Hudson, the crew on deck waving at passing ships, tugs, barges, and—here's the hitch—ferryboats.

It was the evening rush hour. All the big commuter ferries were waddling back and forth across the Hudson, jammed on the westbound leg with commuters heading for the trains in Hoboken. A PT boat racing all-out was a splendid sight so all the commuters naturally rushed to the viewing side of the ferries, which then careened to one side. As we roared past it occurred to me that one of them might, just might, go belly up. But it was too late: at forty-two knots you are gone. As I rounded the Battery I looked back and sighed with relief when I saw that there were no floating bottoms. Since there were no ferries on the East River I maintained full speed until the entrance to the slip at the yard. I then pulled back the throttles, went full astern, made a sliding 180-degree turn into the dock, doffed my cap to the cheering workers on the *Marblehead*, and caught the 6:00 P.M. to Montclair.

On the following Monday, we left for Norfolk to board a tanker bound for Panama. Once we got there, I heard that the New York port captain was looking for me. But we left Norfolk before he found me. When I was in Panama a following squadron officer told me that the port captain was looking for me in Norfolk. That was the last I heard. The thought no doubt occurs to you that anyone who had been admitted to the Bar of the State of New York should have displayed more common sense. By nature I was indeed one who considered future consequences more than most, but the eighty-foot Elco PT boat changed all that. Her drag racing power, brutish indifference to slams and bangs, and just her macho look changed men's personalities. I was the norm among PT captains. For one reason or another, cautious PT boat people faded away.

Squadron Five, the first of the eighty-foot-boat squadrons, had ten months together before entering combat. We assembled at the Brooklyn Navy Yard, shipped on tankers to Panama, and spent seven months there and in the Galapagos Islands. We then spent another two months aboard tankers and in Noumea, New Caledonia, before at last proceeding on our own to Guadalcanal. We had far more time than most other squadrons to become combat ready. Unfortunately, there was a peacetime mentality that cautioned, "whatever you do, don't make a mistake," and it pervaded our training.

We had plenty of time to operate under simulated combat conditions. For starters, this meant operating at night. Our squadron commander attempted only one nighttime maneuver; we all got lost. I got the most lost. I ran so far down the coast of Panama by myself that I ran right off the chart. The CO then decided that these maneuvers were unsafe. He was right but these same conditions (getting lost and losing visual contact with the other boats in your division at night) were even more unsafe in combat. You became a blob to be fired upon by both the Japanese and American navies, particularly the erstwhile members of your own division. Listen to this: "Whoever is circling me, identify now, or I open fire!" Answered by, "Don't shoot! Don't shoot!

23   PT Boat Captain

It's me!" I overheard this panicky exchange between two PT boats in another division, as I was leading my division to its station. I looked around at my three trailing boats and chuckled as each of them closed the interval, snuggling up close to Gunga. They had heard the same transmission and were not about to get lost.

We fired torpedoes in training only once because this required installing training heads that were supposed to bring the torpedo to the surface after its run. They were uncertain devices that sometimes failed. And finding a spent torpedo at the end of its run was chancy. A lost torpedo meant reams of paperwork in which lurked the possibility that the record of the officer in charge would be blemished. Our torpedoes were of World War I vintage. They ran at twenty-seven knots and so were not much of a threat to Japanese destroyers and cruisers, which could tool along at speeds in excess of thirty knots.

We believed that if these torpedoes hit anything, they would explode. We assumed this because early in 1942, a PT boat captain in Newport accidentally leaned on a firing button and launched a torpedo down the harbor. The poor fellow went up to top speed and passed the torpedo, hollering "Fore!" over his radio, to no avail: the torpedo hit a moored freighter and sank it. Later studies showed that over half of these torpedoes were duds.

We had reason to be suspicious of torpedoes. One day we were shown the new, secret, magnetic exploder, which was supposed to detonate when it passed under the hull of a ship. If a torpedo exploded under the hull, the total force would be directed up through the bottom. This was far more damaging than the usual force of a torpedo hitting the side of a hull, most of which dissipated into the air alongside the ship. I watched in naive awe as the demonstrator slid the prototype under a piece of metal and it clicked. This meant, he said, that if there had been a charge in it, the warhead would have exploded. Through scuttlebutt, we later learned that our early sub commanders had watched in frustration and rage as their fancy torpedoes had slithered under targets and out the other side without detonating.

In early 1942 fifty-caliber and twenty-millimeter ammo was in short supply, so we seldom fired our guns and then only in short, aimless bursts. On the way over to the Solomons, aboard an Esso tanker, the commander decided we would have real target practice against two-foot balloons. Balloons were launched from the bow and when they had risen about two hundred feet, each boat in turn would open fire. Nothing happened. A half-dozen balloons floated off into the sky without a blemish. The merchant seamen on the tanker found this very amusing. I, for one, was appalled, less by the fact that we didn't hit the balloon (we weren't going to fire at balloons) than that our fifty-caliber guns had jammed after very short bursts. The gunner cleared the jam in a few seconds but that would be too long when a plane was coming in on us.

I took Gunner's Mate Brown aside and told him that he and I were going to spend the rest of our days aboard the tanker figuring out what caused the guns to jam, and that was all we were going to do. Thereafter and for many days I watched Brown taking the guns apart and putting them back together. Right then, Brown hated me. I hung over him for long days, breathing down his neck. He finally found the problem: the oil being used in the firing mechanism was too gummy and some of the tolerances were too tight. Brown added some thinner to the oil and loosened the sliding parts a bit. With permission from the squadron CO, we proceeded to fire the guns into the air in a continuous burst that ran through five hundred rounds. We only stopped when the CO ran up, screaming at us to cease this senseless waste of ammunition. Thereafter in combat we rarely had a gun jam. Come to think about it, one night the ammo belts caught fire, probably from the solvent mixed in with the lubricating oil. Some gunner's mates from other boats came aboard the 105 and asked me, not Gunner Brown, how I got the guns to fire like that. I referred them to Brown but didn't exactly reveal *who* had solved the problem.

I also made myself a pain in the ass with Miles, my chief engineer. I made twice-weekly inspections of his engine room wherein I inevitably found a grimy spot and said, "Miles, clean engines run, grimy ones don't." I could hear his molars grind. From the start Miles was clearly a dedicated engineer, obvious by the fact that the engines ran flawlessly. I soon stopped snooping around Miles's engine room.

PT 105 never had a disciplinary problem and there were none of consequence in all of the squadron, except once. A chief came aboard the tanker drunk on the night before we shoved off for the Solomons. What mattered was not that he had a load on, but that he made the error of taking a swing at Charlie Bernier, exec on the 107, who was checking people off at the gangplank. The chief missed Charlie, which was lucky for the chief because Charlie might have reflexively swung

back, and Charlie was not one to mess around with. Assaulting on officer is a court-martial offense, but in this case all it provoked was hilar-
ity. We never even had a captain's mast, the disciplinary procedure for
minor infractions that could occur weekly on ships with a complement
equal to a PT squadron. This may have been due to the fact that over
half of us lived together on the boats in units of a dozen, so each boat
became a family. I also think PT enlisted men, being volunteers, were
a good cut above average. Finally, the boat captains, either on their own
or following the example of our regular Navy CO, maintained a mar-
ginal aloofness that was essential to discipline. One boat captain was an
exception to this. He espoused democracy. The crew called him by his
first name and, for a while there, I envied him. But when his boat got
into the stresses of combat, she had more breakdowns than any other,
and an unhappy crew. The 105 avoided mooring alongside her because
she had bad luck.

However, on the tanker ride from Norfolk to Panama, I did have a
disciplinary problem that I did not know how to handle. Since the boats
were on the tanker it was easier for outsiders to come aboard to shoot
the breeze with crew members. One enlisted man from off the boat had
been a fleet welterweight boxer of some renown; aside from this ac-
complishment, he was a bully and a pain in the ass. The crew, out of his
hearing, dubbed him the Weasel. I was at the point of telling him to
stay off the boat (which could have been resented, as an intrusion into
the personal lives of the crew, even by those who disliked him) when
my first boat executive officer, Junior Duckworth (John C. Duckworth), solved the problem for me.

I was blessed to have Junior along during the first few months of life
aboard the 105. He was classically handsome, of slight build, with the
manners of a young man from one of New Orleans's best families,
which is what he was. Junior came aboard on a hot June day when the
105 was tied up at the Brooklyn Navy Yard. I was doing my snooping
in the engine room and had dressed for the occasion in denim cutoffs
and sneakers. Someone called down the hatch that I had a visitor so I
climbed out, straightened up, and there was Junior. He was dressed in
immaculate khakis, complete with cap and a two-blocked tie. He
snapped to attention. This was the first time I had ever seen anyone on
the 105 snap to attention. Junior then saluted me: "Ensign Duckworth
reporting aboard for duty, sir." I had been taught never to salute without a hat on. With most of my crew and the crew of the boat moored
alongside watching—Junior was a vision rarely seen in this part of the

navy yard—I decided against just pulling my forelock, straightened to my full six-foot-three, and saluted him back.

I was not at all sure about Junior and was so nervous myself about handling the boat that for the first few weeks the poor fellow stood around watching. By the time we shipped aboard the tanker with the 105 for the first leg of our journey to the Pacific, from Norfolk to Panama, I had gained some confidence in him. He solved my problem with the Weasel while we were on the tanker. I only saw the end of the problem solving. I was returning from my afternoon chess game with Dave Payne in the tanker's wardroom. I looked down at the bow of the 105 and there was the fleet welterweight, flat on his back, staring sightlessly up at the sky. I thought for a moment that he was dead, but then he rolled over and slowly got up. He was wearing boxing gloves. A silent group clustered by the charthouse, gazing in wonder at the Weasel and then at Junior Duckworth, who was in the process of removing a pair of boxing gloves. Meanwhile he was talking in soothing, almost apologetic tones to the still glassy-eyed Weasel. Junior then turned to the watching audience and said, "I don't think boxing is a good way to spend our time, fellows, somebody might get hurt. Ever play charades?"

While Junior attempted to explain charades to the still bemused crew, Mechin pulled me aside and gleefully filled me in. The Weasel had found the gloves on the ship and had come back to the 105 to have some fun, which consisted of tying the gloves on with each of the young seamen and giving them a walloping. He then challenged the rest of the boat's crew, including big Torpedo Brown, to make a try at him. Boxing is an art and a semi-pro like the Weasel could probably have beaten even Brown unless the bigger man connected right at the beginning. Brown was too embarrassed to ignore the challenge and was about to put on the gloves when Junior casually walked on deck and said, "Boxing? That looks like fun. Can I try?" He took the gloves from Brown and put them on without removing his shirt or even rolling up his sleeves. The Weasel was not so sure about fighting an officer but settled down when Junior, smiling, circled around and said, "Come on." The Weasel threw a left, Junior slipped it and caught him flush on the chin with a right hand, sending him down and out. Among his other carefully hidden accomplishments, Junior had been an intercollegiate middleweight champion. Junior left us two months later to join Squadron Two. He was killed in action at Guadalcanal.

SIDETRACKED
IN PANAMA

We were offloaded in Panama in August 1942 and joined Squadron Two with fourteen boats that had been there for some months as part of the canal defense force. When we heard about the Guadalcanal landing I assumed that our group, Squadron Five, would keep right on going, but that was not to be. The Navy command decided that we weren't experienced enough. For some reason that escaped us, instead of sending Squadron Two they ordered the creation of a new Squadron Three, made up of eight boats from Squadron Two, which then got six boats from Squadron Five, leaving us with six boats.

The jockeying among squadron commanders for officers, crews, and equipment elevated the art of pilfering to a new height. When forming Squadron Three, the creators in Washington forgot to inform the supply people. There was already a Squadron Three on the books, Bulkeley's famous unit that had been expended in the Philippines. So when the new Squadron Three routinely applied for base force material they were turned down because the books showed that "Squadron Three" had already been issued this equipment. The new Squadron Three supply officer was thereupon put to the test, and I was witness to his greatest achievement.

The first four boats of Squadron Three were loaded aboard a tanker at Balboa. I was loafing on the dock, listening to the commanders of Squadrons Two and Three in earnest and loud conversation, the frightened supply officer of departing Squadron Three standing beside them. The gist of the argument was that the base radio of Squadron Two had disappeared during the night and was now, the indignant Squadron Two commander alleged, secreted in the hold of the tanker. I expected the Squadron Three Commander to deny said allegation, but, on the contrary, he admitted that the unlawful taking had indeed occurred, without his knowledge or consent. He said that his people had gone too far and, glaring at his supply officer, assured his brother commander that, as soon as they departed, stern measures would be taken against the miscreants. As we all watched, the ship's crane swung a large crate, labeled Base Radio, over the side and deposited it on the dock. The tanker then departed. I pitied the luckless supply officer but felt that he indeed had gone too far. I was wrong. Two days later the supply chief of Two grew suspicious over the odd location of some of the nails in the base radio crate and he had it opened. It contained an assortment of junk. The base radio was now two days' sail out of Panama on its way to Guadalcanal.

During the remainder of the month we stood around and watched the rest of Squadron Three, and then Two, depart for battle. We were reduced to six boats with the ignominious assignment of guarding the Panama Canal. In October 1942, we were ordered to the Galapagos Islands as pickets against attack on the canal.

The voyage to the Galapagos proved beyond a doubt the seaworthiness of PT boats. We were underway for fifty-four hours through seas that were, for the first day and night, gigantic. The intervals between wave crests were a hundred feet or more, not because of a storm—the weather was clear and balmy—but because the waves in that area were formed from storms thousands of miles away, and as they traveled over the world's largest expanse of ocean they merged with one another to form huge swells. We proceeded at twenty knots, matching the speed of the seaplane tender assigned to us as the refueling vessel. The 105 rode as though on an endless rollercoaster, riding up one side of a wave and pausing at the top with her bow out of water, then sliding down the other side to nuzzle her bow into the next wave, only to begin the climb again. In the trough of the wave, we disappeared from sight so those on the tender could seldom count all six of our boats at once and had to be reassured by our base force aboard the tender that there were indeed six boats out there.

We stood two-hour watches. At the end of the second watch I headed below for a nap. Mechin, who always stood my watch, lay down on a pallet that he had stretched across the ammunition canisters stowed outside my cabin. Through my open door I saw him lying on his back, sound asleep only a minute after hitting the sack. I saw a phenomenon never seen other than in a magic act. As the 105 rose to the top of a wave, Mechin was suspended in air for an instant, with space visible between his body and his pallet. Then he would settle back down. He slept on, snoring comfortably.

Before we'd left Panama, I had spent many hours practicing celestial navigation. The more I had practiced, the more frustrated I had become. The closest I ever came to my location in Panama Bay was some place in Costa Rica. I assumed that the seaplane tender escort would undoubtedly have a competent navigator, but what if I lost the escort during the night? When we met the heavy seas, the possibility of getting lost became even more substantial. I comforted myself with the belief that my exec would prove to be a good navigator. He had been a math teacher before the war, was on friendly terms with trigonometry, and had practiced alongside me—with far better results than I produced. I therefore gave him the twilight watch.

When I came topside at 2000 to relieve him, I asked confidently, "Where are we?" "I don't know." I looked at him in surprise. He was staring glumly ahead. I noticed that his mustache drooped at the corners. "Did you get a fix?" I asked. "Yep. Got a fix. Then threw up all over the chart." Our ups and downs had gotten to him. I could go into the charthouse and wipe off the chart but I decided this would not be prudent, so I sent a young seaman down to clean up and the poor kid merely added to the mess. So, with only the foggiest idea of where we were, I snuggled up close to the lead boat, so close that the CO blinkered to me, "Increase distance." When we were in the Galapagos he took me to task for staying so close with an admonition not to repeat it on the way back.

I resumed practicing star sights and suddenly one day it came to me that my problem was not trigonometry, but misidentifying at least one of the three stars. From that point on I became a good navigator and, running among the Galapagos Islands, an expert pilot. I became so confident of my ability that later I ran aground on the only marked reef in the Solomon Islands.

WE FINALLY
ARRIVE IN
THE COMBAT
ZONE

In early March 1943, the Navy decided that Squadron Five need no longer guard the Panama Canal. We were loaded aboard a tanker for the long voyage to Noumea, New Caledonia. I knew that many wonderful things were in store but there was one detail that puzzled me; how were they going to get us off the tanker? When we were in Norfolk and Panama the eighty-foot, fifty-ton boats had been placed on cradles and unloaded by two of the largest cranes in the world. Those who performed the operation assured me that there were no cranes as big as these anywhere else. While I had some doubt about this claim, it did make me wonder how we would manage in a primitive port like Noumea. In my musings on this problem, I saw us coming all the way back to Panama, still on the tanker.

We reached Noumea at night. Near sunrise I was awakened by volleys of shouts and curses coming from overhead and alongside the ship. I went up on deck and peered around. Above my head was a man attaching some lines to a boom that looked like a misplaced telephone pole. This boom canted down to a large platform with a little house at one end. A Seabee was leaning out of the little house shouting profanities at the Seabee above my head who replied in kind while two others stood idly by. I was so impressed with the vituperation I hardly noticed when the 105 began moving off its cradle, slithered between the tanker's masts and stays, hung suspended in perilous balance, and then descended gently until it floated on the sea. At no time during this epic performance did I hear anything sounding like a direction pass between the two performers, who continued hurling insults at each other.

After several weeks of final outfitting in Noumea, we left for Guadalcanal and the war in the Solomon Islands. We came into the PT base at Tulagi after dark and stood off the harbor entrance until a PT officer came out to pilot us in. I had been operating PTs for almost a year but I had never experienced such darkness. From our place in the six-boat column, all I could see was the wake of the boat ahead and the outline of the twenty-mm gun mounted on its stern, which I used as my distance gauge: if all I could see was the wake, I was too far away; if I could see the gunner, I was too close. The darkness was so complete that I saw nothing else, even when we stopped and I heard voices coming from what I figured was a dock. The voices told us to tie up there for the night and I very slowly slid the 105 next to the boat ahead of her and secured.

An officer on the dock, boarded the boat next to me, and the PT boat captains grouped around him. Without preamble he told us that the base was under almost nightly bombing. "When the condition red siren sounds," he said, "get your boats away from the dock, get as close to shore as possible. Run aground if you have to." I thought this a bit extreme. Here we were after over nine months' training, ready to engage the enemy, and we end up purposely running aground? I silently decided to stay put. We did, and nothing happened that night or for the rest of our stay at Tulagi—except for stray bombs and several daylight air attacks directed at targets bigger than PT boats. I never saw that officer again and assumed that he had been shipped out as a mental case. We never heard any advice from seasoned veterans, although we did get lots of advice from people who looked like seasoned veterans. We eventually found out that almost all of those who'd fought at Guadalcanal had shipped home, and we were listening to replacements.

33   We Finally Arrive in the Combat Zone

It was while in Tulagi, just before the start of the New Georgia campaign, that I ran aground on the only marked reef in the Solomon Islands. I was leading another boat on a routine night patrol when I made
the inexplicable blunder. The reef had two range markers on it and I
simply cut too close. The result was that the 105 had to be hauled off
by a large ramp lighter, which mangled all her screws and shafts. She
was towed into drydock by Jack Kennedy. I remember two things about
my first meeting with JFK: With his 109 he towed the helpless 105 into
a floating drydock with such skill that I mistook him for an old hand;
he was also the only boat captain at Tulagi who did not make a funny
remark about my running aground. Nothing about it was funny to me.

A court of inquiry was convened, an ominous portent. I could see
myself removed as captain and reassigned to some job like laundry
officer. That particular spot was already filled by a former boat captain
who had run into a large buoy in broad daylight. I happily remained
captain of my beloved 105 for two reasons. First, my squadron CO supported me, bless him forever. Second, I was a graduate of Columbia
Law School, and I was directed to write a complete report of the
grounding for the court. My report ran five and a half pages. The first
brief paragraph stated that I took full responsibility; of course I did,
since I alone ran the boat onto the reef. George Cookman, my squadron
exec and a close friend, had hoped to blame it on one of two replacement boat execs who'd been assigned to me for training.

These officers had come out as replacements. They were unusually
incompetent, partly because their training had been in the winter
months at Newport when it was difficult to get in practice at sea. The
squadron CO thought that assigning them to me for training was a
compliment—I didn't. I missed Joe Roberts, who had been promoted
to boat captain. I had my hands full trying to get the boat ready for combat without him and, after a few days of trying to bring the two replacements up to speed, I gave up and did little but snarl at them.

As the 105 left the harbor at dusk on that fatal night, I was at the
wheel, holding to a course I estimated would take me out of the harbor. There was still some light, so I could make out the range markers—well enough, I thought, so I could do this without carefully plotting the course on the chart. This was a mistake I never made again, no
matter how clear the visibility. Just before we ran onto the reef holding
the markers, I turned to one of the replacements—who was staring vacantly into space—and asked abruptly, "Do you know what I'm trying

to do?" He came out of his reverie. "Yes," he replied, "you are trying to get on the range." Thereupon, we did get on the range—and also on the reef that the markers sat on. Mechin told me later that while we were all trying desperately to get off the reef, the two replacements had done nothing but hug each other in glee, like two small children getting an unexpected gift.

My report described five methods used to get off a reef. It did not say that I thought of the dereefing methods, or that I actually tried all of them. I did come up with one, Gunner Brown thought of two, a boatswain riding as a passenger invented the fourth and I read about the fifth the next morning in *Knight's Seamanship* and put it in to round out the exposition. My report did not say that any of these had worked. As I have said, the 105 was wrenched off backwards by a ramp lighter. The court of inquiry was composed entirely of the senior staff officers, and I assumed that they knew about the ramp lighter—since every boat captain in Tulagi knew it and laughed heartily about it. On the other hand, senior staff officers did not pal around with boat captains so this detail may have escaped them.

The officers on the court spent long hours discussing the relative merits of my five methods of dereefing while I stood anxiously outside the courtroom. When my squadron commander came out, he told me that while the court thought my running aground was bad, I had shown great ingenuity in freeing the boat. That was the end of it, except for the effect the blunder had on my style of command.

Three months later, I was acting squadron exec when John Iles, the new captain of the 105, woke me one morning. "Gunga," he said anxiously, "I scraped the reef coming in. Got over it but I bent a prop, maybe two." His eyes rolled as he moaned, "Dammit! It was just stupid!" I answered sleepily, "You hit a sunken log, John." His reply was quick: "No, no, you don't understand. I hit a reef, that damned reef at the entrance." I raised my head. "Iles," I glared at him, "You hit a sunken log." He looked at me and comprehension flooded his face. "Yeah? Right. Sunken log. Big bugger. Yessir!" And that was the end of that.

At the start of the New Georgia campaign in June 1943, the 105 went up to New Georgia alone. We stopped for two nights in the Russell Islands, halfway between Guadalcanal and New Georgia. The Russells had a squadron of PTs under the command of Jack Searles, one of the

heroes of Guadalcanal. The boat captains all lived in a former plantation owner's house, sleeping on netted cots on the broad porch. Located on a hill two or three hundred feet above the shoreline, the house
had a gorgeous view down Starlight Channel, which separated the two
Russell Islands. It was the one and only truly beautiful place I saw in
my year of travel though the Solomons. We who were there believed it
must have been the spot that inspired Michener's *Tales of the South Pacific.* When I saw the movie it certainly reminded me of the PT base in
the Russells.

Expecting combat, the PT squadron had arrived in the Russells
about two weeks earlier, but the Japanese had abandoned both islands
to retreat to New Georgia, so the boat captains had adapted promptly
to peace and tranquility. I am sure that sometimes they visited their
boats tied up under palm trees by the shore, but the main afternoon activity seemed to be volleyball on the lawn. Each afternoon the base doctor filled a water cooler on the porch with alky screamers, a mixture of
medical alcohol and grapefruit juice, and the party was on.

When I checked in with the duty officer on that first afternoon, I decided that I should try to stay ashore with these people whom I assumed were all veterans of Guadalcanal. They certainly looked like veterans, with their grommetless caps and khakis that were the pale color
that comes from washing in saltwater. I told my boat exec and Morgan
Brown, my senior crewman, that I could learn a lot from these men and
"take good care of the 105" while I was up at the planter's house. I asked
the duty officer if I could be assigned a cot for the night. He replied
pleasantly, "Sure, take any cot you want."

That first evening all I learned was that they played poker for big
stakes but that no one had any money, and I finally withdrew. Looking
around the porch I counted the number of officers and the number of
cots; there was one cot fewer than there were men. I picked the one far-
thest from the poker game and turned in.

When I awoke the next morning, I looked at the cot next to me. Underneath it was Abraham Lincoln, lying in his casket. I knew it could
not be and that I had drunk a lot of alky screamers, but he sure looked
like Lincoln. After a few moments of staring at the body, I put two and
two together, so to speak. Since there had been one cot less, the last one
to turn in had stretched himself out on his back underneath the cot
next to mine, carefully tucking the mosquito netting down around him.
He was Lemuel Skidmore, who bore a striking resemblance to Lincoln,

Al Webb and Lennie Thom, members of the "happy few." Thom was PT 109's exec, and both men were close friends of JFK and the author. Note the thick jungle background, typical of PT bases. (Al Webb)

particularly when asleep, stretched out like that, with the cot looking like a coffin through the mosquito netting. Lemuel gave me a real start.

The Russell Islands base was the closest thing to R and R that I ever had. It was where I wanted to spend a couple of days and nights if I had a choice, even though Tulagi offered movies and an officers club. The Russells, in the first days of the New Georgia campaign, also offered a collection of highly entertaining PT officers: people like Al Webb, Lenny Thom, Lem Skidmore, Barney Ross, Al Cluster, and Jack Kennedy. The latter was an active member of the group. He was amiable, always the first to laugh at someone else's joke, and a pleasure to be around.

On my second afternoon, I thought I was going to have my first experience with night combat. The word went out for all boat captains to assemble with Jack Searles. He had been ordered to take all boats out to engage a flock of barges that had been spotted heading for the Russells. This seemed like a splendid opportunity to learn from these seasoned veterans. After being assigned to one of the divisions, I ran down to the 105 and enthusiastically told the crew about our mission. Morgan Brown cooled me down when he said, "Skipper, I been talking to guys stationed here. These are all replacements." "You mean the officers too?" I asked. "Yessir, they arrived about a month ago."

So when we went out, I knew what to expect. Everybody got lost. Within a half-hour, the radio waves were jammed by boats trying to find each other, and this went on for the balance of the night. No one found any Japanese barges because there weren't any. A coast watcher had mistaken one of our own supply groups for the Japanese. I left the next morning for the front lines.

WHERE WE
WERE

The Solomon Islands were far from anywhere: three thousand miles south of Japan and six thousand miles southwest of the United States. Before World War II, the American and Japanese navies had played hundreds of war games, each with the other as the enemy, but I'll bet there wasn't even one scenario staged in the remote Solomons.

For a place that no one (except faithful readers of the *National Geographic*) had ever heard of, the Solomons covered a big area: a dozen large, mountainous islands, hundreds of coral islands, and thousands of reefs running over 550 miles on a southeast-to-northwest line, six hundred miles northeast of Australia. They were sparsely inhabited by Melanesians who'd been joined by a small number of missionaries, coconut plantation managers, traders, prospectors, and storekeepers, mainly Australian and British citizens, who shared government of the islands.

Barely south of the equator, the islands were hot and humid all year round. The coastal areas, where the airfields and naval bases were lo-

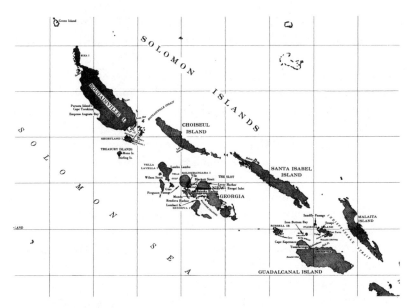

The Solomon Islands, from Guadalcanal to Bougainville. (from Robert J. Bulkley, Jr., *At Close Quarters*)

cated and where most of the land fighting took place, were rich breeding grounds for malaria, dengue, and dysentery, along with fungi that caused severe trench foot, skin rashes, and excruciating earaches. A Marine friend of mine caught elephantiasis on Bougainville.

The Japanese prized the Solomons for their location. Planes flying from the southeastern island of Guadalcanal would threaten the sea lanes to Australia. In February 1942 the Japanese established a big naval and air base at Rabaul on New Britain, just to the northwest of the Solomons. Then they moved down the island chain, planting air bases on Buca Island and another at the southeastern tip of Bougainville. In May 1942 they set up a seaplane base at Tulagi on Florida Island twenty miles to the west of Guadalcanal and began construction of a major air base on the northwest coast of Guadalcanal. You'd think that they would have put their base on the southeastern tip, nearer to Australia, but the topography dictated otherwise. The big islands were the peaks of a sunken volcanic ridge which rose right up out of the sea and, in most places, kept climbing. The area the Japanese chose for their base was the only large flat area on the islands, a huge coconut plantation.

We saw the Japanese activity at Guadalcanal as both the threat the Japanese intended it to be and as an opportunity to counterattack where the Japanese might not expect it and which could not easily be defended. We had already established bases at Noumea in New Caledonia and Efate in the New Hebrides, good jumping off places for an attack and the starting point of the leapfrogging offensive that brought the war to Japan.

In August 1942 our Marines landed at Guadalcanal, and from there a land, sea, and air battle began that lasted more than fourteen months. The Marines and Army successively assaulted Guadalcanal, New Georgia, and Bougainville. Success in the island land fighting was dependent upon control of the seas. There were a half-dozen major sea battles in which the combined tonnage sunk exceeded the total for all naval battles in recorded history. So many warships were sunk off Guadalcanal that the waters there became known as Iron Bottom Sound. Between the big battles, sea fighting continued on a smaller but no less intense scale. Sometimes U.S. and Japanese destroyers fought it out, but more often we used PT boats. In the early stages we attacked enemy warships and transports, and in the later stages we attacked the seagoing amphibious craft that the Japanese used in great numbers to reinforce and supply their troops.

Squadron Three reached the Solomons first, arriving at Tulagi in October 1942. Squadron Two joined them in November. Ownership of the base radio that Squadron Three had liberated in Panama became a moot point as the two squadrons entered the toughest fighting ever experienced by PT boats. For over four months, from the middle of that October through February 1943, they sneaked out at night into the waters off Guadalcanal to attack enemy convoys intent on landing troops and supplies or on shelling Henderson Field, the airfield vital to our air support of the ground action. During much of this period the boats of Squadrons Two and Three were all there was of the U.S. Navy involved in the battle.

It was disheartening for the PT people. Most of their targets spotted them when they crept in to attack and they often were forced to fire their torpedoes under the glare of searchlights and exploding shells. They scored some hits, although fewer than they thought, and then they spent the rest of their nights being chased, shelled, and bombed, laying smoke in puffs to fool their pursuers, trying to shoot out the relentless searchlights, or hiding against the shore where they were dead meat if they were spotted. Although they did not score often, as a result of firing slow torpedoes at fast-moving ships, they accomplished their mission better than they thought.

Look at it from the enemy's perspective. Their ships had a task to perform which, by its nature, required that they stop to unload men or provisions, or slow down to maintain a steady fire platform in order to shell Henderson field. They could do neither knowing that somewhere out in the darkness American PT boats were prowling around, waiting for them to make good, slow targets. That threat often disrupted Japanese plans and was the great achievement of the PT boats at Guadalcanal.

In late February 1943 when Squadron Five loaded aboard the Esso *Lackawanna* for Noumea, New Caledonia, I knew nothing of this larger picture. Our lack of knowledge was incredible: we had no information on the Solomons; on our Toboga Island base in the Bay of Panama we didn't have any charts of the South Pacific, or even a Rand McNally map of the world. There had been fighting since the previous August but no one had thought to send us any intelligence reports. I suggested to our CO that he dub me "intelligence officer," which he did, and with that title I went to Navy headquarters in Panama to obtain the charts and reports on the Solomons which I was sure were there. But I returned with only a small pamphlet by a Marine sergeant that described how to fight the Japanese in the Guadalcanal jungle. I was not encouraged. I didn't even know that all PT boat operations were at night. We still ran around Panama Bay in daylight, to the tune of flag signals hoisted on the lead boat.

For censorship reasons, personal letters from our friends in the squadrons out there hadn't contained any operating information. But they did name some chilling losses: John Chester and my wonderful first boat exec, Junior Duckworth, two of the officers transferred from our squadron, had been killed, as well as J. J. Kelly, one of my Newport roommates, a cheery Irishman with such a zest for life that I could not think of him as gone. We learned from the careful letters only that these men had been killed in action, not how or why. The only information of substance that got through the censor was an account of shark attacks on men in the water that I could have done without.

By the time we finally arrived at Tulagi in April 1943, the American forces had already driven the Japanese from Guadalcanal. Nevertheless, I saw years of fighting ahead and the prospect of ever going home seemed so far in the future that I put it out of my mind. My attitude about war had been formed during World War I, when contending forces had fought endlessly over the same piece of ground and I think my view was shared by most of my peers. We still felt the effects of the misinformation ladled out to us, first about Pearl Harbor and then about the Philippines. I had believed the "Praise the Lord, and pass the ammunition" hogwash that reporters wrote when there was no good news. As the truth slowly leaked out, and in my disgust at being taken in, I went to the other extreme: I didn't believe reports of American

The crew of PT 105. *Left to right, standing:* Attilio Zichella, cook; Enoch Emory, engineer; Thomas Mechin, quartermaster; Charles Brown, torpedoman; Morgan Brown, chief gunner; M. W. Ellis, radioman; and Martin G. Rabel, engineer. *Kneeling:* George Miles, chief engineer; the author; and Warren Harmon, gunner. Not shown are those who joined the crew later, including James Essex, steward's mate; William Monk, torpedoman; and Paul Winters, gunner. Also not shown are the 105's executive officers: John Duckworth, killed in action; Joe Roberts; Phil Hornbrook, killed in action; and John Iles, who succeeded the author as captain. (author's collection)

victories, not even the accounts of our decisive win at Midway; I considered the Japanese navy equal to our own and better than ours in night combat; I thought, if our radar was such hot stuff, how had the Japanese scored the first hits at Savo? I was wrong of course but, as Hamlet stated it precisely, "There is nothing either good or bad but thinking makes it so." I had my own reality. I never dreamed that I would be going home in little more than nine months. As late as November 1943, when Bougainville seemed to be drawing to a close, I asked Westholm, the PT flotilla chief of staff, how much longer he thought we (meaning I) would be out there. Without hesitation, he said "At least another eighteen months."

So as I describe our daily life in the Solomons, keep in mind that we expected to live this way for years to come, moving from island to island, not always in forward gear, but sometimes in reverse.

THE BOAT

She was eighty feet long with a twenty-foot beam just forward of the cockpit that tapered down to fourteen feet at the stern. She weighed fifty tons. From a distance, she looked smaller than she was because her lines were those of a racing boat. She was as big as a luxury yacht but that was where the resemblance ended, because engines and gas tanks took up nearly half of her belowdecks. Those engines were so critical to her existence that I find it easier to describe her insides by starting at the stern.

The aftermost compartment or lazarette (so named because that is Italian for storage compartment) housed engine parts and a worktable for the engineers to use for repairs, but no one ever worked there. It had less than six feet of headroom and was almost always very hot because the exhaust stacks passed through on their way out of the stern.

Forward of the lazarette was the engine room where the three 1,250 horsepower engines resided, along with the heat exchangers (which cooled the engine water by running it through small pipes immersed in constantly changing sea water), a two-cylinder engine generator (the power for the lights, stove, and refrigerator), and two vee drives that took the drive shafts of the wing engines—which faced forward in order to fit in the boat—and reversed the shafts so they exited to the stern. The center engine was the only one with its drive shaft facing sternward. The result of this space-saving arrangement was that the center propeller was about five inches lower in the water than the wing propellers, and this created an unforeseen phenomenon: the center propeller created noticeably less wake than the wing propellers. Since roaming enemy bombers were attracted by our highly fluorescent wake at night, when we were just creeping along, I liked to run only on the center engine while keeping the wing engines in neutral. Jack Kennedy also liked to idle along in that manner, and some critics claim that's why he couldn't evade the enemy destroyer that ran him down. Nonsense! That destroyer would have hit him even if he'd had all three engines engaged.

Those engines were the product of two decades of development by the Packard Motor Car Company. It started with World War I's famous Liberty aircraft engine, which Packard engineers and Gar Wood, America's ace speedboat racer, converted to a marine engine for high-speed racing boats. This engine generated enough power to propel an eighty-foot, fifty-ton boat across the water at over forty knots. This then created a need for overspeed cutouts, so that if a boat flew out of the water and its propellers came clear, the engines would stop before they burned up. All ships have overspeed cutouts, since propellers can come out of the water when a ship is pitching in high seas, but a PT boat could come completely out of the water! I am not putting you on. I know of one case where a PT boat crossed the wake of a battleship and sailed out of the water, landing with such force that half the crew was stunned. The boat was fine, but a dazed engineer had to restart the engines. On the 105, Miles taped down the overspeed cutouts, which were set to trip at 3,000 rpms, because he suspected that his engines could turn up much more than their rated max of 2,400 rpms—and it's a good thing he did. Once when we were running for the nearest exit, I saw the needles flickering at 2,900 rpms!

PT boat engines had unforgettable voices, ranging from a low, bubbling rumble at idling speed (mufflers on the exhaust came out underwater, hence the bubbling) to a pitch and volume at full throttle that sounded like giant, howling tomcats. In the engine room their sound

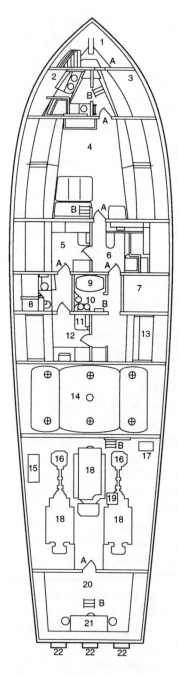

A.	WATERTIGHT DOORS
B.	LADDERS TO BELOW DECK
1.	FOREPEAK, ROPE LOCKER, ANCHOR
2.	CREW'S HEAD
3.	STORAGE
4.	CREW'S QUARTERS
5.	EXEC OFFICER
6.	GALLEY
7.	WARD ROOM
8.	OFFICERS' HEAD
9.	FRESH WATER TANK (200 GALS)
10.	RADIO/RADAR EQUIPMENT
11.	DESK
12.	CAPTAIN
13.	AMMO LOCKER
14.	FUEL TANKS (3000 GALS)
15.	HEAT EXCHANGER
16.	VEE DRIVE
17.	AUXILIARY GENERATOR
18.	ENGINES (1250 HP)
19.	SEAT FOR ENGINEER
20.	LAZARETTE
21.	WORK BENCH
22.	MUFFLERS

Diagram of PT 105 below deck.

occupied the whole spectrum, so that speech was impossible. The engineers wore earplugs while working in there and so they never knew what was going on topside, and didn't give a shit. Except at general quarters, there was only one engineer down there when we were underway. He was seated on a perch over the starboard engine with the three long levers of the gear shifts and buttons to start and stop each engine right at hand. Ahead of him was the instrument panel and a signal panel which indicated whether the engines should be in ahead, neutral, or astern. He sat there for a two-hour watch, staring at the panels, enclosed in a cocoon of heat and sound. He was a boy of eighteen or nineteen, probably from a farm in the south or midwest with a childhood full of tractors, trucks, and pumps. Sitting there sweating in the stink of oil and grease, clad only in cutoffs, Army shoes, and no socks, he was in charge of the greatest marine engines ever built, his idea of heaven.

Forward of the engine room were three thousand-gallon tanks holding one-hundred-octane aviation gasoline. The engines ran on a lower octane gasoline, but not at the efficiency needed to get the boat up and planing. Carrying so much highly volatile fuel fostered the impression that the PT boat was a bomb ready to go off. We were extremely careful about sparks. Smoking, for example, was only allowed topside and then only from the cockpit forward. However, PT boats were tough to blow up. A boat leading the 105 in an intense firefight was hit in her tanks so many times that gasoline was sloshing around in her bilges. While she triumphantly returned to base, her crew stayed prudently on deck because the fumes were too strong to go below. Her engineer only dropped into the engine room to shift gears when she docked. But she didn't blow up.

Above the tanks was a low cabin, labeled on the blueprints as the "dayroom." The idea behind this was for the off-duty crew to sit in there when underway. I never saw anybody sit in there. Mechin and Gunner Brown finally appropriated it for their private sleeping quarters, which cured the overload in the crew's quarters.

Forward of the tanks was my cabin and the ammunition storage area, then the officers' head, a two-hundred-gallon fresh water tank, and the two-man wardroom table, then the exec's stateroom and the galley. The galley was well equipped with an electric stove, oven, and an eight-cubic-foot refrigerator. Food supplies were so poor that the cook seldom had a chance to cook anything worth thinking about and gave the fridge an honored status because cold drinks and ice cream were all there was in the way of luxury. After one boat had its fridge done in by a dose of machine gun bullets, several other boats promptly installed armor plate in back of their own refrigerators.

The crew's quarters were in the forepart of the boat. With its eight bunks and a table amidships, it reminded me of the forecastle in *Treasure Island*. Forward of the crew's quarters was the crew's head; but not on Joe Roberts's boat, where the head was fully occupied by a raisin jack still.

A PT boat was practically unsinkable. All the compartments were watertight and the bulkheads were strong. The bow of the 109 continued to float long after it had been rammed, run over, and blown up by an enemy destroyer, providing a haven for Jack Kennedy and his crew until they prudently decided to swim ashore rather than float out there in full view of the enemy.

On the way to the Galapagos, the 105 put on her own display of unsinkability. We were running through huge seas, which did not faze her as long as I was careful. Sure enough, I got careless on the down slope of a monster wave. The succeeding wave came along while her bow was still sliding down. All I had to do was "quarter" it, turn her bow so she could climb the oncoming wave at a slant, but I was gabbing with Ellis, the radioman. Too late, I watched in stunned amazement as the bow disappeared in solid blue water, like a diving submarine. Water slid over the bow deck and rushed through the cockpit, yanking at my legs. Ellis saw it coming and ducked into the charthouse and shut the door. The water rushed onward to the stern and down the open engine room hatch. For a terrifying instant the 105 was underwater. Then she popped out of the other side of the wave. The engines, sitting for a time in a half-foot of water, continued running without a cough or a sneeze. My fright was nothing compared to that of the kid in the engine room who sat on his perch and watched as seawater cascaded down in front of him. The 105 forged ahead as if going under, rather than over, the waves was all the same to her.

Development of the 105-type PT (Patrol Torpedo) boat began in England in 1935, when Hubert Scott-Paine produced a seventy-foot torpedo boat for the British navy. Scott-Paine had made a fortune designing and building aircraft and then had switched his remarkable talents to designing speedboats, which had come into their own with the development of the internal combustion engine. Scott-Paine not only designed and built these boats, he raced them as well. As a young boy I had seen newsreels of those spectacular contests with Gar Wood and Sir Malcolm Campbell.

The seventy-foot boat that Scott-Paine built was the first large craft ever to achieve and sustain forty knots in the rough waters of the English Channel. For irrelevant reasons the British government chose another design but American boatbuilder Henry Sutphen, of the company commonly known as the Elco Boat Works, recognized a winner when he saw one, bought the boat with his own money, and shipped it back to the United States. Scott-Paine himself piloted the boat through trials that so impressed the Navy that Sutphen was awarded the major contract, winning out over at least eight other boats that had been built by Americans. The size of the Scott-Paine boat was later increased to allow for heavier armament and to give the boat better sea-keeping qualities.

The U.S. Navy came late and reluctantly to the torpedo boat which had been used extensively in World War I by the European navies. Our Navy saw our forces engaged in battles on the high seas too far off our coasts for the limited-range torpedo boat. In the late 1930s, however, the Navy became interested, persuaded by Gen. Douglas MacArthur, who was at that time commanding the forces in the Philippines. Knowing that the United States could not permanently station enough capital ships there to defend against Japanese attack, MacArthur believed that a large number of torpedo boats in the restricted waters of the Philippines could deter the big Japanese warships long enough for our own big ships to arrive. His foresight was in one sense astounding. He had just six PT boats at the time of the attack on Pearl Harbor but two of them, the last two still operating, took him and his family off Corregidor, to live to return another day.

I watched the first eighty-foot torpedo boats being built at the Elco plant in Bayonne, New Jersey. Built upside down, a torpedo boat looked more like an Indian longhouse than boat. One of the carpenters explained to me that it was easier to build that way. First the bulkheads, prefabricated of spruce, oak, and mahogany and made watertight by a marine plywood covering, were lined up athwartships on a template laid out on the floor of the building shed. They looked quite thick for what I thought of as walls because, more than just walls, they were main strength members built to absorb the violent shocks of high speed running. A framework of latitudinal and longitudinal battens were then fastened to the bulkheads. Nothing was nailed. There was not one nail on the entire boat. Everything was fastened in place with screws, bolts, glue, or a combination of the three. The keel was attached to this framework, flush with the bottom except where it curved to the bow; there, a thick hardwood chine connected the bottom and sides. Next the hull planking was fastened to this framework: two layers of $\frac{5}{8}''$ mahogany planks set diagonally and held together by a layer of thin airplane canvas impregnated with glue.

Looking at it upside down, the radical design of the hull became apparent. The bottom of the boat was flat for over two-thirds of its length after which the keel and bottom curved up and became more knife-edged. The hull had a "hard" chine, or pronounced angle, where the bottom turned into the sides. This shape of hull adapted well to both slow and high speed: at slow speed it knifed through the water like any other ship; at high speed it planed along like a small speedboat. Getting this shape right was both an art and a matter of trial and error. This became uncomfortably evident to Henry Sutphen and his chief boatbuilder, Irwin Chase, when they began manufacturing boats based on the Scott-Paine design. The blueprints bore little resemblance to the actual boat. Apparently, Scott-Paine had made changes as he went along and hadn't bothered to revise the plans. Sutphen and Chase finally abandoned the plans and began to painstakingly measure the boat they had brought over from England. In the process, the ingenuity of Elco's boatbuilders came into play so that the final product was a combination of the skills of British and American boatbuilders.

Naval historians say that Elco PT boats were turned out on an assembly line. This was not what I saw. I saw a group of boatbuilders, mostly middle-aged with a sprinkling of old codgers, building boats by hand. If a builder who had crafted clipper ships had been resurrected, he could have joined that group with no problem.

I tend to shortchange the contribution of our own Navy people because the basic boat design came from private British and American boatbuilders, but even though our Navy may have gotten into the act late, they brought some important improvements. The European concept of a torpedo boat was of a small boat that darted out from shore at some nearby target; their boats seldom exceeded fifty feet in length and the crews lived ashore. The U.S. Navy foresaw that this was impractical for American purposes, that crews would have to live aboard for extended periods of time and that the boats would have to be able to defend themselves. Therefore, they increased the size of the boats and added enough machine guns to make them tough opponents for any aircraft. What they did not foresee was that the primary mission of the boat would change from torpedo to gun attack. However, they made a boat that turned out to be big and strong enough to carry even forty-millimeter guns when the time came.

I also tend to forget that there was another American PT boat, the Higgins PT, built by amphibious craft designer Andrew Higgins. This boat was not quite as fast as the Elco, was less comfortable to live aboard, and was definitely wetter in heavy seas—but she had a tighter turning circle. The capability of reversing direction a few seconds faster was nice to have. There were moments with the wheel hard over when I wished the 105 would transform herself into a Higgins PT. People like Stanley Barnes and Ed DuBose inflicted more damage to the enemy in their Higgins boats than most of us did in what I think of as the greatest PT.

The 105 had four torpedo tubes, two on each side, that were trained out slightly when it was time to fire them so that the torpedoes could clear the deck when they were launched. Later, aircraft torpedoes were installed which were simply rolled over the side. The guns were originally installed as protection against aircraft. It didn't occur to the designers that the main mission of the PT boat would be attacking small enemy ships with guns. The conversion happened on my watch, sometime in July 1943, when we had sufficient big warships in the area to battle the enemy's big warships, and after that there was little need for torpedo boats whose job was essentially to delay and harass. However, as our big ships began driving the enemy's large ships out of the area, the Japanese resorted to using thousands of small amphibious craft which traveled substantial distances under their own power and did a good job of reinforcing, provisioning, and removing troops from the islands on which they fought. U.S. destroyers were effective against these barges when they found them but that was the catch: they couldn't continually patrol an area that was within easy range of enemy aircraft. So PTs became gunboats and gradually added more guns. By 1944 they had forty millimeters on their sterns, thirty-seven millimeters on their bows, and the original two twin fifty-caliber machine gun turrets. The 105 only had a twenty millimeter on the stern, the two twin-fifties, and a single fifty on the bow, but at optimum gunboat range, equivalent to a long putt, she could blow a barge apart. The boats outfitted later were truly terrifying at short range.

Even after all the trials and adjustments that went into her making, the 105 had some characteristics of a balky racehorse. In the beginning, the summer of 1942, she developed a speed problem that might have been fatal. She had a critical speed, at about twenty-seven knots, when her stern was down and her bow was up. If and when she got going over twenty-seven knots her stern would come up, her bow would go down, and she would gradually assume the flat out planing posture that took her to over forty knots. All of our boats, even though they consistently ran at over forty knots for the first month, suddenly slowed down to twenty-seven knots. We had bad thoughts about Henry Sutphen and Elco. Later on in Panama we experimented for months, with all the help the Navy and Elco could muster. My favorite theory was that all the trials had been held in the cool and dry climate of the north, and the boat's poor performance was due to the heat and humidity. This theory depressed my superiors and I was told to think of another reason. We tried to lighten the boat by removing the armor plate around the cockpit. It had no effect, but Squadron Five boats left it off anyway; six months later Phil Hornbrook was killed by shrapnel that might have been stopped by that armor. When lowering the weight did no good, we were stumped—until a civilian engineer proposed we try slightly smaller propellers. I thought this ridiculous, but we tried it and it worked. I watched in delight as the rpms rose steadily, hardly hesitating as they reached the critical speed, then the bow started down and suddenly the 105 was planing flat out. She never again failed to reach forty-two knots or better.

She had her own foibles, however. When following another boat on her way to a patrol station she tended to lag behind, but when returning from patrol she won every race. This sounds as if I'm talking about a horse, not a collection of wood and steel. PT sailors, however, were quite adamant that these boats had distinct animal characteristics that set each one apart from the others. Once, the 105 decided on her own that she had gone on enough patrols—ten out of eleven nights, often in place of other boats that were signing off to fix something—so she started to sink at her mooring. We couldn't figure out where the water was coming in so we went down to Tulagi to use their dry dock. We stayed there two days, during which no one could find anything wrong. When we put her back in the water, she had stopped leaking, and we went back to Rendova convinced she had just gotten tired and bored.

The 105 was surprisingly comfortable to live aboard. Let me amend that: I never saw a fat man on a PT boat. If you were in your twenties or younger, lean and agile and indifferent to soggy heat, she was surprisingly comfortable. In any kind of sea she bounced up, down, and sideways in a manner that raised suspicion of her bona fides. It came as natural as breathing to always have a hand on something fixed, to have your legs slightly flexed, and to hold anything spillable out in front so that you, not it, went up and down. Passengers who were strangers to her ways tended to get hurt or spill things on themselves. Her reputation as a seagoing Doberman started when the Navy tested her effect on humans by sending out a doctor with a gravity meter of the kind used on dive-bombers. Now, I am not putting you on: the gravity meter broke and the doctor busted an arm!

In our first days in training we heard the disturbing rumor that prolonged riding on PTs would render us sterile. A delegation of concerned students, including Dave Payne and me, checked this out with a doctor at the Newport Navy Hospital. The doctor's unequivocal opinion was that this was nonsense, but as we left his office and walked down the hall, Dave muttered, "How does he know?" Once we realized that sterility had no connection with impotence, the matter was dropped.

My cabin was upscale for a junior officer. I had a broad bunk I could stretch out on full length, a small closet, bureau, and a desk with a chair fixed to the deck. In the next compartment was a nifty little wardroom table for two. I had my meals there, used it as a writing table, for reading, and for nattering with my exec or a crewmember, usually Zichella, our cook, while he worked a few feet away in the galley.

In the oppressive heat of the Solomons we slept on deck most nights in port, the crew under a canvas canopy stretched over the forecastle deck and I beside the port forward torpedo tube next to the cockpit. In my Brooks Brothers pajamas (a Christmas gift from my two loving older sisters, making me the only PT man who wore pajamas) I rolled out my pallet, covered myself with a narrow cotton sheet, lay my helmet and weapons belt between me and the tube so no one would trip over them, put my head on my kapok life jacket, and went instantly to sleep. My ability to sleep whenever and wherever I wanted astounded me because I had been an insomniac in law school. I also discovered that I could wake up in a hurry. Perhaps I should not have been surprised since men in combat must do this or they don't last. I think loss of sleep caused more cases of combat fatigue than shellfire.

Every night at about 0200 it would rain. I then picked up my belongings, walked forward to the hatch, dropped my belongings down the hatch, climbed down, picked everything up, shoved it all through the narrow door of my cabin, rearranged the lot and went instantly back to sleep. Some nights the rain came early, cooling belowdeck enough so that I slept the entire night in my cabin, which was a bonus, except for one night.

On my back in my bunk, I was gazing at the overhead when I thought to myself, there is something on my right shoulder. I suddenly had the answer to the mystery of the chewed chocolate bar on my desk—the thing on my shoulder was a rat! I was scared shitless of rats! With my eyes riveted on the overhead, I refused to look at him, and only saw his belly when he ambled over my face, dragging his tail across my nose. I lay there, stiff and still, until his tail vanished, then I executed a smart sit up and yelled. I do not recall *what* I yelled but it must have been an urgent message because the entire crew materialized in my cabin, pulling up floorboards and flailing away with clubs, machetes, a broom, a frying pan, and, briefly, a forty-five until Gunner Brown hollered, "For Chrissake, stow that gun!" The rat skittered in and out of the bilges and finally scrambled straight up a bulkhead and disappeared through a ventilator. In full cry the crew took off topside and I brought up the rear. On deck we were abruptly reined in by the silent, raised arm of the man on watch. With his other arm he pointed meaningfully at the 106, moored alongside. Quickly I sized up the situation, turned to Miles, and gave the rotating hand signal for "start engines," then wheeled to Gunner Brown and gave him, palm up, the signal for "cast off." Both men quietly disappeared to their appointed tasks. Mechin swung into the charthouse and recorded in the log our "departure from mooring." Zichella started coffee in the galley. The three young sailors ran along the deck securing fenders.

When the engines started I saw the 106 rouse and my dear friend Dave Payne come on deck. "What's up?" he asked, standing by the port forward torpedo tube and watching us slowly depart. "We're moving moorings," I replied. "What for?" he asked, walking up the deck of the

106 to keep pace with me. "Just decided to move," I mumbled. "What's the matter?" Dave called as we moved alongside the 104, fifty yards away. I couldn't bring myself to tell Dave, my dear friend, that our rat was now his.

Bob Shearer, the captain of the 104, came aboard and over a cup of Zichella's great coffee, along with Mechin, Miles, and Brown, we discussed whether, when, and how we should tell Dave that a rat had joined his crew. But the longer we discussed it, the harder we laughed—which was not right and we were punished for it. The rat crawled under the 106's center engine and died there, probably when the engine started. Three days later the smell was so bad no one could go below. The 106 went all the way down to Tulagi to get the engine hauled. Dave and his crew managed to stretch this out for three nights, during which they saw three different movies, ate cutting meat, and generally had a grand time. Dave returned looking even more like Hamlet with a bad hangover.

DAILY LIFE

PT forward bases in the south Pacific all looked the same: a collection of sagging brown tents, one or two small metal quonset huts, some palm-thatched shacks, a sick bay and command dugouts with only their sandbagged roofs showing above ground, and lots of slit trenches. The layout seemed haphazard since as many palm trees as possible were left standing to provide some concealment from the air. PT boats at both Tulagi and the Russells tied up against the shore, hidden from the air by overhanging trees, bushes, and occasional camouflage netting. Rendova, in the New Georgia Islands and Torokina at Bougainville both had sloping beaches, so the boats were forced to moor in the open and the men hoped for the best.

Rendova Island was one of the major islands in the New Georgia group, which, in turn, was part of the Solomon Islands. On the western side of Rendova was a good harbor, created by a string of coral islands that ran a mile offshore. Our PT base was on one of these islets, named Todd Island after a young PT sailor who was the first to be killed in action there; but we mostly called the islet Rendova. The main island Rendova lay about five miles from New Georgia, where heavy fighting went on far longer than expected, first a battle to wrest the half-built airstrip at Munda from the Japanese and then a struggle to push the Japanese off of New Georgia. The Marines and Seabees had landed on Rendova several days before the PTs arrived. Their mission was to set up 155 howitzers to support the attack on Munda. They saw several days of fierce action against enemy troops, in larger numbers than expected, and they bore the brunt of air attacks for a week; but they got their guns in place and began shelling the Japanese lines five miles across the water. The noise of those big shells overhead made me feel as if I was living under the Sixth Avenue elevated during rush hour.

Rendova was mountainous, like all of the big islands in the Solomons, rising to over three thousand feet, with a brooding, inhospitable look. In times of peace they may have had their beauty, but to my eyes in the summer of 1943 the Solomon Islands were monotonous hulks of dark green, mainly cloud covered with wisps of rain hanging down here and there since it rained somewhere in view all the time. The rain dropped in funnels and seldom stayed long in one place. There was little point in using rain gear—the most we wore were light rubber ponchos that went on and off quickly. As soon as we put them on the rain would stop, so we just got wet and then steamed dry after the rain had passed.

The only relief PT boats and their crews had from life on the forward lines was when something went wrong on a boat that could only be fixed at a rear base, and that was rare. Once an area was secured, PTs were the first to move up the line, where there were no movies and no USO shows. From April 1943 until February 1944, I didn't see a woman. I never saw any sports played, except during those few days on eccentrically idyllic Russell Island where volleyball was played on the lawn outside the planter's house. Even swimming went out of fashion when people came down with excruciating earaches from fungi in the water. The sound of music was seldom heard, although one base force officer had a wind-up phonograph. His record inventory was thin and his selection curious; over and over he played "I Found a Peach in Orange, New Jersey, in Apple Blossom Time." I told my brother officers that I too had found a peach in Orange, New Jersey. Nobody cared.

The fresh water supply was so limited that bathing in it was out of the question—unless it was a sponge bath out of a pan. I tried using a product that someone had sold the Navy called "saltwater soap." I used

Dick Keresey (*right*) with close friend and favorite wingman David Payne, captain of PT 106. (author's collection)

it only once, and then Zichella patiently poured buckets of seawater over me to remove the sticky stuff. All of us went for weeks without baths. I don't recall missing it much. However, I can still feel a shower I took behind the planter's house in the Russells. The former owner had constructed the shower, fed by a large, suspended, wooden tub which collected rainwater from the roof. This water collection system was not efficient and showers were rationed. I had been up the line for three weeks, and when I stopped by the Russell base to check in with my duty officer, he generously suggested I might wish to take a shower. He then went even further and said that I should take a good one. The water was cool, with the unique softness of rainwater. The shower head was as big as a pie plate so that when I pulled the string, water poured over my head and shoulders and down my body, washing away weeks of sweat and grime while I just stood there, luxuriating. I made lots of suds and it was splendid. That a simple shower stands out as a great sensual experience provides a measure of the amenities in our life in the Solomons.

I first met Barney (George H. R.) Ross in the officers' shower at Tulagi. It was an encounter to remember, like a scene from a Marx Brothers movie. I had finished my shower and was standing on one leg to put on a sock when Barney—six feet, two inches, and two hundred pounds—strode in, greeted me with a friendly grin, took off his hat and shoes, stepped under the shower and pulled the cord. Water from the pie-plate wide, overhead shower poured over him and, of course, over his shirt, pants, and socks. He took the soap and vigorously lathered and scrubbed said pants, shirt, and socks, removed them and scrubbed himself, then put everything back on, gave himself and his clothes a good rinse, put on his shoes and hat, and departed with another friendly grin and wave of his hand—soaking wet, of course. I was still standing on one leg, mesmerized by the performance. Those of us who knew Barney well may quibble over whether he had a hat, but otherwise agree that this was classic Barney Ross. He entertained us, without ever telling a joke, simply by the ludicrous spin he put on some mundane act like taking a shower.

I know Jack Kennedy enjoyed his company even during the week they were hiding from the enemy. When they made the movie "PT 109," President Kennedy's sole request was that they find a part for Barney. When it reappears on TV, or you rent it on video, watch for the scene in which the actor playing Kennedy throws a bucket of slops over the side and accidentally douses a chief petty officer about to come aboard. Barney (too old to play himself) plays the chief and steals the scene.

Knowing this bit of movie trivia will also show you a side of Kennedy that may be new. He never forgot his PT buddies and always had time for them. Even I had a ten-minute visit in the Oval Office. He saw my name on a White House visitors' list and invited me up for an aimless, happy chat about our days together on Rendova. Kennedy had a caring side to him. He sent money to the widow of a PT friend who died without leaving much.

Al Webb in his postwar life became V.P. of sales for Cavanagh Hats. When he visited the President at the White House he jokingly told the President that his refusal to wear a hat was hurting the hat business (true). Kennedy met the challenge in his own way. The next day he greeted former President Eisenhower at the Washington airport and thereafter sent Al a picture of the great occasion: it showed Kennedy leaning forward, his right hand extended; in his left hand he held a hat,

President Kennedy greets former president Eisenhower—while surreptitiously advertising a hat for his PT buddy Al Webb. (courtesy of the John F. Kennedy Library)

the lining facing out toward the camera. The Cavanagh Hats label was plainly visible!

There was no library and books were scarce, handed around until they fell apart. Before leaving Panama I had foreseen the lack of reading material and, in addition to a few paperback westerns and the chess book that I used to great effect against Dave, I acquired a two-volume set of Gibbon's *Decline and Fall of the Roman Empire*. I expected Gibbon to be difficult and dull; on the contrary, he proved a good companion, taking me back to a time when most men were born, lived, and died without ever seeing war.

Days at the mooring were vacant. The enemy air force, after giving up on dislodging the Marine howitzers, concentrated their attacks on the ships supporting our ground forces—except for one dive-bombing attack on us, which I will get to. That once was enough. If the radar people reported a single bogey at ten miles and closing, we went to general quarters with our engines running, prepared for a quick exit. Most of the time we sat on our moorings, watching nothing happen.

My day started shortly after daybreak when I attended a debriefing session on the beach. Even if I hadn't been out the night before, I often went to hear what had gone on so I would know what might go on. On the beach, breakfast was served like all of our meals, on trestle tables under a tarpaulin that kept off the rain but not the flies. To fend off the flies required eating with one hand and swishing with the other. So I usually skipped the breakfast and took a whaleboat back to the 105, where Zichella served me breakfast of scrambled powdered eggs, bacon, and toast. Then I would spend the morning censoring letters. I tried not to read them but simply looked for place names. The reading went very fast and was very dull. Once I decided to further Rabel's education by informing him that there was no such word as "nexted," that the word was simply "next." He seemed to listen attentively but his next letter contained "nexted" twice, which was enough to tell me that it was none of my damn business how he spelled words.

When that chore was done I poked around the deck, inspecting the guns and ammo for cleanliness. My tolerance level for neglected weapons was zero. In Panama I once found some green mold on a cartridge belt and Gunner Brown spent the day cleaning all four thousand rounds himself, with no help from his striker, while I watched. After this incident he and the rest of the crew reconciled themselves to my unswerving belief that clean things worked, and the 105 was always spotless by 0800. If Willie Monk was working on a torpedo I stood by and tried to appear interested, but this brought back nauseating memories of Newport Torpedo School. I never inspected the engine room after my first six months aboard without an invitation from Miles, which was rare and usually involved admiring a new paint job. Sometimes I inspected the smoke-screen generator. The only way I could assure myself that it would work when we needed it was to have Gunner Brown crack the valve, so that the generator gave off a puff of smoke. I was to regret this deeply later.

It was still on the near side of 0900 when I joined Gibbon for an hour or two. The way to read Gibbon was not to take him too seriously, not to worry that I couldn't tell the difference between a Scythian and a Sarmatian. Having learned from other reading that Gibbon was a pretty relaxed fellow himself, I concluded that I was just the audience he had written for, someone with lots of time on his hands. After Gibbon, I rummaged around for a western and pigged out. My favorite reading spot was topside, sitting on the bow deck with my back against the charthouse. By this time of day I found it too hot below deck; besides, I liked to be able to stand up and look around at the sky, just in case.

Late in the morning, my puritan instinct urged me to do something useful; I ducked into the charthouse and practiced estimating firing angles on a maneuvering board. Radar was being installed, and presumably there would come a time when I would pick up a target on the scope at, say, five miles. By plotting the target blips, my course, speed, and my torpedo speed, I could calculate the torpedo firing angle. All of this was kid stuff to a regular Navy man but I had nearly flunked this sort of thing at midshipman school. Now I was someone else; I had already fired four torpedoes at the enemy and missed. I was determined not to miss if I got another chance. It took a lot of effort to work out a plot in a charthouse that was going up, down, and sideways in combat conditions. Nevertheless I felt that the more I practiced the better I would be at estimating target angles in the cockpit, with Ellis calling up changes in target range and bearing from the charthouse. I became so adept at this exercise that I taught it later in the war.

I can't remember a single good meal. I praised Zichella for his scrambled eggs, but I lied. We depended on Army supplies and our basic fare consisted of Spam, Vienna sausages, C Rations (which I think became dog food after the war), strange looking canned string beans, powdered milk, powdered eggs, dehydrated shredded potatoes, and a mix that made thick, plasterlike pancakes.

Dave Payne's 106 always moored alongside us. After lunch he and I would sit on the forecastle deck and play chess until it was time to go ashore for the briefing at 1600. On nights when the 105 was going out, my body clock told me what time it was. I got a dull pain just below my rib cage ten minutes before the whaleboat drew alongside; this pain sometimes lasted only a few minutes, sometimes longer, but always disappeared as the 105 got under way.

Chow time in the crew's quarters: hot, crowded, and lots of laughter. (U.S. Naval Institute photo collection)

I spent some days on the beach with other boat officers and Robert D. Woodward, our supply officer. Woody was very tall, thin, amiable, and, in his job of supplying Squadron Five, larcenously efficient. With the base force, he departed from Noumea a week ahead of us to set up logistics at Tulagi. George Cookman, our squadron exec and leader of the six-officer cabal of boat captains, told Woody half jokingly that his first mission was to find lodgings for us equal to the Hotel Tivoli in Panama, a beautiful retreat that looked like a scene from a Somerset Maugham novel. Tulagi was on the lowest rung of habitability. Latrines sat over the water, close to the dock where we landed. Paths were gooey mud. For some reason I've forgotten, boat captains at Tulagi lived ashore, not on their boats, and we were profoundly depressed the first time we walked off the dock with our duffel bags into the mud and saw nothing but sagging brown tents. We followed Woody up the trail. At the top, around a bend, Woody stopped, waited for us to reach him, and pointed his long arm in triumph: "Fellas, voilà! The Tivoli!" He was gloriously close to right. There in front of us was a little house on stilts with plywood halfway up the sides, then stout netting rising to a peaked roof. Inside were eight cots for the six boat captains plus George and Woody.

We had no "Tivoli" at Rendova but after three months in the Solomons we were quite at home in the sagging brown tents. We sat on

The Tulagi PT boat base, a typical ramshackle collection of huts huddled under palm trees. (U.S. Naval Historical Center)

cots in the division leader's tent and talked and laughed about simple things, like watching Flower Pot, a massive ex-pro lineman try to get his hand far enough into a jar to pry out a piece of candy. To those of us with normal hands this was easy but Flower Pot's finger wiggled a good inch away from the stuck-together candy balls. Flower Pot, so called because his neck was so thick that his head looked like an inverted flower pot, was a gentle and amiable gorilla. I watched him give up and hand the jar to Al Webb.

"Al, gimme one of them, will ya?"

Al turned and glared at him: "Get your own candy!" I thought this was not only rude but dangerous. Flower Pot patiently took back the jar and tried slamming the bottom with his hand. Bully Barrett quickly reached over, took the jar, and pried loose one of the balls. Flower Pot leered in triumph at Al Webb and said "One of the green ones, Bully."

Once or twice a week Doc Freeto ran his "psychiatric clinic." After an early supper we would repair to his tent for cocktails. The bar fare was limited to alky screamers, no ice, but they were very tasty. It was a rare night indeed without something untoward occurring at the good doctor's meeting, which he, in all sincerity, intended as group therapy, perhaps with a bit of spiritual guidance from Father Webster.

Bully Barrett had emphatic views, which he emphasized by jumping up and down in his chair. On one of Bully's particularly energetic landings, the chair (a homemade job of nailed-together boxes) collapsed. Two nails pierced his buttocks, pinning him to the seat. He rolled over onto his hands and knees, the chair clinging to him. He yelled for someone to take the thing off him and demanded to know what was so funny. No one was capable of useful movement. Barrett said, "Come on Doc, this is no joke, dammit, do something!"

The doctor seemed to realize he'd better behave more professionally, so he had Joe Atkinson, who was as large and strong as Flower Pot— PT boats were overrun with ex-football linemen—lift Bully onto the surgery table still in a kneeling position with the legless chair mounting him. In the meantime, the doctor had put on a surgical gown and now he began laying out instruments.

"What are you doing?" Bully asked suspiciously.

"I am preparing to operate," replied the doctor.

"Operate, my ass!" cried Bully and this unintended pun increased the laughter level. The pinioned victim then realized he had better take charge. "Will someone," he asked patiently, "pull this damn thing offa me?"

Someone did just that. The doctor pulled down Bully's pants and patted his behind with sulfanilamide, giving him a couple of extra pats. Barrett was a tough little guy. He climbed from the table, sat in another chair, and basked in the glow of praise for providing such high comedy.

Our entertainment was homemade and simpleminded and yet, with all the vacant hours and carefully concealed dread of what the next patrol might bring, there has never been a time in my long life when I have known so much laughter.

Father Giles Webster didn't look like a Franciscan priest. He looked like the hockey defenseman he'd been in college, and he walked with the swagger of a Princeton man, which he'd been before getting the call to the seminary.

Ecumenism flowered briefly during the war, a time when mutual intolerance between Catholics and Protestants was about the same as it had been since the Reformation. I was raised in the Roman Catholic religion, which taught me that it was a mortal sin to attend a Protestant service. And when I asked for my wife's hand in marriage, her Protestant parents turned me down because I was Catholic. We married anyway, after I returned from the Pacific, but we could only be married in the rectory because "mixed" marriages were not permitted in the church proper. When my older brother, who was also my best man, came into the dreary room where we were to be married, he looked around and asked, "Where did they put the body?"

The barriers between faiths disappeared in the Solomons. Father Giles performed Protestant services as well as Catholic. Out of curiosity, I asked what kind of Protestant service he gave. "Southern Baptist. I love it," he replied, promptly and with conviction. This surprised me since I knew that he was a conservative Roman Catholic. But Father Giles was a man of surprises. He never drank but he tended bar like a Boston bartender, justifying his enthusiasm with the argument that "the Bible says 'give drink to those who thirst' and this is the thirstiest bunch I know."

He believed deeply in the sacrament of confession. Tom Hayde and I postponed getting in the line until just before mass, when we knew that Father Giles (glaring at the two of us and obviously frustrated) would have to grant everyone still in line "general absolution."

And Father Giles had another problem which he once brought up during a sermon: "I know I have dispensed with the condition of no breakfast before communion, but the other morning one of you was so drunk he almost fell on his face." Hayde whispered to me, "Listen to the monk—it was him serving the drinks!"

Although he did seem confused by his efforts to apply the rules of his church in these peculiar circumstances, Father Giles was a great comfort and source of strength to us, many of whom were not Catholic or even Christian. His emphasis on the sacrament of confession was shrewd; he knew that there were those who needed to talk to God through him, or who needed just to talk to someone about private things. I didn't appreciate then what he was about. One morning I prepared to lead a division of four boats from Rendova to the new beachhead at Bougainville. I was impatient to get going because I would only have an hour of daylight left when we arrived, and there was no way that I would approach an area like that in darkness. I was on the outermost of the four PT boats tied to the dock and told the captain to get under way.

"Got a problem, Gunga," he said, "Father Giles has a line of guys on the inboard boat." I looked over and sure enough our good chaplain had decided to hear confessions and had set himself up by the stern twenty millimeter. I called over to him, saying that we had to get under way, but there was no response. I walked across the two intervening boats and, standing at a respectful distance, engaged in discourse with the confessor, pointing out that I really had to get under way now or risk getting shot at by all the nervous people up in Bougainville. I suggested that he grant a general absolution, and in frustration pointed out that most of those guys in line weren't even Catholics! Nothing worked. Father Giles proposed that we all take off while he continued to hold confessions there on the stern. How could I explain it if I took the chaplain with me? In the end I waited nearly an hour for him to finish and barely made it to Bougainville in time to be visually identified as friend!

I had drifted away from the church during college and law school but in the summer of 1943, I found that living in the presence of death made me feel the presence of God. At a certain moment He was there. I prayed that He would give me the strength to face the night's patrol. Once or twice I prayed that He would let me survive, but in this I had a sense of futility. Prayers couldn't prevent death, the province of that strumpet Fortune, giggling as she took the best or the most unlikely. She seemed to take special delight in striking the unlikely.

The night that I brought the 105 back to base with Phil Hornbrook, my boat exec, lying dead on the dayroom canopy, an intelligence officer came aboard. He was a man in his mid-thirties with the cultured accent and manner of someone who had taught in a university before the war. He and I sat on the deck, against the dayroom bulkhead, talking until nearly dawn. I learned about his wife and two small children. I also realized that he was there to give me comfort, but I was not in the state of shock that he assumed. I was sorry to lose Phil but these things happened and this nice guy was costing me some sleep. Still, I enjoyed hearing about his life back home and his family; and I was glad for him that he had a nice safe job on the base and I thought I wouldn't mind having one like that myself. Two days later he was killed on a PBY that disappeared while making a run to Guadalcanal.

A major American strength in World War II was our technical support force. We outnumbered the entire world in people who could fix things and things in the Solomons broke down a lot. Mechanical and electrical things designed and built in the temperate climate of the United States did not adapt easily to the damp, salty heat where green mold began growing as soon as you turned your back.

Life on the base force was hard and dangerous. Night bombers dropped their bombs more often on the little island where the base force was located than on PTs moored offshore. In the first place, the base force made an easier target, and in the second place, it didn't take much intelligence to figure out that the quickest way to put PTs out of action was to knock out their maintenance.

Most of our base force personnel were older than our boat crews. The work each of them performed required prior experience in his particular craft in civilian life. The skills needed to operate a PT could be learned in three months, but fixing one was another matter. Our chief carpenter's mate, Pop Dieteman, could fix five-foot-wide holes in hulls while standing in a dinghy. I saw him do it, wobbling back and forth while a crewman lay on the deck of the boat, ready to grab him if he started to go over the side.

Pop carried the age differential to an extreme. We started out with the assumption that he was somewhere in his early forties, which was old for anyone connected with PT boats. The longer I knew Pop, the more suspicious I became about his real age. He was a great storyteller and talked about public events he'd witnessed well before World War I. Then at Bougainville his real age came out. A bomb had exploded close to Pop and he lay paralyzed. He was conscious and trying to joke about his paralysis when they carried him down into the sick-bay dugout. The doctor who examined him sat back, looking puzzled. "Pop," he said "something tells me you have the wrong age in your record. How about it? I need to know in order to help. How old are you?" Pop looked up at him and grinned, "Sixty-four or maybe it's sixty-five." Everyone in the dugout cheered. A day later most of his paralysis disappeared, but Pop got orders back to the States.

He was not the only one who brought a treasure of skills that takes years to accumulate. One of the Navy's advantages over the Army was in the quality of the food—except in PT boats, because we depended on the Army for supplies. There was one exception to our normally dreary menu; our squadron was blessed with a baker who had over twenty years' experience. I can't remember his name or figure out how we got him; Woody probably stole him. The man was a genius. He took an empty fifty-gallon drum, cut holes in it here and there, set it on a couple of logs, lit a fire under it, and turned out not just good bread, but Parker House rolls, delicious buns, croissants! Name it, he could bake it. We realized how lucky we'd been when Squadron Five moved up the line from Tulagi to Rendova. Tulagi was now a rear base with movies, showers, and so forth; but when our baker departed, Tulagi found itself back on pasty white bread. Then, a terrible thing happened: when we left Rendova for Bougainville the Rendova base commander forbade Woody to take our baker. Knowing Woody as he did, the base commander posted a watch at the dock to make sure the baker didn't leave. At Bougainville we went back to pasty white bread.

In the close quarters of a PT boat, Navy protocol was somewhat relaxed but onshore the base command followed the book as if the shabby collection of tents and huts were a battleship. We boat captains did not question this adherence to tradition, but the choice to use first or last names was always a puzzlement. In general, the rule seemed to be that, if the base command called you by your first name instead of your last, you had passed upward through an invisible ceiling in the hierarchy.

Take the case of Lt. (jg) Huck Wood and the squadron command. Soon after the New Georgia campaign started, a PT force was sent to Lever Harbor on the north side of New Georgia to operate in the Kula Gulf. Land fighting was going on to the south where our forces were attempting to push the Japanese north and off the island. Lever Harbor was therefore behind enemy lines and the farther our troops advanced, the more dangerous it became for the PT base.

There were two PT squadrons at Lever under Comdr. Bob Kelly. For a variety of reasons Huck's squadron found itself without a squadron commander. It had nothing but junior boat captains.

After he returned to Rendova from Lever, Huck told me of his strange encounter with the first name/last name protocol.

"I found out I was acting squadron commander when Kelly called me Huck. He said, 'Huck, you are now acting squadron commander.' Before that he always called me 'Wood' if he called me anything. Not that he gave me any responsibility. He ran both squadrons." As Huck told me about this sudden rise to the top, he paused and said, "It had only lasted a few days when, out of somewhere, a lieutenant commander showed up to take over. I found out I was demoted when Kelly came out of his tent and yelled, 'Wood!' Then you know what happened?" He looked at me. I hadn't heard. "The new CO?" he asked. It still meant nothing to me, in Rendova we never heard anything about what went on at Lever. "What about him?" I urged Huck on.

"Every day the Japs were getting pushed closer and closer to us. We had a detachment of Marines but they wouldn't do much good if the Japs arrived in force. A couple of days after what's-his-name, the new CO, showed up, about noon the alarm goes off and people are shouting the Japs are coming in. We take off from the base tents and run for the dock with the Marines running in the opposite direction. As I'm galloping out on the dock I hear Kelly holler, 'Hey, Huck!' I turn around and Kelly is waving at me to come back, so back I go. Our new CO is out flat on the ground. The guy had fainted! I should have known when Kelly called me 'Huck.'"

I looked at Huck inquiringly. This had only been a couple of weeks earlier. Here he was, a boat captain readying himself to go out in a division I was leading that night.

"They finally got another squadron commander. Kelly is back to calling me 'Wood'," Huck grinned at me, "some career, huh?"

8

THE BATTLE
OF BLACKETT
STRAIT,
OR, THE
NIGHT WE
ALMOST
LOST JFK

The time was high noon, 2 August 1943. All twenty PT boats based at Rendova Island were moored in nests of two or three boats. About fifty yards separated each nest. Shelving beaches prevented the boats from mooring close to shore. There was nothing for it but to moor out in the open and hope that the Japanese air force would pick on bigger targets in the area or that we would get sufficient warning to get under way and scatter.

All of the 105 crew was aboard and most were flaked out on the bow. However, our two twin fifty-caliber and stern twenty-millimeter guns were manned because there was a sporadic air battle in progress only ten miles away over New Georgia. I was lolling in the cockpit nattering with Mechin, my twenty-one-year-old quartermaster. Tommy Mechin had transferred to PT duty after almost three years of naval service, part of a very small core of experienced hands. The 105 was lucky to get regular Navy petty officers to man its engine room, torpedoes, guns, and radio. With experienced men in these key jobs, boat

PT 164 lies on the beach after a dive-bombing attack on 1 August 1943. The author saw the bow fly fifty feet in the air. But the 164 stayed afloat and was towed to the beach. Most of it lived to fight another day—as parts of other PT boats. (U.S. Naval Historical Center)

officers could be trained in a few months. Boats with both inexperienced captains and crew were floating embarrassments.

Mechin provided more than experience, he was a pleasure to have aboard with his almost constant good humor—and he seemed to like my company as much as I did his. He was also a highly persuasive man; he extracted a three-day leave from me just four days before we left Norfolk for Panama: he came to me with a letter from his young wife, the gist of which was that she was going to leave him; so he had to get home and "straighten things out." I was puzzled as to how he would straighten something like that out in two days. I had also recently seen a British wartime movie with the identical story line, but I gave him the leave anyway, which I didn't have the slightest authority to do, this being a matter for our squadron commander.

Like many others, our conversation on that August day was relaxed and disjointed, with both of us watching the sky. In my peripheral vision I suddenly caught sight of a flock of Japanese dive-bombers wheeling around the northern end of Rendova. Their fixed landing gear made for instant identification. For a second I thought they were heading for an ammunition dump a mile or so away but then the leader waggled, sideslipped and adjusted his course right for us. Mechin screamed, "Jap planes! Dead ahead! Jap planes!"

I looked to my right and astern and saw my two twin fifty gunners and my stern twenty-millimeter gunner already tracking but watching me at the same time. We'd practiced this daylight air-attack drill, but never had one for real. In the three previous air attacks, the enemy had always found better targets than PT boats. I raised my right arm and watched the planes close. They were in groups of three, gliding down as if they were coming in for a landing. I heard the familiar whine as Miles started the engines. In the time I took to raise my arm, Miles had gone from sitting flaked-out on deck to his engines, with his fireman Rabel right on his tail. Some boats were already firing, their tracers streaking out at targets still a thousand yards away. What a waste, I thought: by the time the planes were within effective range, those guns would be reloading or, more likely, jammed.

The 105 and the 106 were on the same mooring, as usual. I glanced over; the 106 was silent but tracking. Dave had his hand raised but he had his forty-five automatic in it, pointing. I thought that was a nice touch, he'd likely shoot himself. At about a thousand yards, it was clear that the dive-bombers were going to have PT boats for lunch. They had passed right over two LSTs (Landing Ships, Tank, which we referred to as Long Slow Targets). I saw each vee of planes head for the moored nests of PTs scattered over the half-mile-square anchorage. I should have felt honored that the lead vee was heading right for us, but at that precise moment I felt nothing at all. The planes seemed to throttle back and waggle from side to side as if to cut their airspeed. They were intent on placing their bombs on target, contemptuous of our firepower. They're close enough now, I thought, and I brought my right arm down in an exaggerated sweep. Mechin whirled around to face aft and make sure the stern gunner got the signal.

I know that I yelled "Commence firing!" but I couldn't hear myself because the starboard twin-fifties began firing in my right ear, then the port twin-fifties opened ten feet behind me, the twenty-millimeter racketed away on the stern, and the 106 was now hard at it. Dave hadn't waited for me nor I for him; we just thought alike about waiting until the target was big in our sights. We knew from embarrassing experience that the twin-fifties sometimes jammed after the initial five-second burst, so those first five seconds had to count. I glanced over at Payne and, sure enough, he was firing his forty-five skyward. I shifted my sights to the planes. They veered to their starboard, I think to avoid the concentrated fire from our guns. Then came the bombs.

I never saw them. My senses were stunned by the staccato crack-whangs of the explosions. For a moment, I was held in place by con-cussions, unable to move and staring vacantly over the bow at the now-empty sky. I thought, it's raining, how could it rain? I looked down at my hands saw that they were speckled with sawdust—it's raining saw-dust? I looked up to port and fifty feet in the air was the bow of a PT boat, blown sky high. It seemed stuck up there like the tail in a game of pin-the-tail-on-the-donkey. I didn't understand, then or later, how a bomb could land on a PT boat just forward of the cockpit, propel the bow up in the air, and leave the aft two-thirds of the boat afloat. The dogged down hatch that led to the vanished crew's quarters now looked like a front door. Then the planes were gone.

They had hit the nest of PTs next to ours, destroyed that one boat, and killed two men. Somehow the other men on the ruined boat sur-vived. A dozen or more Japanese dive-bombers had attacked at least twenty PT boats, moored in pods of two or three in broad daylight, and their score was only two boats. We had done even worse than they had. I could not believe it. Our two boats had eight fifty-caliber and two twenty-millimeter guns throwing lead at three planes that were so close that I had seen one pilot's droopy Charlie Chan mustache. Other than that strange veer to our port, which may have been to avoid our fire, nothing had happened. I heard Mechin, who stood with his back to me facing aft to watch the planes disappear, mutter to himself, "Shit, nuthin?"

That attack should have destroyed most of our boats, which when nested together formed forty-by-eighty-foot targets; and most of the planes should have flown straight into the water, their pilots riddled from our fire. Any war game would have called it that way. I suppose probabilities work out in the big picture, but in the thousands of snap-shot moments from that war, probability gave way to luck. Believe me, luck exists—and we treated it with great respect. When it comes to in-dividual survival, luck outranks skill, experience, and cowardice. Nonetheless, back to high noon.

The 105 was alive and well, her engines turning over. We parted company with the 106 and headed for the channel and open water. I expected orders from the base radio but none came. Some of the other boats were casting off their moorings, but I seemed to be the only one rushing for the nearest exit. Once I got into the channel, I lay to. It seemed like a good spot because it lay between our base island and another island we used for refueling. An attacking plane would have a problem getting at us. Then we were given a second chance at an enemy plane.

Our own planes' bombing attack was still on over New Georgia; there were Zeros after our dive-bombers and Corsairs after the Zeros. One of our bombers dropped out of a cumulus cloud in a vertical dive, chased by a Zero. I thought our guy would go right into the sea when, just a few feet off the water, he flipped from vertical to horizontal and came in our general direction with the Zero still on his tail. We managed to get our guns bearing right behind him, and darned if that Zero didn't run into our fire. The range must have been over five hundred yards but this time we scored; the Zero dove toward the water. I immediately started scanning 360 degrees, for fear there were other Zeros or dive-bombers coming in from God-knew-where. Others saw the Zero splash, and Torpedo Brown in the forward gun turret and Winters in the aft turret exultantly screamed "Hot damn!" The men on deck were pumping and waving their arms. After being bombed and shelled a half-dozen times and rarely getting a chance to shoot back, even turning the Zero away would have been a major triumph.

I thought that we had saved one of our planes but the thought was short-lived. Later that afternoon I stopped by an LST to scrounge some real food; when I told the supply ensign how we picked off a Zero chasing our dive-bomber he said ruefully, "Yeah, well we shot down the dive-bomber." The poor guy thought he was gaining a refuge and of course every gunner in Rendova Harbor had just seen the dive-bombing and was of a mind to shoot at anything that came in their direction. After about an hour of quiet, word came over the radio for all boat captains to report to the base. I brought the 105 back to its mooring with the 106 and Dave and I took the whaleboat into the beach. The base commander's greeting to the boat captains was, "You people were not supposed to be moored together like that." Where the hell had he been? We'd been moored like that for the past two weeks. I was smart enough to keep my mouth shut. No one else said anything either, not even the two other squadron commanders.

Later the base radioman told me that shortly before noon they had received a message from Guadalcanal headquarters saying, "Jap dive-bombers will attack Rendova PTs at 1200 hours today." While the base commander was contemplating this message, the bombs started falling. I deduced from this incredibly accurate prediction that the coast watcher at Rabaul was somehow listening in on conversations at the Japanese air base—how else would he have known the attack would be precisely at noon? It had never occurred to me that this kind of detailed intelligence was the result of our having broken the Japanese code. All that splendid work was for naught.

The loss of only one boat from a couple of dozen meant that we could still send out a sizable force. However, all the boat crews were particularly tired that night. Most of us had been out almost every night for two weeks. On the majority of those nights we'd been in gun battles with enemy barges, bombed by enemy floatplanes, or had a couple of mix-ups with our own forces. Sleep came in two hour stretches. During the day there were things to get done. Refueling from fifty-gallon drums was a long process when a good two thousand gallons were needed. We also had to work on the engines, torpedoes, guns, and radio, all of which needed cleaning and adjustments after a night of bouncing around. With a crew as good as mine, I had less to do than most of the other boat captains, but I still had to be up and looking lively. Replacement captains like Jack Kennedy had it much harder because they had replacement crews and, therefore, more mechanical break-downs.

When we went out that night, the boats were divided into five divisions. Our division consisted of the 105, a radar-equipped lead boat from another squadron, and the 107, captained by Joe Roberts. At that time radar had been installed on only a few boats, so division leaders rode on these boats. This tended to mix up squadrons so that the divisions lost some of their cohesiveness. On the other hand, radar provided a critical advantage. As it turned out, however, the base command gave orders that canceled out this advantage.

The five divisions of PTs idled out of Rendova Harbor about 1700. In an effort to confuse any Japanese who might be watching from Rendova Hill, each division fanned out on a different course. Joe and I joined up on the port and starboard quarters of the lead boat. This vee formation had become regulation at cruising speed after combat experience had showed that cruising in a column increased the chance of a bomb hit; after spotting our highly visible wake, night-flying Japanese planes would come in astern, fly up the long single wake, and drop bombs. They had a three-times-better chance of scoring than when the boats were in a vee, or echelon, formation.

Our division cruised south that night, down the Rendova coast. It was early evening and I was already tired. I had been out on a mission the night before so this should have been my night off, but every operable boat had been called out. I looked at Miles and thought how nice it would be if he would just say, "A fuel pump is broke, Skipper." But that didn't happen. How did the story ever start that PT engines were unreliable? The 105's engines ran fifteen hundred hours when the book called for engine changes once every five hundred hours. They ran so long that the propeller diameter was worn down by an eighth of an inch. I'm wandering. Back to the night the world almost lost JFK.

After about thirty minutes and shortly before I had figured we'd reach the southern tip of Rendova, the lead boat turned to port, toward the coast. When we slowed to ten knots, Joe and I folded into line astern from our cruising vee. With little hesitation due to his radar, the division leader found the entrance to a small cove and we coasted in, stopped, and dropped anchor. I had no idea why we were there and did not ask. As far as I was concerned, we could stay all night.

The Solomon Islands are a curious mixture: Guadalcanal and our base at Rendova were dreary and sullen but then elsewhere there were pretty little spots; this cove where we stopped for perhaps an hour was one of the unexpected gems. Lush tropical foliage came right down to the water's edge and there was a faint scent of something like honeysuckle. (I still remember that scent, so different from the smells of engines, damp life jackets, stale coffee, and sweat that merged and created the unique smell of a PT boat at anchor.) I had the rare experience of noticing nature, viewing the scenery, instead of examining the shore for signs of a hidden gun battery.

There was an Army detachment there, sent down a month before at the start of the New Georgia campaign. One young enlisted man swam out to the 105 and the crew showed him around the boat. He was fascinated but claimed that his current detail was the best ever; his unit had been sent to secure the south end of Rendova and had not seen even one Japanese. The Americans had made themselves comfortable and hoped that the U.S. Army had forgotten they were there. We promised not to tell.

We left after about an hour. I didn't know why we were there or why we were leaving. The lead boat lit up its engines and we followed her out. From our course heading of 290 degrees I knew we were heading for Ferguson Passage which led into Blackett Strait. The strait was bordered on the north by Kolombangara Island, a round cone that rose steeply to over six thousand feet. To the east of Kolombangara across six miles of water called Vila Gulf lay New Georgia, where our army was painfully gaining ground against dug-in Japanese forces. Kolombangara appeared to be an enemy way station for supplies and reinforcements coming down from Rabaul. The southern border of Blackett Strait was a string of coral islets, broken by Ferguson Passage. On our frequent night patrols we either entered Blackett Strait via the passage or went further west around Ghizo Island, which marked the southwestern entrance to the strait.

After we'd been heading toward Ferguson Passage for about an hour and were, by my estimate, maybe four or five miles off, we had an "untoward event"—our term for being shot at, bombed, or otherwise molested. A bomb exploded on the water right in the middle of our vee formation. Like most of them at night, it came out of nowhere. Since we were traveling at a cruising speed of twenty-seven knots and showing mile-long wakes, I cursed myself for not having ordered my crew to watch skyward rather than seaward. It was a particularly dark night—no moon and heavy cloud cover—which made me think that a bomb attack was unlikely. I learned later that the Japanese planes had been mustered in force that night for the express purpose of attacking PT boats, so they were flying low, looking for us.

The bomb caused no apparent damage. It had exploded in the exact center of our formation as if the bomber had intended to get all of us with just one bomb. Bomb fragments must have whistled by but the blast itself smothered any other sound. It did unnerve us. The crash of bomb near-misses was very hard on the nerves, more so than shells from ships or shore batteries, because they so often came out of the dark without warning. The lead boat continued on course with the 105 and the 107 on each quarter. We passed through Ferguson Passage at about 2100, slowed to an idling speed of seven knots and began a slow cruise eastward, gradually turning north.

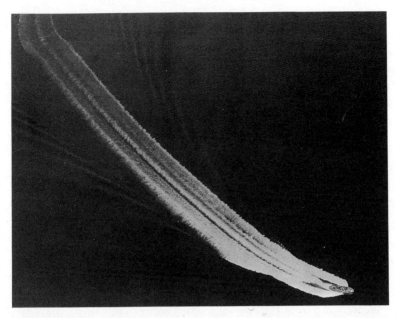

The PT boat's long, fluorescent wake, easily visible to enemy planes and ships at night, explains why Jack Kennedy's PT 109 was running only on its center engine at slow speed when run down by an enemy destroyer. (Fred Freeman Collection, U.S. Naval Institute)

I put the 105's mufflers on. These mufflers, like those on autos except bigger, were attached to the stern and took the engine exhaust downward so it was released underwater. This cut down the decibel level from that of a B-17 bomber to a remarkably subdued bubbling. I liked the mufflers, less for their value in reducing the risk of detection than for increasing our chances of hearing bombers at night. At more than ten knots we changed over (by opening butterfly valves) to allow the exhaust to vent above the waterline. If we failed to do this either the mufflers would have blown off or the exhaust gases would have blown back to kill the engines. I had the wheel. If things started to happen, the few seconds gained by personally being able to go hard over and shove up the throttles might have meant the difference between a hit or a miss for something coming out of the dark.

At this speed I had my center engine in gear and the wing engines idling in neutral. This somewhat reduced my highly phosphorescent wake and therefore the risk of detection from the air. Not by much, mind you, but when the very first out-of-nowhere bomb had missed us on an early mission, a paranoia about light had taken hold: For instance, our compass had no light; the dial was phosphorescent and its faint glow could only be seen by a night bomber if its pilot flew over us ten feet off the deck—and upside down. Even so, we taped the compass so that only a narrow slit showed my heading.

I spent my time keeping station on the division lead boat and staring into the darkness ahead, occasionally glancing to starboard and astern to make sure the deck crew was alert. It was just force of habit, because every man was doing his job. They all knew that every man on the boat depended on every other man. How changed these men were! During our nine months of training I had nagged them incessantly to stay alert. Now I never had to say a word. Three months earlier I'd been overtly obeyed because they knew I was quick to punish; now there was a bond of mutual trust forged by the pressured heat of combat. Why do I call them men? They were "not old enough for a man nor young enough for a boy." I think that's Shakespeare.

We were in a sort of cul-de-sac formed between two small coral islets that lay about one mile to the east and another string of islets two miles to the west, which formed the western boundary of Blackett Strait. Four miles north was Kolombangara. I couldn't see it because the night was so dark, with a heavy cloud cover, no moon—or just a sliver. Which was just fine. I hated the moon; it left us naked to the shore gunners who waited for us to come within killing range, and left us nowhere to hide from the prowling night bombers. Hide? An eighty-foot PT in open water? Yessir, I knew where to hide: under low clouds laden with water. Planes don't like them. Better yet, there was always a rain squall around. I had my eye on one.

This was our first chance to attack using torpedoes. I should have felt excitement but I didn't. For one thing, we'd been out four nights in a row and each time had been cautioned to expect the Japanese navy. All we found were occasional barges trying to sneak supplies into New Georgia. There'd been vicious firefights at close range but nothing remotely of the size worth wasting a torpedo for. And with that last bomb blast still ringing in my ears I was more worried about night-bombers than the much-talked-about-but-never-seen Japanese destroyers. And finally, I was just too tired to waste energy on excitement, I just had to get through the night.

A stray thought had a cheerful tinge to it: we cannot go scooting around too much, or we may scoot up on a reef if we come under attack; on the other hand, enemy destroyers will not try to chase us far because of the same risk posed to them by the reef. And our division leader has the new and magical radar, so all I have to do is stay on his tail like part of a conga line. As I pondered this cheery thought, I heard a burp from the radio. For some reason beyond my subnormal technical mind, our TBS radio always gave a prefatory burp or two before emitting anything intelligible. Often the burp was all it managed because these were tuned frequencies and the bouncing of the boat created tuning problems. This burp alerted us that someone was out there saying something. I heard Ellis in the charthouse as he scrambled to the dial and worked it like a safecracker to find the sender's frequency. He succeeded. The radio blared out in the middle of a sentence delivered in the hysterical tenor of a very frightened someone "under heavy fire-blatt-hiss-blatt-ships-blatt-running." Over the westward horizon lights flashed rapidly; anywhere else those gun flashes might have been sheet lightning. So began what Joe Roberts called "that farce in Blackett Strait."

As Joe says in his poem, the radio was "a screaming fright." Someone was broadcasting to-whom-it-may-concern what he surely believed were his last moments on earth. Mechin crowded next to me to get a look at the flashes. "Shore guns?" he asked. I peered through my binoculars. "Could be. They could be on Vella Lavella." I kept looking westward but with an eye on the lead boat as it continued on course. I waited for him to come up with news on what his radar had picked up. At that close range, his transmission would override that blabber that continued to pour from the radio—now two hysterical tenors competing to describe their last moments.

Our division leader appeared to be increasing speed. In gear went my wing engines, off came my mufflers, and I ticked up my throttles a bit to make sure that I didn't lose him. I noticed Joe Roberts closing the gap on the other wing. Smart guy, Joe, not about to lose contact and spend the rest of the night wondering where the hell he was, and knowing he was as likely to be shot at by us as by them. The radio blather and light flashes stopped just long enough for me to think that whatever had happened to the west was over. Then the flashes started again—much closer, four miles away at most, broad on our port bow—and with them, the crack of shell fire. "Not shore guns!" Mechin and I chanted in unison.

"Prepare for torpedo attack," I called, needlessly since our tubes were already trained out and the torpedoman was standing by with his mallet, ready to fire manually if the electric firing buttons at my right hand failed. Paul Winters, my youngest crew member, was in the starboard gun turret. He raised himself up as far as possible by kneeling on the ammo canisters at my instructions—the better to take advantage of his particularly keen night vision.

The westernmost division leader had made the first contact with the enemy. He led a four-boat division, including Kennedy's 109. When blips appeared on his radar screen, he mistook them for barges and started off on a strafing run, leaving the 109 and another boat in the lurch. His boat and the second boat in his division were greeted by salvos from four Japanese destroyers on their way down Blackett Strait to New Georgia. So the two PT boats fired torpedoes and left the scene. The division leader never rejoined the two boats he had left behind. Since the 109 had no radar and her radio never picked up the panicked transmission that I heard, Kennedy knew even less than I did.

The Japanese destroyers continued down Blackett Strait and appeared on the radar screen of the second division leader, who fired his torpedoes and departed, hitting nothing. The other three boats in his division did not know what was going on until the destroyers opened fire and then it was too late for them to launch their torpedoes. The destroyers kept on down the strait and popped up next on George Cookman's radar. He also led four boats, all from my Squadron Five. His division was south of Ferguson Passage so they were further away from the enemy destroyers than the rest of us. George was one of the best: capable, courageous, and a lot of fun to be around. So when the blips showed up on his screen, what did my hero do? He took off at high speed through Ferguson Passage to join the attack, but he left his three other boats behind! The boat captains sat on their thumbs, wondering where George had gone. Then there was an immense display of pyrotechnics as two destroyers, alerted by his high speed wake, brought George under fire. Since George was only about two miles to the east of me, I could see the destroyers' foredecks pop out of the darkness as their guns flashed and I thought, now, finally, we've got our chance.

We needed more speed to get a good target angle. I pushed up my throttles and drew abreast of the division leader, figuring he would be taking off at high speed to attack. But he held steady at ten knots and I had to pull back. Since the flashing gunfire had stopped about five minutes ago, I could see nothing but blank darkness. I thought I might have lost some night vision from watching the flashes. It doesn't take much light to have this happen. "Winters, do you see anything?" I asked. "No sir," came the reply. "Want me up on the bow?" asked Mechin, who was bouncing up and down on his toes beside me. "No way. Try to keep track of where we are." Mechin needed something to do besides jiggle next to me. As quartermaster, he was the one man who had no set job at general quarters torpedo attack. I noted that I would have to think of something for him to do just so he would stop jiggling.

I looked at the lead boat in astonishment. They were firing their torpedoes! First the starboard aft torpedo whooshed out of its tube, then the starboard forward torpedo. I knew the port torpedoes were fired simultaneously. "Skipper! They fired their fish!" yelled Rabel from the port aft gun turret. "Winters, look off the port bow!" from me. I thought that the leader must have fired at a blip on the radar screen because he had no visual contact, those gun flashes were miles away. "Maybe I should let mine go in the same general direction," I thought. Then: "no, I'll see them in half a mo' and get my own target angle." With our slow twenty-seven knot World War I torpedoes, the lead angle needed to be big, and those destroyers were probably doing thirty knots. My only decent chance for a hit was to get close, something I could never do at our slow speed. As possibles chased each other through my mind, I saw the lead boat turn to port, followed by the 103. Standard procedure called for me to follow the leader so I started putting the wheel over. Then I stopped and pulled my throttles back. I felt the engines go into neutral as the engineer obeyed my bizarre signal ordering all engines out of gear in the near presence of the enemy.

I watched the other two boats disappear in the dark astern heading toward Ferguson Passage. Bright rooster tails fluoresced from their sterns as they went to high speed. A few seconds later the sea was brightly lit around them by exploding bombs. Instantly our radio came alive with a loud-and-clear message from my division leader to base. In the shrill voice of a man gripped by fear he called, "I have fired torpedoes! I am under heavy fire from Jap destroyers! I am under heavy fire! Shells all around me!" Mechin and I looked at each other in astonishment.

"What the hell is he talking about?" I asked no one in particular. None of this made sense. He had just been bombed by planes. Those were bomb bursts, not shells. Bombs make a shattering noise, like a load of glass hitting pavement. Shells go whump, I guess because they tend to explode farther underwater than bombs. Besides, I was between him and the destroyers; I would have heard the shells pass overhead. Then I had the chilling thought that maybe destroyers were sneaking up through Ferguson Passage *behind* us, that maybe I didn't know so much about shell bursts and bomb bursts. I felt Mechin looking at me and Winters looking at me—in fact, the whole crew was looking at me. I had to do something so I grabbed the radio mike: "Oak Leader, this is Oak King. Where is the target, over?" A few seconds of silence followed, during which I assumed that our leader had discovered that I wasn't behind him. Then came the screaming response, "Oak King, get out of there, you're in a trap, you're in a trap! Get out!"

Sparky Ellis had his TBS right on frequency and this forecast of doom was heard by the entire crew, except for Miles down in the engine room, who couldn't hear anything and cared less, just so his engines were giving their usual faultless performance. Mechin echoed my thought, "There must be something astern of us." I thumbed the mike, "Oak Leader, are there targets in Ferguson Passage?" I used "targets" meaning destroyers because even though we had a rudimentary code, with words like "potato" for engine and "crystal ball" for radar, I had forgotten the code word for destroyer. Base command got upset if we called things by their right names. A couple of nights earlier Dave Payne had called me to say that he had to stop because he had a cold "potato." When I'd asked him what was wrong with his potato, he'd replied, "I think it is the fuel pump," which, according to base command, gave the whole thing away. I got blamed along with Dave. Meanwhile, there I was, worried about what to call a destroyer when the whole radio world knew that there were Japanese destroyers and U.S. PT boats having a go at each other in Blackett Strait.

"Oak King get out of there, you're in a trap," resounded from the speaker: The same words, same shrill hysteria. My confusion turned to anger. He had me and my crew in a state of nerves and I was beginning to see what had happened. "That son of a bitch fired his torpedoes and ran," I snarled. "Yeah, skipper," said Mechin in a soothing tone. The last thing he needed was an overwrought captain. He said, "They're up ahead. They didn't fire. Those were bombs." Then came the stunner, a transmission from base command in the dugout on Rendova. Fifty miles from the scene, base command decided to take over; "Oak King, get out of there!" was delivered with measured menace.

I was getting a direct order from base command to carry out the orders of a dingbat who'd done a complete funk, had fired torpedoes from

A bow-deck gunner and an ammo handler look for enemy barges. (Fred Freeman Collection, U.S. Naval Institute)

out of range, and then had run away, leaving me without radar guidance. I could have followed the leader, which was standard operating procedure. I could still do it, turn around and get the hell out. I was under a direct order to do just that from the commander of the whole shebang. But it would be wrong. "Don't do it," I said to myself. "What the hell does he know sitting in a dugout fifty miles away? There are enemy ships to the north of the 105. If I carry out his order I'll miss the chance to do what we came all the way out here to do. But if I don't turn around I may find myself court-martialed. Well now!" That last transmission had been pretty weak. I had heard it, but nobody else could have except for Mechin and Ellis. As long as I gave no "Roger," I could say I never heard the order. I knew that Mechin and Ellis would back me up. To hell with it, I decided, I am going it alone to the north.

"Now stay still, Fear," I said to myself. Never before under fire had that mind-choker struck. Sometimes before a patrol fear grabbed at me but never when I needed to think quickly and coldly. I felt it start, "Hail Mary, pray for us now and at the hour of our death." Fear sank back, grinning. He knew his time would come again. I raised my speed a few knots, compromising between the need to get a decent firing angle and the risk that my wake would call in the bombers.

My thoughts raced: the division leader has drawn the bombers south, maybe they'll stay there. I cringed at the prospect of a flare popping over my head. That's what they'll do—light me up for the destroyers and at the same time kill my night vision. If a flare pops I will crank the wheel, shove up the throttles, and get the hell out—live to fight another day.

There was no flare. This was a new dimension for me, going it alone toward a darkness made complete by the mass of Kolombangara. Anyone between me and that backdrop would see me before I saw them. Maybe they already had; maybe their guns were already training toward me; maybe the first star shell was on its way. "Mechin, give Winters the glasses." Mechin handed the glasses up to Winters, who raised them, began searching, and said calmly, "I see a ship off the port bow." Wordlessly, Mechin took the binoculars back from Winters and handed them to me. We moved around each other, Mechin taking the wheel while I climbed on the side of the gun turret to take a look. Once Winters had shown me the line of sight, I made out a small flurry of white and, a few seconds later, the bow and bridge of a destroyer. She was making thirty knots at a range of a thousand yards, angle on the bow sixty degrees—all wild guesses. She'd open fire any second.

"Come right twenty," I ordered, still watching through the binoculars. Mechin cranked the wheel and the bow swung right. "Steady," I said, and Mechin cranked the other way to bring her back a little. Good enough. I pushed the aft torpedo tube buttons and the torpedoes whooshed out of their tubes into the water. For the first twenty yards I saw their wakes hesitate, wiggle, and then straighten out on the target line. Good for Torpedo Brown. There was no flame from excess oil in the tube to give us away and the gyros had started strong to bring them on course. I was about to press the forward firing buttons but the disappearing image of the torpedo wakes against the now-visible stern wake of the target didn't look good. They were going to miss astern. Firing the other two would be a waste so I decided to wait for a better shot. I yanked the throttles back to bare idling speed but kept the bow on target. My wake could be seen at this range just as I had seen his bow wave before I had seen him. For two minutes I pooped along with all engines idling ahead, a hand on throttles ready to shove them to the wall and go hard over if the enemy opened fire on me. I was watching along the line of my torpedo tracks and hoping against the odds that I would see the flash of a hit. Nothing.

I turned around and headed back toward Ferguson Passage; I was hoping to find my division leader with his radar and to persuade him to be my eyes for another shot. He was likely hanging around at the entrance to the passage. Maybe he had gotten hold of himself and I could coax him back up here. What goes in has to come out and I bet those destroyers would sashay back this way in a couple of hours. With radar we could get our asses up against Kolombangara and they would never see me. How to prevent my division leader from firing at me, though? In his state he would likely take me for the destroyers. I had it! I would break radio silence, which had already been violated like the rape of Nanking. I would tell him that I was coming down the road to join him just like base command wanted me to, thereby solving my legal problem. "You are a smart one, Gunga," I told myself.

As I reached for the mike, the speaker burped and then issued the dumbest order in the entire dumb-ass operation, "Boats that have fired torpedoes return to base. All others return to station." This stupidity meant that the four division leader boats, all of which had fired their torpedoes, went home. That left an assortment of radarless boats groping blindly around Blackett Strait. My plan to get the radar-equipped lead boat to act as my eyes was dead. Oh well, I hadn't had much hope that I could get him to rejoin the war. God! I suddenly thought that maybe I could get Cookman. "Oak George, over." Nothing. Then, "Oak George has gone home. This is Oak Peter, over." That was Dave, floating somewhere south of me. Maybe he had gotten radar in the last day or two and I hadn't noticed. "Have you got a crystal ball?" I asked, not giving my call sign for fear the base command would order me home for a summary court martial. "Negative. All crystal balls rolling home." Dave's resigned tone conveyed his own predicament.

Why in God's name didn't I fire all four torpedoes? I could be on my way back to base. I could get some sleep. What could be better than to flake out next to the port forward torpedo tube? The crew is in as bad shape as I am so there is nothing for it but to look busy. A flare popped overhead. Shit! I was lit up like Macy's window. Reveille Gunga! Get out of here.

It wasn't a star shell, thank God, but a plane up there had spotted my wake. *Varoom* went the 105 as I jammed the throttles up, her stern settling in the water and then kicking up like a crazy drag racer. She went from ten to forty knots in, what, thirty seconds? Time is relative; it seemed like an hour. But I took about as much time thinking about what to do as a chipmunk, racing for his hole ahead of the fox. Once I was seen, I wanted *speed.*

A bomb shattered in my wake fifty yards back. I was running flat out. Where the hell was Ferguson Passage? Somewhere ahead, yes, but there were also dozens of flanking reefs. The passage was only a half-mile across and I could be off on my position by at least a mile. All right, now do what you planned. You've been here before, don't let fear grab you. I crouched down and cranked the wheel hard to starboard. The 105 careened sideways before heading in at ninety degrees to my long, high-speed wake. Then back came my throttles, out of gear went the wing engines, and I coasted out of the flare-light into a dark made even darker by the contrasting light from the flare. The pilots of those planes would see nothing outside the illuminated area. That was my theory, anyway. I heard at least two planes throbbing over the flare but they didn't spot the 105, squatting nearly motionless outside the light. Check my gunners.

With barrels up, all gunners waited to open up on the first shape that appeared overhead. I left it to them. It was better to risk a trigger happy gunner than to have them wait for a command from me; a second in time might be lost and that would be a second too many. I waited in blessed silence long enough to be sure that the planes had wandered elsewhere and then swung into the charthouse. I guessed we were a mile from the Passage. I would go north to the Kolombangara coast and then head east close to the shore line. Those destroyers must have stopped in the narrow strait that separates Kolombangara from New Georgia. Maybe I could get the inshore advantage, see them silhouetted against the sea's horizon instead of the other way round. I had about four miles left to go north.

Back in the cockpit I headed north at a crawl, using only the center engine—anything more and that wake would have brought back those planes. Once they knew I was heading toward their charges, they would never let up. It was about 0200; another twenty minutes and I should be close enough to the shore to turn east. Another fifteen minutes and I should be close to where I thought those destroyers were stopped. If I got a shot at one dead in the water—Winters suddenly hitched up on the gun turret. "Off to starboard! See it? Movin' slow," he half-whispers, as if someone out there might hear him. "Ship. Speed ten knots," from Mechin. "Thirty degrees starboard." I still saw nothing but swung twenty degrees to port so as not to fall behind whatever it was Winters and Mechin saw or thought they saw. It could be an illusion born of a hope that I fire the two remaining torpedoes so we can return to base. Better yet, we go down the line to the Russells for a reload and a beer.

I trained my glasses toward where Winters was pointing, thirty degrees off to starboard, and saw nothing. Well, maybe a blob, but hell, I wanted to get rid of those torpedoes as much as Mechin and Winters did. The blob must have read my mean suspicions. It said, "Here I am," with a flash of its forward turret that revealed the outline of a destroyer from broad on its bow, moving slowly with hardly any bow wave. A whump over my head was followed by a gun-crack, then another flash, and the sea shot up in a white pillar some yards ahead of me. If I was going to fire, it had to be then. I pushed the buttons for the forward torpedoes and waited a long two seconds for them to rush from their tubes into the water. I saw the wake boil up at the stern of the destroyer. The Japanese captain saw me fire, or else he had already decided to go to flank speed, and he opened fire. Until then he had been just creeping along, using the backdrop of Kolombangara for concealment.

As fear nibbled at the nape of my neck, I bent down and cranked the wheel counterclockwise as fast as I could for a port turn. I shifted my right hand to the throttles and started pushing them up gradually. The 105 turned quicker to port than starboard because the clockwise-spinning propellers helped it on a port turn. Briefly I was running in the same direction as the destroyer. He was already walloping along at twenty knots and climbing.

The torpedoes will miss astern. A startled yell from the twenty-millimeter gun crew as a shell whumps over the stern so close they can feel it. God, he'll get us with the next one. Hail Mary, full of grace.

The shells stopped. He either thought the last salvo hit me—the rooster tail of an accelerating PT at night could look like an explosion—or maybe he was afraid of illuminating himself to other PT boats, not knowing it was just me out there for miles around. I was bouncing along at forty knots; then, mindful of the planes up there, I went hard over ninety degrees to the east, where I guessed I would have more running room. Once on the eastern course I did my quick-stop and lay doggo. Sure enough, a flare popped and drifted down my high-speed wake now a couple of hundred yards away. No bombs dropped.

I took a quick bearing, swung into the charthouse, and plotted a course to Ferguson Passage. Then I went back to the cockpit, traded places with Mechin at the wheel, and the 105 was off for home.

"Well, we must have scared them, Skipper," Mechin said, always the one to look on the bright side. I remembered I had sent no contact report so I grabbed the mike and called to anyone who might be listening, "This is Oak King. I have fired at a target. It is going west fast. Over." I waited. Silence. Not even a burp. I tried once more with no response. Mechin said, "Shit, Skipper, we're probably the only ones still out here." I did feel that way. It felt kind of peaceful as we slowly traveled south. I knew I had missed the destroyer astern. His boiling wake told me that my twenty-seven knot torpedoes would find him long gone when they crossed his course, so I didn't even look for a hit. If a miracle happened, the eagerly watching crew would let me know. About ten minutes after contact I saw what looked like a flare that had failed to open burning on the water a few hundred yards away. My right hand went to the throttles. The light flamed up, flickered wildly for a few seconds, then disappeared. "What in the hell was that?" I asked Mechin. He shrugged. I heard no alien sound above us. There was no successive pop of a flare so I stayed on course.

Sunrise 3 August. The 105 returned to Rendova and moored alongside the 106. Dave Payne and I took a whaleboat in for the debriefing. I was more than somewhat worried that the base commander would rise up in his well-known wrath when I reported my solo wanderings and torpedo attacks, all of which were contrary to his commands. I was prepared with my "What message, Commander?" speech, which I had rehearsed with Mechin to get just the right ring of sincere stupidity. But not a word was said. There was a surprising lack of recrimination for what was without question a completely loused-up operation. Thirty torpedoes had been fired without one hit. Some captains claimed hits, but it was clear that no one believed them. I listened to my division leader report that he fired four torpedoes from a thousand yards and observed two hits. Joe Roberts, whose 103 had been right beside the lead boat, said that he had fired at the same time from two miles and had hit nothing. I waited for the intelligence officer to ask how one boat could fire from a thousand yards and another—right next to it— could fire simultaneously from two miles, but all he did was write it down. For once I refrained from educating the assemblage.

In his ode to Gunga Dick, Joe Roberts captures the night in one verse:

> I hope to forget the date
> Of that farce in Blackett Strait
> When the Express was running into PT confusion.
> The radio was a screaming fright
> And the flares a fearful sight,
> So Gunga fired twice to be amusin'.

When the lead boat fired its torpedoes, Joe Roberts and I made split-second, opposite decisions: Joe fired with the leader and I waited. When I had time to think about it, I decided that Joe had been right, much as it pained me to admit it. Eight torpedoes (even at two miles, which was Joe's conservative but more accurate range estimate) created a spread in which a ship should have been hit by at least one torpedo. Maybe one was hit but the damned torpedo just butted the hull and failed to detonate. When I later taught torpedo tactics I emphasized simultaneous attacks by three or more boats, instead of the lone wolf effort that I had made. Of course I continued to dream of the carnage I would have created if the 105 had been able to get up close after those destroyers had stopped.

I had been awake for twenty-four hours. I was beginning to hallucinate from fatigue so when I heard that the 109 had been run down and sunk I thought it was just another dream spinning around the briefing tent. "What boat was that?" I asked the boat captain next to me. "The 109—Kennedy and Thom and Barney Ross." Ross had no boat assignment so he had volunteered to ride with Kennedy. I felt as much shock and grief as my dulled senses would permit. Although none of them were in Squadron Five, I'd known and liked each of them. Intruding on this grief was the thought that this was a lesson to be learned: never volunteer and don't accept volunteers. Barney had volunteered; volunteers bring bad luck.

I listened to the captains of the two boats that had been with the 109. They were remnants of two divisions whose leaders had returned to base, leaving them without radar. The three boats had been puttering around together at the western end of Blackett Strait when a destroyer had come out of the dark at high speed and rammed the 109. All they had seen then was an explosion of flame. Both captains who had seen Kennedy run down said they had fired their torpedoes and escaped under heavy fire. Then I understood the strange flare we had seen. It hadn't been a flare at all, but the 109, some five miles to the west, exploding in flames. My times were only approximate, as were my distances, but I was quite sure the destroyer that had gone to flank-speed to avoid my torpedoes had still been going all-out when it had come out of the blackness and had run over the 109. I had seen no gunfire, however. Our boat captains said they had retired under heavy fire. At that moment I felt too tired to think straight and wondered what difference any of it made, anyhow.

I heard someone say, "Commander, do you want to send some boats back to look?" The commander looked at the two boat captains who'd been with Kennedy and asked, "What do you think?" One of them answered flatly, "Commander, there was nothing left. The boat went up in a ball of flames." The commander then terminated the discussion. Meanwhile, Kennedy and the rest of his surviving crew were left hanging onto the severed bow of the 109, expecting or hoping that we'd come back for them. They had no idea that by 0900 that morning all the boats that had fired torpedoes were on their way back to the Russells for re-arming, and the rest of the boat crews were sound asleep. When Kennedy, Thom, Ross, and the other survivors returned a week later, they came back from "forgotten land." During that week I never thought of them nor were they ever mentioned. This was normal; when a man died in combat, he was banished from mind and conversation as if he'd never lived. It made no difference even if he'd been a close friend. Kennedy, Thom, and Ross had been consigned to the dead.

I saw a lot of all three men after their ordeal. I never heard one of them say anything about the fact that no one came back to look for them. The morning they came back, I went to the sick bay to visit Barney Ross, who was being treated for various burns, cuts, and sores. Barney was being interviewed by reporters. He had an unflagging sense of the ridiculous and described scenes of impossible derring-do, which the reporters might have believed except for the laughter from the boat captains around him. Dave Payne told me that, on that first morning, he had heard Jack Kennedy berate one of the boat captains for leaving him, but I think this brief flare-up was the end of the matter as far as Jack was concerned.

The tragedy of the 109 was not that she was lost, and certainly not that blame could be attached to Jack Kennedy or any of his crew. On the contrary, the 109, although completely out of the loop because its radio did not pick up the brief and garbled radio messages, went to where the action was. If luck had not chosen to put the 109 directly in the path of the onrushing Japanese destroyer, if the 109 had been a few hundred yards to either side, then that Japanese destroyer might have been the victim of the 109, instead of the other way around.

The tragedy was that the comrades of the 109 did not go back to look for survivors, even though we saw the search as hopeless. We had not yet learned that hopeless searches should still be made, so that those of us who still had to go out night after night would know that, if we did not return, our comrades would look for us and would fight to save us beyond any reasonable expectation.

We should have gone back.

THE
TWENTY-YARD
SHOOT-OUTS

Who would have thought that a boat carrying three thousand gallons of gasoline, with no armor and guns intended for defense against aircraft, would do most of its fighting in point-blank battles like the *Monitor* and *Merrimac?* Certainly not the designers of the PT boat, and certainly not me. After the campaigns in the Philippines and Guadalcanal, PT boats became mostly gunboats—a mission for which they were dramatically unsuited. During my training days, when I daydreamed of my role in things to come, I saw myself in grommetless cap like some flying ace, gallantly saluting the bridge of the flagship as I roared toward a distant line of enemy battleships. Incidentally, I always saw myself coming back triumphant. In reality—except for one night when I fired torpedoes fruitlessly at barely seen Japanese destroyers—my sea battles turned out to be quick and nasty nighttime firefights against Japanese barges.

How they came to be called barges I never knew. They were mainly amphibious craft about sixty feet long, with a low freeboard but still capable of making quite long interisland trips. Thousands of them were increasingly used to transport men and material after the Japanese had lost control of the seas and could no longer risk regular transports. Our first encounters with barges were unexpected. We were looking for either transports or destroyers, which had been the usual torpedo targets at Guadalcanal. Instead we found from two to a dozen low-slung, shallow-draft little craft against which torpedoes were useless. I think I was in the first battle with barges that was finally more than a sudden and inconclusive burst of gunfire followed by each side losing the other in the dark; it was a bad night.

Our squadron exec was George Cookman, Yale '37, captain of the Yale squash team, and my idea of the complete PT officer. Like most of us, he was arrogant, but he reserved his arrogance for the poker table, darts, and the like. In squadron matters, I never heard him do anything more than make suggestions, which we boat captains followed because we respected his ability. While making my way down to the dock for the night's patrol on 5 August, two nights after the Blackett Strait battle, I was surprised to find George walking alongside me. He had been out the night before, so this should have been his night off. "Where are you going?" I asked grumpily. I didn't mean to be grumpy but I was so tired that's the way everything came out. "On patrol with you, old pal," came the reply. "You were out last night." George grinned at me: "Sure, but I like to go out. Besides, somebody has to keep you off the reefs." He was referring to my idiotic running aground a month or so earlier. I gave a grouchy "Fapp!" and we got in the whaleboat. George got off at a Squadron Nine boat, captained by Bill Battle—normally he would have ridden in one of his own squadron boats, probably mine, but he was a last-minute volunteer substitute for another division leader who said he had a stomachache. I solemnly said that I thought I had a stomachache coming on, too. George laughed. That's the last memory I have of him.

George had our four boats patrolling in column, and the 105 was second behind him. We were moving slowly up Blackett Strait, with no mission except to shoot at anything we saw. After the wild torpedo action a few nights before, we were looking for more Japanese destroyers. George's boat was the only one with radar so he made the first contact. "I have targets," he said quietly over the radio. I then called general quarters, also quietly, and Mechin repeated it after dashing to the stern.

A PT boat crew discusses operations onshore before a night mission. (Fred Freeman Collection, U.S. Naval Institute)

In less than twenty seconds the off-watch, who'd been flaked-out on deck, were up and at their places for the expected torpedo attack. After half a minute, George came back again, "The targets are barges, half a dozen. We are attacking with guns." Hearing this, Torpedo Brown moved from his position next to the starboard forward tube to the starboard gun turret, replacing the less-experienced Winters.

I moved the throttles up slowly but George was increasing his distance from me, a bright rooster tail flaring up at his stern. I jammed the throttles to the wall, risking a crap-out rather than lose him. Even so, the interval between my boat and his had become a good five boat lengths; I kept willing the 105 to get up to speed. We had never discussed gun attacks but it made sense to get right up on his tail so that my guns could open up with his. Abruptly the darkness ahead lit up in crisscrossing streams of tracer fire, with George's boat right in the center: He'd run into the middle of a column of barges. (I felt as if I were in a bad dream, where I was running in place.) I saw him being destroyed and could not seem to move. I thought that the fire from both sides would ignite his gas tanks at any moment and he would disappear

A gunner in a port twin fifty-millimeter turret checks his weapon before a night patrol. (U.S. Naval Institute photo collection)

in a ball of flame. The next thing I knew, his boat, or its wake—which was all I could see—disappeared on the other side of the barges.

By the time the 105 caught up, all of the barges appeared to have crossed my bow. I saw the stern of one disappearing in the dark on my port side and yelled, "Open fire!" My port fifty-caliber turret opened up on the retreating barge. My starboard turret gunner could not fire at a surface target to port but he opened up on his own side, spraying the night in case there was something out there he could not see. Nothing came from the stern twenty millimeter. "Open fire!" I screamed, "Mechin, get back there! Tell them!" Mechin scrambled back and yelled at the gunner. I could see he was aiming but not firing. My port gunner was now full on the barge, which started emitting sparks like a Roman candle. A good dose from the stern twenty millimeter and we had him for sure. But where was the twenty millimeter? Mechin was back, saying, "He thinks it's one of ours." I was enraged that anyone would question an order at a time like this. "Dammit, Mechin, tell him to open fire!" I yelled. Mechin scuttled back and the gunner opened up with a halfhearted burst but the target had disappeared.

The 105 was now either through the enemy column or across the tail of it. We were right on George's stern, so I eased back. The two boats following us had lost even more distance and were completely out of the action. Surprisingly, George's boat looked okay. I expected him to come about to pursue the barges but the boat continued on for about five minutes. Then Bill Battle's voice came up on the radio, "Charlie Two, this is Battle, over." Although his voice was calm, I knew that not hearing George's voice meant problems. "I hear you five by five, over," I replied. "Charlie Two from Battle. Take command of the division. We have casualties. Returning to base. Over." The heavy fire from the Japanese barges had obviously hit home. "Roger, wilco," I acknowledged. I began calling the other boats, "Charlie Div, come in please." Being experienced boat captains, they replied in order so as not to blank each other out. "We are going barge hunting," I told them. I didn't know the other two captains or they me, but each replied with a reassuringly emphatic "Roger."

I turned around and headed back. It was my first job as a division leader and I decided to do it my way. When I looked back and saw the two boats spaced at three boat-lengths away, I came up on the radio again, "Close up, please." That was the first and only time I used "Please." They got up so close that the bow of the second boat loomed over my stern and I saw the third board jamming up tight. These men were good boat captains. They were not about to miss out the second time. Satisfied that anything that showed up would get a terminal blast, I swung down into the charthouse. During the last ten minutes I had been following George blindly, so I needed a better fix on where I was and a course back to where the barges might be. I noted my approximate position and grabbed the parallel rulers to plot my course. That's when I learned that I had a *problem.*

My hands shook! I couldn't hold the rulers steady! I looked in disbelief at my hands, which seemed to have separated themselves from me. I didn't feel scared or even nervous, but my hands were terrified. "What do I do now?" I thought. My boat exec was a "bum of the night" replacing my regular exec, who'd been killed a few nights ago. Mechin could lay on a course but I couldn't let him see my shaky hands; whatever else he thought of me, he had to believe that I was a cool customer in combat, otherwise the 105 would fall apart. "To hell with it, eyeball a course!" I muttered to myself, "There's plenty of water around us and you couldn't plot an interception course within twenty degrees anyway." I climbed back into the cockpit and set a course a bit to starboard of the reciprocal course we'd been on when we ran into the barges.

I increased speed to twenty-five knots, heedless that the wake might attract night-bombers; the gunfire of ten minutes ago would have brought them if they were anywhere around. We searched the area for the rest of the night. I was sure at least one barge was probably dead in the water but we found nothing. Where in the hell could half a dozen barges have gone like that? They probably laid doggo, and with their low silhouettes, we probably went right by them, maybe a couple of times. Frustrated and angry, I called off the search and headed home while there was still an hour of darkness left. Because fliers on either side tended to shoot first and ask questions later, we had to clear the area before pilots could see us.

I called the twenty-millimeter gunner to the cockpit on the way back. I was at the wheel and did not look at him, but I could tell he was tense. Slowly and precisely, to be sure he understood each word, I said, "Do not ever again fail to fire when I say fire. I don't give a shit what you think you see. Fire on it!" I waited for him to say he thought it was a PT and to ask whether he should fire at something he knows is ours. There was silence. I thought he was concocting an excuse or he was expecting me to say more—because I usually did. Finally he said, "Okay, Skipper." We left it at that. He was a good man. I had some misgivings and wondered whether he had frozen through fear, stress, or whatever causes buck fever. But he never again failed me, even when the 105 fired at a U.S. Corsair that had changed course to fly right at us and then changed course again when the pilot saw our tracers arcing toward him.

We got in at daylight and I stopped at the fuel dock before going in for the debriefing. I was down in the charthouse rolling up a chart when someone stuck his head in the door and said, "Mr. Cookman is dead." I did not look up. I turned and dropped down the ladder to belowdecks and sat at my wardroom table. I was paralyzed by fear, not grief, at losing one of my closest friends. Fear had shoved grief aside. Fear whispered, "If it can happen to him, it can happen to you." George Cookman had seemed invulnerable. He was one of very few men I had met who seemed born to lead. If a bullet or bomb could find him, one of them could sure find me. I sat and stared at the table. Two nights before I had lost Phil Hornbrook, the 105's exec and I was still trying to cope with his death, which might have been avoided had I listened.

We'd been returning from the night's patrol. The 105 was tail-end-Charlie in a four-boat division led by George Cookman, riding in Dave Payne's boat. Phil had the wheel and I was standing next to him. The patrol had been uneventful and I was looking forward to the next night off. A new engine sound intruded on my thoughts. There was, of course, always engine sound on a PT boat but this sound was different. Perhaps somebody had opened the engine room hatch. I wasn't really listening. I was thinking about getting back to base and then there was a blinding light, followed a millisecond later by a shattering crash and concussion. I did not see Phil drop from the wheel, the space next to me was simply empty. Phil was on the deck behind me, screaming, "My legs! I can't feel my legs!" I reflexively stepped to the left, took the wheel, steadied the boat on course, and told Mechin to check the stern for casualties. I knew that the bomb had exploded off our starboard quarter. Incredibly, no one at the stern twenty millimeter was hit. Phil was our only casualty and he died minutes after the bomb hit. Torpedo Brown picked him up off the cockpit deck and stretched him out on the dayroom canopy. After I was certain the plane was not going to make another pass, I turned over the wheel to Mechin and stepped back to see about Phil. I put my ear to his chest and heard no heart beat. I couldn't think of anything else, so I held his hand and said the Lord's Prayer.

Afterward I went through my usual process of figuring out what went wrong and decided that I had not listened. If I had been listening, I would have known in an instant that the sound I heard was not the 105's engines but the sound of a bomber flying up our wake. I counted out the interval between when I first heard the sound to the bomb blast—it was five or six seconds, time enough to yell "hard left," and for Phil to whip the wheel over, moving the 105 a few feet away. I was still blaming myself about losing Phil when I found myself confronted by the loss of George Cookman. I grieved for Phil but did not connect his fate with mine. On the other hand, once death had happened to George Cookman, I felt it staring me in the face. The statistics also looked bad, two squadron officers gone in how much time, three nights? Or was it two? I could not keep track. At this rate my chances for survival looked slim.

After awhile I got up from the table and went ashore to the debriefing. I stayed outside the tent until Bill Battle had completed his account of the devastation that occurred when the enemy crossfire ripped his boat. When it was my turn, I could see the base commander was shaken by what appeared to be a clear defeat in the first real test of PTs against barges. My account of seeing the stern of a retreating barge blown apart by my port fifty-caliber guns openly produced a few skeptical grunts, then the conversation turned to installing heavier armament. We received no credit for a barge. So many tales of torpedo hits

PT boat and crew at the dock. Note boats tied up under trees for concealment. (U.S. Naval Institute photo collection)

by PTs in the early days of the Philippines and Guadalcanal had turned out to be hallucinations that it was assumed we were making things up. Later in the war, I read reports based on captured enemy documents which showed that PT boats did far more damage in barge battle than we were given credit for. One reason why the Japanese sent bombers out on nightly runs against PT boats was that they were seeking to protect their convoys against what they called "devil boats."

Battle and I talked briefly later. It startled me to realize that here was a man who had had half of his crew either killed or wounded and he was trying to comfort me for the loss of my friend. Bill told me that George had been standing on the cockpit step, the highest place in the boat, so he could see better. Most gunfire at night was high, at least for the first few seconds, and it caught George first. Well, I knew one way to exorcise his ghost. I joined the other boat captains in Doc Freeto's tent, where Father Giles Webster was doling out alky screamers like communion wine.

I was just settling in when the base radar officer came into the tent with the news that he had seen George's helmet and it was "just full of holes and we should come take a look." Except for a sharply indrawn breath, there was a moment of silence before someone said, "Why don't you mail it home to his family?" I watched the radar officer consider this suggestion and come to the realization that he had said the wrong thing at the wrong time to the wrong people. He turned and left. He was a good radar officer who did a splendid job. He must have led a miserable, lonely life because he was not accepted into our lives. I did not think for a moment that he understood that we were all frightened by a bullet-riddled, blood- and brain-splattered helmet. What he saw was a group of hard-faced, cold-eyed PT captains sitting on cots, sipping alcohol and grapefruit juice, and bantering with a big Franciscan priest-bartender.

It was now an hour since I'd come in and I was acquiring a mild buzz from Doc Freeto's screamers when my problems got worse. The junior base doctor came into the tent and asked if he could speak to me in private. We stepped outside, where he told me, "Your man Smith has combat fatigue and I've had to take him off the 105." I reacted sharply, "What in the hell are you talking about?" I was angry that any doctor would think he could interfere with my boat at all, no less remove one of my best men. "Where is he? Let me talk to him." Here I was, just getting past George Cookman, beginning to feel I could manage my-self, and I hear this hokum that Smith has combat fatigue. He was the steadiest man on the boat. We had been together more than a year and he'd already proved himself in combat.

The doctor took me over to an isolated tent where Smith was sitting with a base staff officer and a couple of pharmacist's mates. Nowhere in training had there been any lessons on what to do when you're faced with a man who is too scared to fight but can still function. I knew what people with combat fatigue looked like; they were clearly unfit. Some went into a trancelike state where they sat and stared vacantly. Others hallucinated. One officer had begun sleeping in the charthouse, cra-dling a submachine gun with the safety off. Another had begun digging a foxhole and had dug himself in over his head before they got him. In other words, these were clear nut cases. But Smith was quite rational. I could see he was listening to what I said, which was mostly a Knute-Rockne-style pep talk about not letting the good ole 105 down. I end-ed by saying, "Let's try one more time, Smitty." He turned to look at me and said evenly, "I will not go out."

Rage began building up in me. I could lose my crew if this man stayed on the beach. I felt the forty-five on my leg. It seemed to say "Put me to his head and he'll go out." I turned to the base officer and the doctor and said, "I need this man. There's nothing wrong with him." What I meant was that if he was taken off the boat everyone else would put in for combat fatigue. Unfortunately, I was not articulate; I was too tired and scared to be articulate. The doctor looked at the base staff officer and shook his head. The base officer closed the matter by saying, "We'll send out a replacement from the base torpedo force."

I took a whaleboat out to the 105 and said as casually as I could that Smith was off the boat and that we were getting a replacement. It was not news to them. There was no comment except a halfhearted attempt at humor by Mechin who said, "Skipper, how do I get this combat fatigue? Sounds like a good deal." Gunner Brown answered, "You're too stupid, Mechin."

I was trying to think up something reassuring to say when a whale-boat drew alongside and Willie Monk, torpedoman first class, busted to third class for various crimes and misdemeanors committed in Pana-ma, stepped aboard the 105. A big grin lit up his face and in his bayou country drawl he said, "Ain't you fellas lucky, though? You got me, Willie Monk." The cheers that went up startled the crew on the 106 and they all came over to see what was going on. The wonderful Willie Monk saved my day. He had been languishing in sullen discontent on the beach, so coming aboard the 105 was a great prize for him. His swaggering enthusiasm affected the rest of the crew. They forgot Smith and I forgot George Cookman, my friend who had stood in the highest place.

I did not forget, however, that George had gotten up on that cockpit step, had stood as high as he could in order to see everything, and had been cut down by the first burst of high fire. I believed deeply in learning from mistakes made in any combat action or untoward event. I sat down and tried to figure out for myself what I had done wrong and what I could do better. The first lesson from last night's barge fight was, do not stand any higher than you have to. After that first firefight, whenever we tangled with barges I went into a half-stoop, still on my feet and still able to see what I needed to, but reducing my natural height by a foot. I must have looked as if I was craning forward in order to see the enemy better, but I was simply lowering my head to avoid the high fire. The snickering noise of bullets over my head confirmed my theory.

The second lesson learned was to keep my boats very close, much closer than what we had considered a prudent standard distance at night. I accepted the risk of collision in order to maximize firepower during the first few seconds of combat, because that's when it all happened. Barge fighting was like the shoot-out at the OK Corral: We won or we lost in a hurry. Unlike most other warships, we had no armor and sat on up to three thousand gallons of gasoline. That is why I called barge fights "twenty-yard shoot-outs." We had to get close, real close, quickly, for maximum effect. A tracer or red-hot bullet in gasoline vapor can cause an explosion just as easily at a hundred yards as at twenty.

I also adopted the echelon formation in place of a column. My theory was based on the fact that the barges were usually close inshore: the instant they caught sight of us, they would turn and run at right angles toward the beach; I would then deploy my boats, in echelon formation, in the direction that they ran so that each boat closed the range. Joe Burk improved on this tactic over in New Guinea. He would lurk within a few feet of shore, invisible against the land background, and wait for the barges. He terminated more than thirty this way. Joe had a high tolerance for risk. One night he got stuck on a reef and went down himself to free an embedded propeller. The Japanese sent out an armed barge to destroy his boat; Joe climbed back aboard and destroyed the enemy barge while still aground. He then dove back under his PT, freed the propeller, and went home. That was Joe Burk, the greatest gunboat captain since John Paul Jones. This was Gunga Dick, ordinary mortal.

PTs seldom operated alone. They patrolled in divisions of two to four boats. I once tried to lead a division of six boats, but it was a complete bollocks because one or more of the boats kept going off frequency. Division leaders were experienced boat captains who were promoted off of their boats to lead divisions. I put in about fifteen patrols before I got promoted. Curiously, I was promoted soon after I had done the type of complete balls-up that I feared would again put me in line for laundry officer.

Two divisions of three boats each had gone up to Vila Gulf looking for something to shoot at. The 105 was a wing boat in Division B. Once we got up to Vila Gulf, both divisions stopped; I assumed that the leaders were figuring out what to do next. We floated around for quite some time, enough time to become bored with just leaning against the cockpit, watching my division leader's boat. I relieved my boredom by studying the dark masses of islands around us and speculating whether they might contain shore guns. By taking my eyes off my lead boat, I was about to learn the delusional aspect of relative bearings (a relative bearing is the angle of an object off the bow). In my case, as the starboard wing boat, the division leader's boat should normally have been about forty-five degrees off my port bow while we were under way. But we were not under way, we were stopped, just floating around, and our relative bearings changed aimlessly as the sea moved the boats this way and that.

Suddenly the two division leaders sent terse radio commands to get under way. I joined up on what I thought was my division leader's boat, the boat that was forty-five or so degrees off my port bow. As bad luck would have it, the boat I followed was not the leader of Division B but the leader of Division A. While I'd been speculating on the contents of nearby islands, the drifting 105 had changed her heading, so that the lead boats had changed places relative to her bow. Against all reasonable odds, the boat captain of the starboard wing boat of Division A made the identical mistake. So, instead of being rudely shoved aside so that I could scurry after my own division leader, I joined the wrong division unchallenged. These were long odds, that two boats in two divisions had made the exact same mistake—odds about as long as the possibility of running aground on the only marked reef in the Solomon Islands! When both divisions started out on separate patrols, the one I was in headed to the west, the other to the east, and both division leaders went into column formation at idling speed. I took my usual third place in line as befitted the starboard wing boat. My doppelganger was also running as third boat in my place. If nothing untoward had occurred that night, no one would have been the wiser, but, of course, it did.

About ten minutes elapsed before my original division leader came up on the radio with a barge contact, a good one, three barges in open water miles from shore. I was exhilarated and so was my crew. This was our first good contact since the night we had lost George Cookman. We'd been shot at and bombed, and now it was our turn to do some damage. I started moving up on the boat ahead of me to make sure I didn't lose him when our division went to attack speed. Nothing happened ahead of me.

I thought this fellow, the division leader, is going in too slowly, I hope he doesn't lose the target. Just as I thought this, my rightful division leader's unmistakable voice came on the air, "Baker Charlie, close-up!" I wondered, "What is the man talking about? I *am* closed up." To satisfy him, I moved even closer to the second boat, so close that I could almost see the worried look of the stern gunner as my bow loomed over him. Again, I heard the voice of my division leader: "We are on target. Baker Charlie, close-up!" Simultaneously I saw the eruption of tracer fire about three miles to the east. Then the dreadful truth danced in those flashes on the horizon: I had joined the wrong division. I watched the intense but brief exchange of fire and thought, "You've done it this time."

For the rest of the night's patrol during which we wandered fruitlessly around and then returned to base empty-handed shortly before dawn, I agonized over my stupidity. I could feel the frustration of my crew. My worries became more extreme as the hours wore on until, finally, I saw myself standing at attention in front of the entire base while the base commander handed me a white feather (the Victorian symbol of cowardice) and pointed in the direction of the laundry—or rather its future location, since there was no laundry.

The two divisions returned to base separately, and I found myself in the whaleboat with the two boat captains and the leader of the wrong division. We rode into the base in silence. I expected that any moment the division leader would say to me "How did you get here?" He said nothing so I said nothing. Division leaders sometimes did not know which boat captains were in their divisions. Could it be that he did not know that I was supposed to be with the other division?

When I took my place at the debriefing, I sat with the people I came in with. The boat captain of the boat I had changed places with was already seated with the other division. He looked over at me unhappily. I thought for a moment he was going to get up and change places with me, but, after a move in my direction, he remained where he was.

The division leader who had led the barge attack reported good results, which he said would have been better if his third boat had not lagged so far behind that he never got in a shot. He then delivered a lecture on station-keeping to the unfortunate boat captain who had taken my place. The leader of the division I had erroneously joined, added to the lecture, "You should take a lesson from Keresey, here. He stays real close!"

I thought, they have no idea that the two of us changed places and I am not about to tell them. The other boat captain apparently decided that the heat he was now taking was less than it would be if he confessed to the switch, so he too remained silent. The lesson I learned from this is that mistakes sometimes correct themselves if you keep your mouth shut. A few days later I was elevated to division leader.

It was not unusual for boats in the same division to be strangers to each other and to their division leader. This had been the case in the Blackett Strait battle in which JFK's 109 had been lost and I think it was a major cause of the wholesale debacle that night. The notion of leading a patrol without first meeting with the boat captains did not appeal to me. After finding out in each briefing what boats I was to lead, I scurried about gathering my boat captains for a skull session. Among the patrols that I led, one stands out because we almost carried out a coordinated attack using four boats—without a foul up. We only had a few minutes together before we went out, long enough to explain my echelon theory and to emphasize the importance of staying less than a boat-length apart. They surprised me. "Gotcha." "Will do." "I'll be right on your ass, Gunga." They were just as sick of the screwed-up, every-man-for-himself attacks as I was.

Barge sightings were sparse. The Cookman action and others had caused the barge convoys to change their routes to avoid us. They also ran as close to the beach as possible, so that even our radar could not pick them up. Luckily, that night we caught two barges sneaking down the coast. The radar picked up two blips as the barges came around a point with the open sea at their backs. They were still two thousand yards distant. I came up on the radio: "I have targets, two barges, two thousand yards dead ahead. Over." From my other three boats came a quick, "Roger. Over." I decided to take the barges to starboard, which put us on the seaward side. The barges would be able to see us better than we could see them but there wasn't enough room inboard to come at them in an echelon—and that was what I had told these boat captains I was going to do. I thumbed the mike and gave the order, "Echelon right, echelon right. Execute." I watched the three following boats smoothly fan out in a forty-five degree angle toward the nearby shore. The last boat couldn't have been more than fifty yards off the beach, but the captain didn't appear deterred by the obvious risk. I swear that guy would have tried running along the beach to keep his assigned position.

"I am increasing speed. I am increasing speed." Most of us repeated orders because the first few transmitted words sometimes weren't heard. I also used a sing-song with a high-low tune on the last two words; I thought it made me sound calmer than I was.

I gradually got up to full speed. We must have been clearly visible to the barges and we had to reach them before they got to the beach. We closed with them in what seemed like seconds, and my bow and starboard fifty-millimeter guns got on them, followed by the stern twenty millimeter. Joe Roberts took the wheel while I crouched beside the starboard turret, watching the barges. There were flashes of return fire but, instead of using a machine gun, they seemed to be using rifles. We were past them and turning when the other boats in my division passed inboard of the barges and opened fire to seaward. I had not figured on this. The barges hadn't turned and run for the beach or, if they had, we had come at them too close together for them to cover any distance. When the fourth boat came out from behind the barges, he found himself abeam of what he thought was another barge, but it was actually the third boat, lagging behind with an engine that overheated or froze up just as we started our attack. That boat should have dropped out but, as the boat captain told me later, "After all that stuff about fighting as a team, I wasn't about to do that. Just as we got abeam of the barges the goddam engine melted." Following the maxim that said to fire at anything that wasn't where it should be, my fourth boat gave the third a brief dose of fire. Fortunately there was no harm done, other than making a mess of bullet holes for the base carpenters to plug.

In the meantime I brought my boats in a tight circle, preparing to come in again. We were now three—the third boat's captain had to stand and watch. I was quite sure that our first run had demolished the barges; I'd seen debris fly into the air from the brutal impact of fifty-caliber bullets. I still wanted to get confirmation by picking up debris. Unfortunately, the fireworks brought in an enemy bomber. Any remaining night vision disappeared in the glare of exploding bombs, all of which missed but turned my attention from the barges to this more immediate threat. My boat and the two following boats let off streams of fire into the night sky and the disabled boat pugnaciously joined in as if to say, "Try me." After turning a full circle while staring skyward, I went to idling speed. My two remaining boats followed my every move as if attached to me by strings. Eventually the third boat limped up with its bad engine and we went home.

Base command did not give us credit for the barges because we had no debris and thus no confirmation. However, once again we learned something useful. The captain of the boat with the bad engine said, "Those barges had a gunboat with them! God, what firepower! Must have had sixteen guns. We gotta get bigger guns or somethin'." Gunboat? I hadn't seen any gunboat. As if on cue, his engineer walked in with a handful of made-in-America fifty-caliber slugs he'd picked out of the boat. He held them out for all to see. Everybody laughed. Not only had the fourth boat briefly mistaken the third boat for a barge, the third boat had seen an enemy gunboat. That incident taught us that the firepower of a PT boat was fearsome. It also showed us that we had boats that could fight in close. I had seen this proved a few nights before as well, when I had still been captain of the 105.

I was still without a regular exec, going out on patrols with a different second officer every time and finding out that they were a mostly useless and obviously scared bunch. After Phil had been killed, the 105 had acquired a reputation of being unsafe. On that night I had the singular good fortune to have Finn Percy along as my temporary exec. My crew didn't trust Percy any more than they had trusted the other execs, but there were two differences: Finn was not scared, and he was very good company.

Percy was from an old southern family, with all the charm, good looks and dashing courage that goes with that tradition. I could imagine his great-granddad leading the charge at Bull Run and tripping over his sword. I was delighted to have Percy's company and, on our way up to station, I listened with pleasure to his chitchat. I think Finn was pleased to be on the 105 for the very reason that others were not: he liked the fact that the 105 stepped in it more often than most.

The 105 was second boat in a three-boat division. Sid Hix in the *Li'l Duck* was number three. The division was led by a squadron commander. Another senior officer was also aboard the lead boat. He had led divisions himself, many times; he was competent and very popular among the boat captains, and I was puzzled why he was on this patrol as an observer. It was bad luck to have an observer along and, besides, this was just a usual look-and-shoot patrol.

We were in waters south of Vella Lavella when the division leader spotted a small interisland freighter going north. He gave one warble on the radio announcing that he had a target, and took off at full speed. I jammed my throttles up, losing a hundred yards but easily keeping him in sight. Sid Hix (in the third boat) lost us completely. The division leader had just turned a three boat division into two. We could just make out the blob in the dark ahead of the lead boat. I saw we had a stern chase and plenty of time, since a ship like that couldn't do better than ten knots. Finn was excitedly jumping up and down next to me, as if he were watching a Tulane football game. "Let's fire a torpedo," he said. "Finn," I explained, "we have a stern chase. We'd never hit it." Normally I responded to suggestions from execs with a snarl but this time, it was happily different—here was a guy who at least wanted to fight the war. Then the little freighter opened up with what seemed to be the biggest gun ever put on a ship that size.

The Japanese ship began throwing shells with an astoundingly flat trajectory, almost like a German eighty-eight millimeter. The shells came right at us every five or six seconds, looking like red balls of fire. They passed over the lead boat and then whumped over me. There was a big flash on the lead boat. "He's hit!" yelled Finn in the tone a fan uses when a pass has been intercepted. I had slowly closed and was able to see the lead boat clearly. It didn't appear to be damaged. "Lookit that, Skipper," yelled Willie Monk, "too much oil in the tubes." The lead boat had fired a torpedo and Willie knew the flash we'd seen was caused by excess oil igniting in the tube. He was letting me know that such a thing would not happen on the 105. I was still closing my interval when a huge waterspout erupted in front of me. My bow rose up in the air as if the 105 was trying to stand on its stern, and a shock wave rattled my teeth. "Christ Almighty, he got hit," I thought, half-stunned. When the geyser of water collapsed, it revealed the lead boat intact and charging along. "What was that?" asked Percy. "I'll tell you what that was," yelled Willie Monk, "that was a depth charge!"

If I had been successful in closing with the lead boat, the 105 would have been destroyed. What a stupid way to go, I thought. When his torpedo had—not surprisingly—missed, it had suddenly occurred to the division leader to drop a depth charge under the freighter as his boat went by it. This was a good idea all right, but he dropped it too soon. My guess was that it missed the bottom of the freighter by fifty yards and the bottom of the 105 by twenty-five yards. It did have unexpected results.

The deck gun stopped firing, whereupon the lead boat drew alongside, gave her a blast, and kept on going. I had pulled back on my throttles after the close call with the depth charge because I was afraid he would drop another. Fortunately he did not, but it meant that my speed was just above idle when I came alongside the freighter. For the next half minute the 105 and the freighter went at each other like the *Monitor* and the *Merrimac*. Most of the fire was coming from the 105. The lead boat had taken the brunt of the freighter's small-arms fire but we were in too close for their deck gun to get on us. Willie Monk in the starboard turret had his twin-fifties dismantling the deck cabin and the twenty-millimeter gunner was dosing the freighter's stern area, where the deck gun was located. Rabel on the bow had swung his single fifty-caliber gun around to get at the bow of the freighter. I hoped he didn't get too enthusiastic because the jury-rigged gun had no stop on it and could swivel far enough to do us in, too.

Frankly, I wasn't doing much thinking at all. I was watching in stunned amazement as streams of fire took the freighter's deckhouse apart. Monk's gun barrels glowed red and I noticed a flicker of flame in the ammo canister. Monk held the guns on target with one hand and slapped at the flames, yelling, "Hey Skipper, lookit this!" He wanted me to observe that he was on fire—the thin coating of oil on the ammo had ignited from the red-hot guns. Very interesting, Willie. Zichella

stood in a wobbling crouch on the side of the turret and indiscrimi-
nately whacked at the flames and Willie. This was well beyond my
learning. Nothing in the books had said that ammunition could catch
fire if you kept firing the fifty-calibers long enough. Zichella doused
Monk with a bucket of water. I wondered where the hell he'd found the
bucket; a lot of things went on in the 105 that I didn't know about.

I did not want to be caught alongside the freighter when the ammo
in the turret canisters ran out. We had spares, but fitting them took a
good half minute, during which we'd just be sitting there. I pushed the
throttles up and headed for the lead boat, which was halfway through
a circle about a quarter mile out, apparently ready to make another run.
By now he'd probably realized that he'd almost blown me up but I came
up on the radio anyway: "Charlie One, watch the depth charges. I'm
right behind you." There was a moment's silence, then, " Charlie Two,
disengage." I pulled back to watch the lead boat make another run.
This gave me time to replenish the ammo so that I could make a second run after the leader had done his bit and was somewhere else. We
had not reckoned on Sid Hix, who'd been wandering around looking
for us.

When he saw the shooting start, Sid headed for the action at full
speed. As he began to close in after the leader's second run, the sea
around him lit up with the glare of exploding bombs. This you could
count on: Japanese bombers cruised around with the specific mission
of breaking up our attacks on barges, and they were usually successful;
one run was often all we could get in before the bombers spotted us.
After that we would be looking and firing skyward, to contend with this
always dangerous menace. Sid's boat was brightly lit by the explosions
but all the bombs missed. When the last bomb had come down, I could
see him nosing in to the freighter. "It's on a reef," radioed Hix. "Do
not approach. I am backing down. No sign of people aboard." The occupants of the freighter had gone over the side and taken off for the
beach of Vella Lavella about a quarter mile distant. Since it was very
dark out there, I didn't see any of this, but a friend of mine did. He happened to be sitting on the beach watching the show.

About a week later when I made a midnight run up to a cove on Vella Lavella, which was still in Japanese hands, I picked up a downed
Australian pilot whose plane had been shot down the afternoon of our
gunfight with the freighter. He had been sitting on the beach that
evening, wondering what to do next. The local coastwatcher had seen

him go down and retrieved him the next day. Two nights later the 105 picked him up. On our way back to base he told me about that night.

"All of a sudden the damnedest gun battle started right offshore of me. There were streaks and even big balls of fire shooting off all over. It was something like your Fourth of July. I was sitting there enjoying the sight when someone crawled out of the water not fifty feet from me, and then a whole bunch followed him. I took off into the bush and didn't stop running for a mile or two." It was only because this Australian confirmed our account that we got credit for the freighter. A reconnaissance plane had taken pictures of the wreck, the damage so extensive that it looked like the work of a bomb; until our Australian friend came in, the intelligence people opined that our claimed victim had been destroyed by aircraft.

I couldn't fault this mulish refusal to give us credit; PT boat crews thought that anything they fired on immediately sank to the bottom of the sea. Intelligence was well aware that most eyewitness accounts were heavily laced with wishes. We really nailed ourselves to the wall when we reported that we had attacked four Japanese destroyers and had sunk one, damaged another, and sent the others fleeing in terror. As it turned out they were American destroyers and we had not hit anything. It didn't help us when the destroyers reported back that they had engaged Japanese torpedo boats, destroyed most of them, and sent the others fleeing in terror. They hadn't hit anything either.

It would have been nothing short of criminal to deny us credit for the freighter, but we did learn something. The lead boat had illustrated that a PT boat did not explode easily. She had absorbed at least a couple of hundred hits, so many that below decks was coated in a thin layer of sawdust and there was an inch of gasoline sloshing around in the bilges. The fumes were so strong that everyone had to stay on deck, entering the engine room only to shift gears. With those fumes the boat was a bomb ready to go off at the first spark, even though it didn't.

Regardless of the fact that he nearly blew me out of the water, I gained respect for that leader's willingness to fight. That initial shell fire scared me and, after all, he was ahead of me. After the battle, the division leader decided to go home, but he also decided that Sid Hix and I should continue on patrol. Before leaving, he dropped the senior officer, who'd been riding with him as an observer, off on my boat. The worst role is that of observer. You have no way to occupy yourself when things start happening, so you can't help but dwell on what can happen to *you*. For another thing, there was a widespread superstition that passengers were casualty prone. A courageous officer, the observer was nevertheless white around the eyes when he came aboard. Finn and I then inadvertently made things worse.

I had been telling Finn that these sorts of battles gave me a stomachache and that, at that moment, I had a humdinger. As the senior officer came into the cockpit, Finn was giving me his considered opinion that, no matter what fancy medicines there might be, nothing beat plain old bicarbonate of soda. The observer was dumbfounded: "I have just been through the worst experience of my life and you two stand there talking about bicarbonate of soda?" Finn and I saw no reason to enlighten him so we just shrugged and Finn asked, "Whatcha wanna talk about?"

10

DAWN RAID

"What's a dawn raid?" I looked across at Dave Payne, who sprawled on a spare cot in the base officers' tent. A half-dozen boat captains had been talking about a dawn raid when I'd walked in, newly arrived from an engine overhaul at Guadalcanal. So far I had learned only that our Squadron Five boats were going to attack some Japanese barge installations on Kolombangara at dawn tomorrow morning.

Dave gave me his professorial look and said, "Dawn . . . when night contends with day. That's *Macbeth*, son."

"Yeah, sure, but dark dawn? Light dawn? What the hell are they talking about?"

"Beats me," Bobby Shearer, the 104 boat captain, cut in, seeing that Dave was not going to enlighten me, "I'm supposed to go into Ringi Cove with the 103 and your 105 will cover us."

I looked at Bobby, perplexed. Here was another mystery word, *cover*. I asked, "What am I going to cover you with?" I knew what cover meant but not how it applied to me. Once the two boats I was supposed to cover disappeared into the cove, there was no way I could provide covering fire. "Beats me again," said Bobby, "You'll think of something, Gunga."

I remember that well: it was rare indeed, even as close as we were, for one of us to pay another a compliment or to acknowledge in any way the bond between us. Coming from Shearer, who was one of the very best but not a talker, it was like getting a medal.

After three days in Tulagi, which in the last two months had acquired movies and an officers' bar with real whiskey, I had brought the 105 back to Rendova, moored her as usual alongside Payne's 106, and hailed a whaleboat to bring me to the base—all while I was in a state of relative contentment.

It was now 21 August 1943, and enemy barge movements were getting scarce as the Japanese retreated from New Georgia. I figured future patrols in this campaign would be as quiet as those near the end at Guadalcanal. Clearly this was not to be. Someone had decided we would bring the war to the enemy.

The chart spread on the ground in the tent showed three coves on Kolombangara, the large island just to the west of New Georgia: Ringi was the furthest east and close to the strait between Kolombangara and Arundel; Vovobe was a mile and a half west; and a mile west of Vovobe was an unnamed cove. No doubt, one or all of these were barge installations. We knew that the Japanese were retreating from New Georgia and that their evacuation route crossed the strait to Kolombangara. We didn't know whether they would make a stand on Kolombangara or go further west to Vella Lavella. We had been patrolling Blackett Strait, which bordered the south coast of Kolombangara, nightly for the past six weeks and had fought a number of barges running along the coast. The battle in which Jack Kennedy's 109 had been lost had taken place three weeks earlier; Jack and his crew had been rescued from Kolombangara just two weeks before. PTs had never ventured there in daylight. Now, as the sun rose tomorrow morning, Japanese shore guns were going to see the 105 floating in plain sight as she "covered" her companions who'd be somewhere inside a Japanese harbor.

I hoped no one noticed my relief that the 105 wasn't going into that harbor. Buried under that relief was a resentment that the 105 was being given a secondary role.

"They chose boats to go in that had thirty-seven millimeters on the bow," Shearer answered my unasked question. I had dragged my feet over substituting the heavier, but inaccurate, single-shot thirty-seven-millimeter gun for the single-fifty bow gun. (The far better rapid-fire thirty-seven didn't appear until later.) I liked the fifty caliber best. Even on a pitching bow it got on target fast, the gunner adjusting his aim by the tracers. One good burst from that gun did far more damage than the base gunnery people knew; I had seen the deckhouse of a small freighter start to fly apart under its impact, a job the starboard twin fifties and stern twenty millimeter finished once they could train on the target. The base command had believed reports at a debriefing that fifty-caliber ammo had bounced off the sides of barges. After I'd observed, at that same debriefing, that that was bullshit, I found myself at the end of the list for changeovers to the thirty-seven. What those boat captains had seen bouncing off the barges must have been tracer ends which detached on impact and streaked in all directions.

"Where will you be, Dave?" I asked. He answered, "I'll be on the 108 with Sid. We're hitting the cove next to Ringi." Sid Hix, the captain of PT 108, was sitting next to Dave. Before my arrival, they'd been talking about the problems involved in reaching their assigned cove while it was still dark, but timing it so that they had just enough light to define any docks or buildings against the shore backdrop. I forgot about my own problems as I got involved in theirs. Dave continued, "This chart shows plenty of water in the cove, but how do we know there isn't a sand bar at the entrance?"

"We don't. Gosh, neither did the guy who drew this," said Sid. Sid used four-letter words like "gosh." He was very handsome, amiable, and earnest. He had a beautiful girlfriend he called Li'l Duck and so he called his 108 the *Li'l Duck*—the only boat in our squadron with a name. Sid died the next morning trying to get the *Li'l Duck* into Vovobe Cove. After that, no one in Squadron Five painted names on their boats.

Dave stared into space. "Whoever planned this mission does not know that we do not see tiny entrances to coves in the dark, and if we get into this cove we'll see even less."

"Does anyone know Japanese for 'Show a light'?" asked Tom Hayde, "That would do it. They turn on the lights and boom-bang!"

This brought forth a collective, hysterical giggle, but then we lapsed into silence. Little did we know that Joe Burk over in New Guinea would carry out a raid such as this by finding a Nisei Japanese-American nutty enough to help Joe do just what Hayde joked about. Joe, in his meticulous fashion, had studied aerial photos as well as charts to determine reef locations. In the dead of night he had backed into the cove. He explained to me later that by going in astern he could get out quicker—and he thought his silhouette would look more like a barge. While he backed his boat in, the Nisei talked to himself in Japanese, to give the impression that he was a barge captain unsure where he was going. Once they were well inside the cove, the Nisei shouted in Japanese, "Please show dock location." When the enemy Japanese responded by illuminating the dock, Joe opened up with everything he had, totally destroying the dock, fuel dump, ammunition shed, and many unfortunate Japanese who'd been waiting for what they thought was one of their barges. He then departed. That was Joe Burk.

I thought maybe someone would suggest that someone else suggest to the base command that this mission was insane, but no one suggested any such thing. No one on the base command there ever asked the boat captains whether or not a mission was possible. They thought the missions up. We carried them out. I began thinking that the way out of this was to avoid the cove entrances until it got too light, say "Aw, shucks," and return to base. Then maybe the idea would be dropped. Not bad thinking—until Shearer said to me, "Guess who's leading our division? Our very own squadron commander." My look of dismay brought a laugh. Our squadron CO had not ridden any patrols. For the first few days of the New Georgia campaign he'd remained behind in the Russells, and what he'd been doing there none of us knew or cared; not that we disliked him, we just took him for who he was. He had been our squadron commander right from squadron commissioning. A naturally quiet, reserved man, he went by the book and maintained the same distance from his subordinate officers as a battleship captain. He called all of us by our last names, dined alone or with other COs, and never engaged in personal conversation. It therefore took awhile for us to realize that he hated his assignment to PT boats.

But our CO, bless him, did what he could do best. He trained us in the ways of the regular Navy and that was good. By April 1943, when we reached the Solomons, our crews were expert and disciplined and our boats were ready to go. Our guns fired and our torpedos left their tubes and ran in the direction we aimed—even if they never hit anything.

Incredibly, our CO never learned to handle a PT boat. Once in Panama I watched in fascination as he attempted to dock a PT in a strong tidal current and gusty winds; after several tries, he turned the job over to the boat captain. Gradually he left operations to George Cookman, retreated to his paperwork, and we saw less and less of him. So to hear that he'd decided to lead this mission caused me shock and dismay. "Why?" I asked no one in particular. "He thought it up so I guess he feels he has to be on it," Dave said uncertainly. Tom Hayde, my so-called exec broke in: "I think he's strikin' for a Silver Star."

Let me try to explain Hayde, because without him I wouldn't have this opportunity to explain anything. The next morning he saved my life. Tom Hayde was the warrant officer in charge of Squadron Five's base engineering. Early in 1941, the Navy had scoured the land in search of people who understood high performance gasoline engines and found Hayde, among others including a bunch of ex-rumrunners. He was a Chicago fireman with ten years' experience and knew all about big gasoline engines. He had the black hair and blue eyes of the Irish, big hands, and a five-foot-ten, chunky body that had carried him through the Saturday night brawls that passed for entertainment in his part of Chicago.

We were close friends. That we were both Irish Catholics may have helped in the beginning. He told funny stories and he laughed at my stories. I can't think of anything Tom took seriously, certainly not this war or the people running it. We could sit for hours on the deck of the 105, telling half-true stories of our lives before the war and embellishing on joint tales of drinking and girl chasing in Panama.

How Tom became, for awhile, acting exec of the 105 goes a long way toward explaining him. After my regular exec, Phil Hornbrook, was killed, I was assigned a different second officer on every patrol. Except for Finn Percy, who entertained me during one horrendous firefight, they were all a useless, tiresome and scared bunch; scared because the 105 seemed to step in shit everytime she went out. With one of these "bums of the night" (as Mechin called them) on board, I got even less sleep than usual. On patrol, when nothing was happening, we stood watches two on and two off. When I was off I slept sitting up against the day room bulkhead just behind the cockpit; at the slightest suspicious movement, Mechin—who stood the other watch—would lean over and rouse me with, "Skipper, you betta lookit this." He completely ignored the temporary exec.

When Phil was killed, Tom was down in the Russell Islands running the engine repair shop and growing increasingly restive, because he believed that all the amusing events were taking place at Rendova. So it came to pass one day, when the 105 was at its mooring in Rendova, that a whaleboat came alongside and deposited Tom and his duffel bag. "Well my goodness!" I exclaimed, "what got you up here?" I assumed that base engineering had moved up and Tom was paying me a social visit, but to my surprise he answered, "I'm your new exec." "My new exec?" "Yeah." "How come?" I was feeling a little dense since I knew that Tom hadn't gone through the three months of intensive training required for PT officers. Tom knew all about Packard V-12 engines but not about running a PT boat.

"Well, I'm sittin on my ass down in the Russell when I hear you lost Hornbrook. So I seize the moment. I go to Searles and tell him I have orders to proceed here. He doesn't question it because who in hell would make that up? Then when I get here, I tell them I got orders from down the line to come here and act as your exec and likewise they buy it because who would want to ride with you?"

So I now had an unlawful exec, if there is such a thing, who knew absolutely nothing about PT boats but the engines. I already had Miles, an extremely capable chief motor mac who guarded his engine room like a sullen troll. But I could not have been happier. Tom was great company and that was what I needed. The crew loved him. While they had ignored the "bums of the night," they didn't have to ignore Hayde, because he never gave an order. Mechin even stopped waking me up so often. So there you have Tom Hayde on the evening before the dawn raid.

Since we were to take off at about 0300, we all went out to the boats at 1700, much as we would if we were going on patrol. We were aboard a short while when a whaleboat stopped by and John Iles came aboard.

John, during the course of the next morning, became a lifelong friend. He also succeeded me as captain of the 105. But at that point I knew him as the skipper of an old Squadron Two boat, who was having a miserable time trying to keep the crate afloat. John had come out as a replacement officer about three months earlier and had been shuffled around after getting a boat and then losing it to a more senior boatless officer.

I had first noticed him when I witnessed one of Bob Kelly's classic chew-outs, with John as the victim. While keeping station, moving at cruising speed to reach the patrol area, John's boat glanced off the lead boat, putting a two-foot hole in her port bow. It really wasn't John's

fault, because the leader had turned hard to starboard without allow-
ing enough leeway for his starboard wing boat. Nevertheless John got
the blame and provided a morning's entertainment for the entire base
as we watched Kelly deliver a purple-faced diatribe. When Kelly concluded, John, who had stood throughout at embarrassed attention,
asked what he thought was a sensible question, prefaced by the cus-
tomary groveling: "Sir, I need to get my boat fixed so's I can make
tonight's patrol." Lounging there on a front-row cot, I catalogued that
statement under nice-effort-at-appearing-dauntless, but Kelly reacted
otherwise: "So you need to get your boat fixed, do you?"—at a decibel
level that could dislodge coconuts. Kelly then turned around, grabbed
a piece of plank, a hammer, and some nails, which he had stowed for
just that occasion. He held them out to John roaring, "Here you are.
You broke it, now fix it!"

John Iles, in front of God and most of the Rendova PT base,
walked down to the dock with the wood, the hammer, and the nails,
got into a whaleboat and was taken to the wounded boat. When he got
there he found Pop Dieteman had already fixed the hole—on Kelly's
orders.

I heard later from John himself that he had thought me one of the
"more arrogant sumbitches in the Solomons—along with your snooty
chum Payne. I used to moor alongside you two guys, thinking I could
get some help. There I was with this old boat and replacement crew and
I'd come over to your boat, and there the two of you'd be, squatting on
the bow like a couple of pelicans, peering down at that goddam chess
set, and I'd say, 'Could you give me some help with a torpedo?' and
without even looking up from that goddam board, you'd holler, 'Willie
Monk,' and your torpedoman would get up and amble over to my boat
without even looking at me."

I said innocently, "I don't remember. When did you moor alongside
of us?" and John got mad at me all over again. When he came aboard
that night and announced he was my new permanent exec, I was occupied with our next morning's mission and I barely acknowledged his
presence. And there was one other item of moment. What about Tom
Hayde? He had been officially replaced. He should have packed his
duffel and headed for the beach, where he definitely belonged because
the squadron base engineering group that he'd originally headed had
moved up from the Russells and was open for operations. But he
didn't go. Not that night, not before what was clearly slated to be the

last morning of our lives. I could not bring myself to order him off the boat. I thought I needed him. I was so right.

It was a little past 2000 hours when I decided to pack it in, leaving word with the watch to call me at 0300, which would give me a few minutes before we got underway. I lay on my bunk staring at the overhead, sure that I could never sleep for thinking of what lay in store—and I did stay awake for thirty seconds. At three, I climbed to the cockpit to find Hayde, Iles, and Mechin already there.

We waited until 0400 which puzzled me because at 0600 it would be light and we would have to go like hell to reach Ringi Cove while it was still dark. I fumed over the delay (and never did find out what caused it). Just before we took off, Zichella came up on deck with a breakfast of coffee and baloney sandwiches.

Now I've said that I'd acquired a reputation for coolness under fire. When we actually stepped in it, when some untoward (to use Dave Payne's word) event occurred, a basic cornered-rat instinct took over. It was before and after the event that I sometimes had to mask my fear, and I was good at that. I had to be. A boat captain who showed the slightest trace of fear would lose control of his crew. There had been a boat captain who'd panicked when a torpedo started up on deck, making a fearful racket. He dove off the boat. His crew would not let him back aboard.

This morning, however, the baloney sandwich nearly did me in. I chomped down, began to chew, and nothing happened! My mouthful of baloney sandwich remained as pristine as the rest of the sandwich in my hand. I chewed and chewed. I tried working my jaw sideways like a cow. Nothing happened. Fear, which I prevented from showing on my outside, had taken full control of my insides and had shut down the contraptions that nature installs for the mastication of baloney sandwiches. I was on the brink of disaster until it occurred to me to blame the cook. "Dammit Zichella," I snarled as I extracted the bread and baloney, "that is a terrible sandwich." Poor Zichella looked at me mournfully. Tom Hayde turned to Iles and said, "At a time like this, he complains about the food." No one was the wiser.

Between our late start and some backing-and-forthing to locate the entrance to Blackett Strait (which all of us had found over and over, without difficulty, for the past six weeks), our dawn raid brigade didn't arrive on the coast of Kolombangara until 0630. It was now daylight and we were parading up the enemy-held coast in clear view, nine PT boats in column. I was sure that we were already in the sights of Japanese shore guns, less than a half-mile away, holding their fire until the rest of the invasion force came over the horizon. "Well, well," I thought, "Can we go home now? Try again another dawn?" But, no, we steamed past the first small harbor and the three rearmost boats peeled off. I say "steamed" because I kept thinking of pictures I'd seen of the Grand Fleet at Jutland. We passed the second harbor and Dave Payne's three boats turned into the coast.

It was now a sparkling clear day. John Iles was at the wheel, I stood next to him, Mechin was behind me, and Tom Hayde had assigned himself to watch the stern twenty-millimeter crew.

I wondered what was going through John's mind. After months of shuttling around from one inexperienced group to another, here he was, assigned to the most experienced squadron around. How did he view his first mission with old hands like us? Did he think it just a bit odd that we were casually rumbling up to a Japanese harbor after breakfast? Rather than ask him his views, I decided to give him mine: "John, you are about to do the brashest thing you will ever do in your life."

John continued to stare silently at the stern of the boat ahead of us, but I knew he was considering my observation. After a moment I thought he was going to reply but, instead, he simply nodded. We came abreast of the entrance to Ringi Cove. All three boats stopped and I told John to come up on the offshore side of the 104 in case the commander wanted my advice on the quickest way to get the hell out.

I saw Shearer lean over the wheel and I was surprised when he suddenly went up to full speed. The two boats disappeared inside the narrow entrance so quickly that I was amazed to find myself alone. John took our engines to neutral and there we sat, a hundred yards from the entrance. No one spoke. We waited for gunfire to erupt inside the harbor. Instead, the first sound to break the silence was a familiar whump over my head; a shell burst fifty yards down the shoreline to the west. I stood frozen in place. I looked to starboard, east up the shoreline, saw a flash about a half-mile away, and felt another whump over my head.

John Iles reacted to the first shell by putting the engines in gear, swinging hard to port, and shoving the throttles up for a getaway to the west—back the way we'd come just five minutes ago. I reached for the mike and called, "This is Oak King, we are under fire, we are under fire, shore guns east, when you come out, come out fast." Even as I said it, I thought, "Is this all I can do? Tell them to come out fast? See you later, folks!"

Then, as we began running back the way we'd come, it occurred to me what cover I could provide. We had a smoke screen generator, a cylinder like a propane tank located on our stern with some kind of chemical under pressure, and a small pipe and nozzle sticking up. You turned a valve and it laid smoke. I'd never laid a smoke screen, and the ones I'd seen were on the thin and wispy side, but it would be some sort of cover—even though when the boats came out, they'd be exposed to the shell fire until they caught up with my screen.

"Lay smoke!" I yelled and Mechin, turning to the stern, echoed the order. We were racing straight down a shoreline that was less than a hundred yards to starboard. The shell bursts were now a few yards to port. The 105 had gone far enough down the shoreline and far enough inshore that the guns couldn't reach us, but for some reason they kept firing. Glancing back, I saw no smoke starting from the stern. I knew they'd heard the order because Gunner Brown was bent over the generator. Nothing was coming out and by now we were moving too far away.

"God I can't leave them," I thought, "I just can't run away and leave Bobby Shearer." I could hear him saying "You'll think of something." I turned to John at the wheel and said, "We have to go back." "Yeah." John nodded his approval. I said, "I better take the wheel." "Yeah."

We switched places and John grabbed the binoculars and began scanning the shore for gunfire. I put the boat hard over to port, away from the shore. This would bring us into the line of fire but I had no room for a starboard inshore turn. The firing stopped briefly, probably so the spotter could try to figure out what we were up to. As we completed our turn and headed back, shells again whumped overhead and burst in front of us. The eighteen-year-old fireman, most junior enlisted man aboard, who had the lowliest jobs like washing dishes and making the captain's bunk, now had a chance to shine. His assignment was the bow fifty and there he was in denim cutoffs, his feet splayed, his linebacker legs bent to ride the bounces as if they were part of the deck, and he was firing at the shore a half-mile away. It was too much to hope that he could take out the guns at this range; but I think they either pulled in their spotter on the beach or the bow gunner knocked him off, because there was another lull. I glanced astern—still no smoke.

PT 105 leading a three-boat division in the echelon formation used in barge attacks. (U.S. Naval Institute photo collection)

"Lay smoke!" I yelled, " Lay smoke!" and turned to look again just as Hayde came up to the cockpit. "The thing won't start," he said. I knew what was wrong, and it had been my doing. Sometimes I'd told Gunner Brown to pop the valve to see whether the damn thing worked and we'd gotten a confirming puff; a few days ago I had troubled to read the directions, which cautioned that opening the valve frequently could cause it to clog. Later Hayde would entertain the base with his rendition of my response to this emergency: "He looked at me with his eyes buggin' out of his head and said, 'That's all right—lay smoke any- way!'"

Hayde stared at me, rightly concluded that I was beyond reason, shrugged, and went back to the group working on the generator. By this time the 105 was abeam the entrance to Ringi Cave, but now four hundred yards offshore. I turned and headed in. The 105 now offered itself broadside to the shore guns. I say guns because water-bursts and whumps overhead came too fast for one gun. Now Willie Monk in the starboard twin-fifty turret and Morgan Brown at the stern twenty mil- limeter opened up on the shore gun flashes. I saw Zichella scuttle up to the bow gunner with a canister of fifty-caliber ammo and I watched them reload as smoothly as if they had practiced this a hundred times. Maybe they had; things went on I didn't know about.

At the same instant that the 105 turned into shore, the 104 and 103 came busting out of the harbor entrance as if on cue, and in the next instant smoke billowed from our stern.

Mechin, still facing aft, yelled, "Lookit that, Skipper!"

I looked back to see the most beautiful, barn-sized, thick, white cloud pouring from our stern. This was due to the inspiration of Tom Hayde-the-Magnificent, who had raced back to the stern, grabbed an axe that I didn't know we had, brushed aside Brown and his striker who were desperately jiggling the valve, and in one swing cut a hole just behind the clog. The opening was bigger than any valve setting and therefore made a far thicker and bigger smoke screen than Navy specs called for; and even though I knew that cylinder was going to give out real soon, it was so beautiful that my eyes still get teary at the memory. A few seconds later, at a relative speed of eighty knots, the 104 and 103 roared past the 105 and into the shelter of Hayde's smoke screen.

All of this split-second precision timing must have stunned the Japanese shore gunners because for moments—and these were the most critical moments, when the 105 was broadside at a constant range, like a wooden duck in a shooting gallery—they ceased firing. At least I think they did, or it may have been that the next problem blotted shell bursts from my perception. I was now hurtling toward a beach and, as I cranked the wheel hard over to port, was not at all sure I had enough turning room. Embedded in my memory was the sound and feel of propellers grinding into coral—only those who have run aground, as I had when I put the 105 on the only marked reef in the Solomon Islands, can understand the terror. Fear struck. Now, whenever fear struck me, it did so physically, hitting some part of my anatomy, my hands, the back of my neck, or right under my rib cage. This time it kicked me right in the ass. It was a good thing the wheel was already hard over, because for precious moments I could not move. I was waiting for the disgusting sound and shudder of boat meeting reef.

Nothing happened to stop the sliding turn that brought the 105 within a boat-length of shore. I was so gripped by my fear of running aground that the quick dots in the water (made by a machine gun at the harbor entrance) just vaguely got my attention. But what I did see was the bow gunner and Willie Monk both whip around and give the nearby bushes a sustained burst of fire. In my peripheral vision I saw an explosion of whirling sand, coral and bushes. That Japanese gun must have been set up too late to get our two boats coming out, and it had a very short life.

Now we were curving away from the beach and back into the firing arc of the shore guns, so I turned to run parallel to the shore, but not soon enough. A shell passed so close to the starboard turret that Willie Monk was burned across his bare torso. Then a second shell missed my head by so little margin that the suction it created pulled my helmet up and over my eyes. These shells came through the smoke. Those gunners were able to get on to us even though we were covered by our own screen so I canted back closer to the shore.

It is marvelously strange how men under mortal stress react. Now here we were in shit up to our elbows when Hayde sees Miles pop up out of the engine room hatch. So Hayde strides up to knock Miles back into the engine room with the blunt side of his axe before Miles can go over the side.

"Where did you think he was going?" I asked Hayde later.

"I dunno but I thought he thought he was better off somewhere else. I know I thought I'd be better off somewhere else," my friend and the saver of my life replied in a tone implying that the whole episode was of my making. Hayde stopped from clouting Miles when Miles stopped halfway out of the hatch and signaled Mechin for me to turn around. When I did, I saw Miles pointing down; that meant I should check at my tachometers. This was a signal Miles normally used to tell me to get his engines in sync. So when I looked down at the instrument panel, I saw the three tach needles shivering a bit above 2,900 rpms. Our top rpm was 2,400, or about 42 knots. The 105 was going somewhere in the vicinity of 50 knots!

I looked back at Miles and nodded my congratulations. He pounded his chest like Tarzan and popped back into his engine room. (If a shell had ever hit the 105, I truly believe the good Lord would have sent Miles out of the boat and into the clouds riding astride a Packard V-12 engine.) For a brief moment I too ignored the shell fire and sensed only this splendid boat, racing flat out. The sea that day was perfect for speed: small choppy waves helped the hull break the surface tension, so that little but her props and rudders were in the water. She skimmed over the surface without a bounce or tremor, her engines screaming their wonderful, giant-tomcat howl, and her guns chattering into the smoke astern and the nearby shore.

I had not thought about the attacks we were waging on the other harbors. When did Dave and Sid Hix in the 108 leave our column to carry out their assigned raid on Vovobe cove? Shaken by the shell that had kissed my helmet, I only half-registered a PT boat that seemed, slowly, to be making its way across my course a few hundred yards ahead. A haze hung about her that I couldn't identify. At first I thought she was alone, but then I saw two boats about a quarter mile out to sea, stopped as if waiting. Then my mind cleared enough for me to grasp what was going on. The 108 was under fire from machine guns; I saw the dots and skips in the water. She was in trouble, barely moving. I adjusted course toward the shore. At the speed the 105 was traveling, I must have gone astern of the 108 in a half minute, until my huge smoke screen shielded her from any effective fire. As we went behind her, the air whispered with small arms fire overhead. Streaking across the stern of the 108, we must have startled the Japanese gunners and, like gunners the world over, their fire jerked upward for the time it took for us to squeak by, leaving behind Tom Hayde's magnificent smoke screen for them to gaze upon in wonder.

Unlike the 104, the 108 had never made it into their cove. When they were met by a storm of machine-gun fire at the entrance, the two other boats had turned and run, which was all they could do. Dave was among the first men hit on the 108. Bullets tore away his side. He collapsed through the cockpit door and fell down the ladder to the deck below. Sid Hix was hit in the head but still managed to say, "Take the boat out" to his quartermaster, Cannon, who was hit in both legs but managed to pull himself up, take the wheel, and turn the boat around. Grady Chandler, the exec, was not hit and hurried to the engine room, because the engines had stopped as the 108 turned around. Grady and one engineer scrambled around stuffing cotton wadding into the holes drilled in the heat exchangers by machine-gun bullets. Without those heat exchangers, an engine would seize up quickly. The other engineer, on the engine-control seat, kept restarting each engine as it died. The engine ran for a few seconds, then crapped out, started again, then crapped out, and in this way they kept the boat going at a few knots toward safety. Almost all on deck were killed or wounded. Cannon, the wounded quartermaster, had to hold himself up as he steered the boat away from the punishing small-arms fire.

After we passed astern of the 108, I turned out to join my division. As I did I was gratified to hear the squadron commander come up on the radio with, "105, well done." I was less gratified when he followed with, "105, you may cease smoking." I had no way to cease smoking. My runaway smoke screen was now blanketing a good part of Kolombangara. As my decapitated generator continued gushing smoke, I envisioned myself rejoining my division and engulfing us all, after which we would wander around forever, groping blindly for the exit. I solved this problem by turning to Mechin: "Mechin, tell them to cease smoking." Mechin turned smartly and echoed, "Cease smoking!" Hayde cut the cables holding the generator and shoved it over the stern.

I learned that Sid was dying and Dave was very badly wounded only after we'd returned to base. Sid was lying on a cot in the medical tent, removed from the area where doctor and pharmacist's mates were working on those who could be saved. Sid looked very dignified and calm, as if he was satisfied that he had done his best. I could only look at my friend for a brief moment before I felt myself losing control. I turned and asked where Dave was.

He was down in the dugout used for surgery. I went inside. He was lying alone on the surgery table. Whatever could be done had been done, and they'd left to work on others. For a terrible moment I thought he was dead. When he lifted his head a little and grinned at me, I gasped with relief.

"They left me a bottle of brandy," he said in a surprisingly strong voice, "Pour us a couple." There was a pint of Lejon brandy on the table with him. I found two jars and poured us each a drink. I fed one to him while I sipped the other. In the meantime he was describing how they were going to fly him out and put him on a hospital ship to Hawaii, where he would recuperate in Waikiki and so forth. I could see that the morphine and the brandy were working overtime, so I sat on the other table and listened to him expound upon his future arrival in San Francisco—while helping myself to another brandy. Two sailors came down and gently slid him onto a stretcher. Dave looked at me: "So long my friend. See you in Newport. Just tuck my bottle here." I watched my closest friend being slowly carried to the door. I stayed where I was, clutching the bottle. "Give me the bottle," issued from the stretcher. I watched my buddy as he disappeared through the low entrance. He said "You rotter!" He used words like that. "That's my bottle. Give me the bottle!"

I felt sad so I had another drink, then I tucked the bottle into my pants and left. So much for dawn raids.

THE DECOY

Tom Hayde, my so-called exec, surprised me when he alleged there could be some truth to the rumor that I had gone "asiatic"—a Navy term for a sailor who has been in the Far East so long he wants to stay there; it also connotes a touch of lunacy. "Not true," I said. I did embellish my accounts to make them more entertaining, but the last straw, I suspect, was when I described my stay with the 2d Marine Parachute Battalion as if it had been a great camping trip: the cool mountain stream where I took my evening bath, the Lejon brandy, and those comfy jungle hammocks. Keep in mind that before I left on that excursion I'd been the butt of jokes by the other boat captains who watched me trying to pack, mumbling to myself as I put things in my little haversack and then pulled them out again. "Go ahead, take your pajamas, Gunga"—that kind of remark. So, naturally, when I got back I put a good face on it. While I'd been running around Choiseul, my tormentors back in Torokina had been having a particularly miserable time during the first days of the Bougainville landings. During one of their nightly doses of Japanese bombs, a bomb had blown up the chiefs' raisin jack still, spraying fermented raisins all over. The smell was pretty bad, not to mention that the boat captains' ration of hooch was gone. This made them hypersensitive about anyone being somewhere else.

It all started when, skirting combat fatigue, I suffered some odd symptoms, and then a mild case of malaria pushed me toward the edge. Malarial symptoms, fever and aching limbs, tend to run in cycles—in my case I had a fever every other day so the base command sent me out on patrols on the nights I didn't run a fever. Then, on top of the malaria, I got a mild case of amoebic dysentery. It didn't put me down but I was visiting the head at inconvenient times. One night on patrol I was perched in the head when the 105 suddenly accelerated from idling speed. No one should be sitting on a hard surface when a PT boat starts bouncing. I managed to get up in time to avoid having my bottom permanently framed in a toilet seat. Mechin stuck his head around the door and yelled "We gotta contact, Skipper, you'd better get up here." Flustered, I scrambled up the ladder to the cockpit, my pants and drawers hanging around my ankles, grabbed the binoculars, and started looking for whatever it was. It turned out to be nothing. The story went around, however, that I spent the rest of the night staring through the binoculars with my drawers down. As Joe Roberts suggests in his poem about me, I was untidy but not that untidy.

Between the malaria and dysentery I attained such a spectral appearance that the junior base doctor said, after examining me, "I am going to send you to Australia for ten days' rest. "No." I said. "What?" he said, startled. It was everyone's dream to go to Australia. "No," I repeated. Clearly he was at a loss for words. He didn't consider me to be in bad enough shape to order me off the boat and he thought he was doing me a favor. He shrugged his shoulders and said no more, but the story went around that I turned down a trip to Australia because I liked where I was. I *hated* where I was but I had two compelling reasons for the prompt refusal. First, all of the remaining Squadron Five boat captains were still plugging along and I was not about to leave them, even if they had come to me in a body and said, "Go, Gunga, for our sakes." The second and more decisive reason to stay was that I knew that if I went to Australia for ten days, I would not report for transportation back on the tenth day; and when they sent out a search party, I would be found eventually, cowering in a closet. When I left the Solomons, I would never come back.

During this period John Iles, my successor as captain of the 105, invited me aboard my old boat one night for supper. (This was a nice change because suppers on the beach, eating with one hand while the other swished the flies, were not very tasty.) After supper John and I were sitting at the two-man wardroom table over coffee when he said that he was in a bad state of nerves. He found this very depressing: never in his whole life had he ever been nervous about anything, and he felt that it reflected poorly on his manhood and so forth.

I decided not to adopt the approach that I, too, was nervous and scared. In war movies there's the scene where the young soldier tells the tough-talking-but-kind-deep-down top sergeant that he's scared, and the kindly top sergeant says that he too is scared, and the young soldier, having found that he's not alone in this, leads the charge and gets himself a medal. If I had used this approach with John, he would have shouted, "For Crissake, I don't wanna hear how bad *you* feel!"

So I tried to look at the bright side and changed the subject. In the middle of forecasting that the 105 was due for a five-hundred-hours engine overhaul in a few days I noticed that I'd lost his attention. He was looking at my coffee cup which, from PT boat practice, I was holding up off the table even though we were not under way. The cup was jiggling in tune with my shaking hand. In recent weeks, my right hand had acquired an annoying tremor that came on sporadically for no apparent reason.

John looked up from his inspection of my cup and sighed, *"You're trying to cheer me up?"* I was so embarrassed that I changed the subject and made things worse. I asked, "How is my cockroach?" "You had a cockroach? I mean, you had your own cockroach?" John asked. "Yeah, little guy, came out every night, ran to the middle of the table, stood on his hind legs, and wiggled his feelers at me. I would inch a crumb toward him and he'd pick it up and run back into the crack."

John grinned, "Are you kidding?" I could see that I was not creating the right impression. I did have a cockroach that would appear at supper. Cockroaches were a nuisance, of course, and we squashed them on sight—but this little fellow really seemed to want to be friends. I became acquainted with him a couple of weeks before John had come aboard and I had moved to the beach. John thought this story was hilarious and I left him in a much improved mood; however, he went and told everyone about my cockroach.

About this time I came to suspect that both sides were out to kill *me*. I discovered later that I was not alone in this conviction. Stay in combat long enough and there comes a time when a mission assignment will seem to have little purpose other than to do you in. Yossarian, in Joseph Heller's *Catch-22*, came to the same conclusion. Even today the assignment that raised this suspicion for me seems as bizarre as it did in 1943.

Night-bombers were a constant and deadly threat to PT boats, particularly those with green crews that had not yet acquired the skills that enabled them to hide better—and fight better when the bombers found them. Our barge attacks were frequently disrupted by the arrival of bombers. Pilots could spot the pyrotechnics from miles away and they'd rush to drop bombs into the melee—with no regard for what they might hit. With the bombers' arrival, we were forced to abort the barge attack and we turned our attention to the menace upstairs.

To counter the night-bombers, the Navy first tried sending out Black Cats—PBYs, or patrol bombers, supposedly equipped to fly and fight at night. The idea was that if and when we were attacked, the PBYs would shoot down the attacker. Now, the PBY was a useful flying boat that performed a variety of missions, chief of which was long-range reconnaissance; it even doubled as a torpedo plane early in the war and did do some damage, although how any lumbering PBY escaped being shot down by its target was a mystery to me. What was not a mystery to me was what would happen in a gunfight between a slow, clumsy Black Cat and the agile Japanese night-bombers; my money was on the night-bombers.

The best that can be said for our experience with Black Cats is that no one got hurt. The night that we coordinated with them, the 105 was a wing boat in George Cookman's division. Radio communication between us and two Black Cats circling somewhere in the darkness overhead was terrible. George could talk to one of the Black Cats but not the other, so every message had to be relayed. We'd been on station, creeping around looking for barges, for about an hour when a bomb—as usual from out of nowhere—exploded in the center of our three-boat division. There was something uniquely terrifying about an unexpected bomb explosion at night on the water. First there was intense light as from a giant flashbulb; in the millisecond before the sound of the explosion, I could see the faces of the crew around me in white shock, and the lead boat and the other wing boat would be vividly clear. Then the shattering blast would press me down against the deck. This particular night, there was no damage.

After quiet had returned, George Cookman came up on the radio, calling to the Black Cat above us, " Did you just drop a bomb?" The PBY in contact with him answered, "No, I didn't drop a bomb." "Ask your friend," said George, referring to the Black Cat he couldn't radio. After an appreciable silence, the first Black Cat responded, "No, he didn't drop a bomb." "Then we have company," George observed. No sooner had he said this than tracer fire streaked above us. I couldn't tell who was firing or what their target was. It was a startling and spectacular sight—tiny white and red balls of fire arcing across the darkness. One of the Black Cats came up on the radio with the unnecessary observation, "We are under fire, under attack by enemy plane." I guessed that he'd forgotten to change frequency and the message was intended for his home base—he certainly didn't need to tell us. This prompted George to come up with a classic suggestion: "Bring him down here and we'll get on his tail." When the laughter subsided, we took off at high speed for elsewhere and George asked the Black Cats to please go home. That was the end of that experiment, although about a month later our boats began occasionally using Black Cats as spotters. The planes would drop flares on enemy barges, destroying their occupants' night vision and making them easy prey for attacking PTs. The down side was when a Black Cat mistook a PT boat for a barge and lit up the PT boat.

A few weeks later, the Navy came up with what sounded like an effective solution to the night-bomber problem. A new night-fighter arrived called the Black Widow, a fast and agile plane specially designed for air-to-air night combat using radar and infrared night scopes. I was leading the patrol on the first night the Black Widow was available over at the Munda Airstrip. During our briefing the base commander had announced that we'd have this marvelous new air cover. He looked over at me: "Keresey, you will time your arrival at Ferguson Passage for 2400. The Black Widow will rendezvous with you there. At exactly 2400 go to high speed and head west up Blackett Strait." In a knee-jerk reaction, I asked, "Why would I do that?" The commander looked at me as if I were dense and said, "So your wake will attract enemy bombers and the Black Widow can shoot them down." I stared at him in disbelief. The command dugout became very quiet as the other boat captains saw what the commander had in mind: I was to be a decoy, a tethered goat. I said no more because anything I said would start with

"You son-of-a-bitch." The timing would have to be miraculous. And with a friendly plane up there, the 105 couldn't shoot at any blob overhead the instant it appeared; this was our best defense and it had become a pretty good one as our gunners grew experienced in spotting the vague form of a bomber approaching in the darkness.

I walked out of the dugout, thinking, what a dumb-assed mess. In the book *At Close Quarters* (USGPO, 1962) Robert J. Bulkley, Jr., makes a brief reference to this mission, along with the statement that I volunteered. There was no way that I would have volunteered to put the 105 (and her crew) at risk as a decoy. I was humiliated by the thought that my great boat and crew were not worth as much as a wretched enemy bomber. Outside the dugout, the boat captain assigned to follow me approached, cleared his throat in embarrassment, and said, "Since you're leading this patrol in the 105, perhaps when you start your run I should head in the other direction." I thought about this. We were supposed to be a two-boat mission, out after enemy barges. Splitting up would greatly lessen our effectiveness. On the other hand, the chances of finding any barges after the whiz-bang bombing that lay ahead were very slim; the enemy would see it all, know where we were, and head the other way. But the other captain was clearly sweating on this one, trying to convey the message that it would be better to risk one PT than two. I told him that the moment he saw me go west at full speed, he should head east at slow speed to conceal his wake. "Good luck," I added. " The same to you." he said.

As I boarded the 105 I was trying to figure out a reasonable explanation for this mission to give the crew. I failed, so I said nothing. We took off for Ferguson Passage. At 2300 hours and about eight miles from the entrance, we dropped to idling speed so we wouldn't arrive at the rendezvous too early. I then realized that I had no choice but to tell my crew what was up: if I suddenly pushed the throttles up to full speed they would decide that I had shipped an oar. I turned to Mechin and told him the good news, that we were going to be covered by the wonderful Black Widow. "Great," he acknowledged. I continued, "The Black Widow is going to shoot the Jap plane down when it makes its run on us." "Great," he repeated. "And to make sure the Black Widow gets a good target, we are going to full speed at exactly midnight. That's our rendezvous time." Mechin did not say, "Great." He said, "We are going to do *what?*" I knew the jig was up, so I said, "Mechin, I am under orders to attract the bomber at midnight, so go tell the crew." Mechin worked his way quickly to the stern and back to the cockpit. I was at the wheel and he came and stood next to me.

"Geez, Skipper," he said, his tone conveying fully the message that this was stupid, that I was putting the 105 at risk for one lousy plane, and maybe not even that. I could not think of anything to say. Time dragged by in unaccustomed silence. As we approached the entrance to Ferguson Passage, I was having second thoughts about the other boat. Maybe the second boat should come up to line abreast with the 105 and then we would take off together. If we spotted a plane coming up the twin wakes, we could then hope it wasn't the Black Widow but the enemy, and get on him with double firepower. But it was too late: I could never explain all that over the radio. For a moment I thought the other captain had had the same idea, because he came from my starboard wing to abreast of me. But, no, he had other plans. He veered to starboard and headed northeast, away from me. He was clearing away from the decoy, and I couldn't blame him for that. It was one minute to midnight. Sure enough, I heard the sound of an engine passing overhead. The Black widow was right on schedule. "Skipper, that's a Jap plane." said Mechin anxiously. The sound did resemble that made by Sewing Machine Charlie. I thought it couldn't be, too much of a coincidence. Besides, we'd never heard the sound of a Black Widow's engine, and maybe they sounded the same. "Nah, that's our friend the Widow, right on time." I said, "Here we go." I pushed the throttles up gradually to the wall. The 105, as was her custom after she'd been idling a long time, let out a couple of robust farts, then her stern settled and came up as she began her flat out race. I looked astern and there was that bright wake, pointing right to us, for all up there to see. It occurred to me that the gunners might hesitate to fire at a blob coming up that wake, thinking that it might be the Widow. The hell with that, anything that came up that wake was cutting meat. Without looking at him I yelled to Mechin, "I want all guns to commence firing at anything that they see coming up that wake." Mechin took off for the stern as I shouted my orders to Willie Monk in the starboard turret. I was mad at the world now.

As soon as I had a hundred yards of wake I started a long zigzag for what little good it might do. It was now several minutes after the scheduled rendezvous with the Black Widow. The radio burped and came alive, "Oak King, Oak King, over." I reached for the mike, but the speaker continued without waiting for my acknowledgment, "Cancel exercise. Cancel exercise, over." I didn't waste time acknowledging, Ellis did it for me. I went into a hard ninety-degree turn, pulled the throttles back, and went to three engines ahead idling. I decided against running on only my center engine (to show the least possible wake), because chances were the enemy bombers already had me spotted. With all three engines, I could accelerate a few seconds faster. After a moment, a voice came over the radio that I didn't recognize. "Your friend crashed on takeoff."

Mechin, now back in the cockpit, said, "That plane we heard was Jap." "I know that, dammit," I snarled. I didn't know what to do: the enemy plane or planes up there knew we were somewhere close to that half-mile-long wake still flickering in the waves. They would surely find us, but I didn't want to go to high-speed evasion yet because the roar of our unmuffled engines would hide the sound of their planes coming in on us. With mufflers on, we would hear them a few seconds before we saw them. We puttered along, all eyes skyward. An enemy barge could have tied up alongside without our seeing it.

"What to do?" I thought, "what to do, you jackass?" Whizzer White (later known as Supreme Court Justice Byron L. White) and I had written our own little primer on how to keep from getting bombed; here I was with a chance at a live demonstration and I was coming up short on ideas. Where were those rainsqualls Professor Gunga had said were everywhere? How about just a low cloud to hide under? There was nothing but wispy, high cirrus—had they picked tonight for the exercise to make sure the decoy would be spotted?

Mechin interrupted my musings with, "What do we do now, skipper?" His tone implied that I had gotten us into this mess and more. I had offered up as bait not just myself, but the 105. My first problem was the crew's morale. They had witnessed a complete foul-up, one which had put them at risk for nothing. They had every reason to lose confidence in me. "Well, Gunga," I said to myself "when all else fails, let your cornered-rat instinct loose: brazen it out."

"We are going to fight the boat," I said tightly. I had no idea what I meant but it seemed to satisfy Mechin. "Fight the boat!" he yelled then scuttled back to the stern, repeating, "Fight the boat!" Willie Monk in the starboard turret also heard what I said: "Yeah, fight the boat! I'm gonna splash that shithead up there." He pulled back on the loading levers and they slid forward with their distinctive clack. Winters in the port after-turret echoed the clack. I could see the barrel of the stern 20 millimeter do a 360-degree flourish. The bow fifty caliber couldn't elevate more than 60 degrees, but the gunner was lying flat on the deck with his gun at maximum elevation, ready to catch anyone coming in on the bow. The 105 was no longer running; it was hunting. My brave crew was looking for a fight; I was still looking for a rainsquall.

Three miles to the east the horizon flashed rapidly, and a few moments later I heard the muted crack of bombs. The other PT boat was getting bombed! The planes—it was clear there were several—had flown over me heading east. The pilots must have seen my wake but by the time they had orbited down, they found him, not the 105, and dove on him. For a good three hours that boat was sporadically bombed, two or three bombs at a time. I never saw anything like it, it was as if the entire enemy night-flying force had dedicated their mission to him.

Where we were, nothing happened. At about 0200 I lay down beside the port forward torpedo tube for a little nap and the crew went on port and starboard watches. Gunner Brown woke me about 0300. "The other boat says they're under heavy attack." he reported. "I can see that," I replied. "What do we tell him?" "Tell him he has my sympathy, what the hell am I supposed to tell him?"

Brown shrugged. I heard him mutter to Ellis, who simply acknowledged the other boat's message without relaying my uncharitable comment. About 0400 the other boat transmitted, "Request permission to return to base." I could hear great stress in the sender's voice. It was useless for him to stay out there. There would be no barge targets for either of us, so I told him to go home. I should have told him to go home after he first called.

Two days after my decoy run, the squadron CO showed me a three-page, single-spaced letter from the boat captain who had been the target of the bombing. It was so detailed and so well organized that I thought he must have started writing it the minute his boat tied up at its mooring. The gist of the letter was that his boat was unable to make further patrols. The argumentation was superb, a masterpiece of technical exposition.

"What do you think should be done?" the CO asked. I did not answer immediately. I went back over the letter. I too had composed in my mind letters like this on a couple of mornings after unusually grim patrols. I had never reduced them to writing and, if I had, they would have been sorry affairs compared to this one. It laid out exactly the pieces of equipment, at least a dozen of them, which could fail on the next patrol. If any one of these failed, others would fail, bringing the boat to a permanent halt, drifting helplessly, far from base and at the mercy of the enemy. I was deeply moved, but not about the condition of the boat; it was no worse off than most of the beat up PTs out in the harbor. What the letter said to me was that the writer could no longer cope after the relentless bombing of two nights ago. I looked up from the letter and said, "He would make a good base force officer." The CO nodded his agreement. I lost a good boat captain.

Curious. Even though nothing happened to the 105, I think that mission pushed me closer to the edge than any other—because it was so stupid, because it showed such disdain for the lives of PT sailors, and because I did not tell the base command what I thought of the idea. It was only when I read *Catch-22* that I diagnosed my problem: I hadn't gone asiatic and I didn't have combat fatigue; I was simply convinced that the real purpose of the war was to kill *me*.

GUNGA DICK
AND THE
MARINE
PARA-
TROOPERS

Base command tent, Rendova, Solomon Islands, 0900, 27 October 1943. Me? With Marine paratroopers on Choiseul Island? I couldn't even make it at Camp Wahwayanda! Did these people say paratroopers? Dear God! I have never jumped out of an airplane, either. I saw a movie last week at Tulagi in which a brave reporter on a mission with paratroopers jumps out of an airplane, breaks his leg on landing, and is left to die, but he is brave about it—although he whines a lot toward the end.

I have just described my train of thought following the news that I might be nominated to join a diversionary raid by the 2d Marine Parachute Battalion on Choiseul Island. The objective was to fool the Japanese into thinking that the next landing (after New Georgia) would be Choiseul, when it would in fact be Bougainville. Somebody had the bright idea that we might as well send a PT officer to locate a suitable PT base in case we ever actually took the island, which was occupied by four to five thousand Japanese. This was typical of the might-aswells of some aide back at Guadalcanal who had never seen a PT boat, the 2d Marine Parachute Battalion, or Choiseul Island.

Fifteen minutes earlier, I'd just gotten up after sleeping through what passed for reveille, and I was sitting on the edge of my cot in the division leaders' tent when Essex showed up. Steward's Mate 1st Class Essex was assigned to me, or, rather, had assigned himself to me. We were good friends. He rode with me on several patrols, the only volunteer other than the famous Whizzer White. Essex and I spent one dreadful night huddled together in a foxhole while the Japanese tried to bomb us out of existence. The condition red siren had gone off, sending all present scooting for their foxholes. I was wondering who to impose upon when Essex ran up and asked if I would mind sharing with him; one look at my face told him that was a silly question, so he grabbed my arm and we were in that hole in 1.2 seconds.

The Japanese bombed sporadically most of the night, which meant that every once in a while Essex and I were awakened by the distinctive flutter of a descending stick of bombs, followed by rapid crack-whams as they exploded. Right after the last stick fell in each attack I noticed that Essex wriggled out of our joint fetal position, stood up in the foxhole for a few seconds, and then flopped back down. The next morning I found out what he'd been doing when three mess attendants who'd shared a neighboring foxhole came to me to state their grievance against Essex. One of them announced, "That Essex, he's throwin' a coconut in our foxhole after those bombs goes off and scarin' the shit out of us!" That was Essex, bless him.

Essex never woke me for breakfast unless they were serving something besides pancakes. One morning, he explained that there was not going to be a tasty breakfast; they wanted me in the command tent, now. He said ominously, "Ah—they kinda impatient, wanna know where you at," and then made a show of looking for me in other tents while I dressed hastily and then galloped the twenty-five yards to the command tent. I walked in, sat down unnoticed or ignored, and picked up the gruesome thread of the conversation. I will now relate verbatim the analysis of the situation made by Lieutenant Commander Westholm, who was saying that there were three possible candidates for detached duty with the paratroopers: Lieutenant Commander Taylor, Ensign Manahan, and me. Westholm's next words have always stuck with me: "Commander Taylor knows enough for the mission, but we can't afford to lose him. Manahan we can afford to lose but he doesn't know enough. Now Keresey here—" he trailed off and turned to look at me, as did the base commander and the others. Do you now understand why I can remember his words so clearly? Seeing there was agreement, Westholm turned back to me with, "They go in at midnight. There will be a boat to take you to the Marine base at Vella Lavella this afternoon." I said, "Sir, I would like to start up there now." This reaction was not, by the faintest stretch, born of enthusiasm. My cornered-rat instinct was in full gallop. I wanted as much time as possible to learn how to jump out of an airplane. "What's your hurry?" asked Westholm, a bit disconcerted. "Well, I've never jumped out of an airplane and maybe I can get a lesson." Westholm gave a quick, indrawn breath. "Jump? You're not going to jump. Choiseul is jungle! No one can jump on jungle. No one said anything about jumping. They're going in aboard destroyers." He glared at me.

I could see that he was thinking maybe they should send Manahan after all, and I was glad. Unfortunately, Manahan chose that moment to arrive. He'd already been at the meeting, had decided that he must be the nominee, and had left to get prepared. He entered wearing a Thompson submachine gun, a machete dangled from his belt, and long clips of ammo hung on straps, bandoleer-fashion: give him a sombrero and he'd be Pancho Villa. Westholm looked him up and down and said, "Leave any time you want, Keresey." The ensign was disappointed but took it well and even offered me his Tommy gun and bandoleer. I said, "No thank you, I'll just take my forty-five," the trusty weapon I carried even though I couldn't hit a bull in the ass at ten feet.

I went back to the tent and packed uncertainly, because I had no idea what to bring. I finally settled on a change of socks, skivvies, and shirt, along with my shaving kit. I wistfully rejected my pajamas. Three hours later on Vella Lavella I introduced myself to Lt. Col. Victor Krulak, who was leading the raid. Krulak was small for a Marine. Never confuse size with fighting ability; if there was a correlation, he'd have been seven feet tall. He took me around the battalion, introduced me, and saw to it that I was outfitted with a pack. In my case, the pack contained only rations and a mysterious jungle hammock—I say mysterious because I never figured out how it worked. Whenever it came time to sleep a Marine would appear, wave his arms wildly, kick and grunt, and the thing would be strung between two trees. It had a canopy to keep out the rain, and mosquito netting. Of course it sagged in the middle and once I climbed in, I found myself in a jackknife position. The first time night fell I thought, "Dear God, I shall never sleep," and that was my last thought until daylight.

We boarded old, four-stack destroyers that had been converted for use as high-speed transports. After we loaded, Krulak invited me to join him for the final briefing in the wardroom. The landing plan was simple enough. There were four companies: A, B, C, and Headquarters, to land in that order. Able Company would fan out into the jungle and establish a defensive perimeter. B, C, and Headquarters were to follow. The colonel courteously asked me which company I'd like to join. Considering the order of landing, I opted for Headquarters, which I assumed consisted of typists, cooks, orderlies, and similar noncombatants.

After the strategy session, I went out and sat down on the deck amidships with my back against the bulkhead. Enlisted men sat along the deck on either side. It was so dark that I couldn't see anyone clearly, but I could tell that most of them were very young. They were curious about me, the PT officer. Bulkeley's exploits in the Philippines had made his name as well-known to these kids as Hopalong Cassidy's. They took turns crouching alongside me with their questions, and each conversation was about the same. I said that PT boats went very fast, sixty miles an hour (I went a bit over the max because they all related to a mile-a-minute). Having found out what was important about PTs, they then told me the following: The Marine Corps was the greatest, the 2d Marine Parachute Battalion was the best in the Corps, and the platoon grouped around me was the best in the battalion.

They then told me that each man in this battalion was hand picked. He had his choice of weapon: Browning automatic rifle (BAR), rifle, carbine or even a Thompson submachine gun. Each speaker had been given a choice and felt that his was the best of the lot. Each then showed me his Kaybar knife. (If you saw the movie "Crocodile Dundee," you saw an only slightly enlarged replica of the Kaybar.) It was frightening: a heavy, straight blade, curved at the tip, seven inches long and a quarter-inch thick, tapering to a razor-sharp edge. It could cut down small trees, shave its owner, and do other useful things, but it was a killing knife. That was exactly what the Marines talking to me intended to use theirs for. I was disconcerted, although not at the thought of being in the company of a bunch of throat-cutters; what bothered me was that these were kids who had never been in action. I had grown up on stories in which the hero was always the boy who was modest and shy, while the coward was always the braggart—until the shooting began.

My discomfort increased when a bomb from a wandering enemy float-plane exploded near our ship. One of the Marines said in a startled voice, "What's that, lightning?" Had he never heard a bomb explode? I was entrusting my life to neophytes! How wrong could I be? The Marines were just what they said they were: highly skilled, ferocious fighters; in the next six days I was to see them do everything they bragged about, and I would gain a lifelong respect and affection for the Corps.

At 2400 the destroyers arrived just off the landing site on Choiseul and I clambered down the landing net to the LCVP (Landing Craft, Vehicle, Personnel). Even this simple deed was almost the end of me, but I managed to fall the last few feet into the boat and then found a place at the rear. We took off for shore, only a few hundred yards away. As the landing craft got close, the someone-in-charge whispered, "Down!" Everyone squatted and I followed suit as best I could. Made top-heavy by my pack, I almost toppled over backwards but came up against the aft bulkhead. From my hunkered-down position, knees up against my chin, I wondered what had prompted the "Down!" Enemy troops on the beach? If so, it wouldn't make much difference whether we were down or up because we were done for.

When the bow slid up on the beach, the ramp came down, and the Marines in front of me rose and charged off. I fully intended to rise and charge off with them, but I couldn't seem to move. My pack was just heavy enough to keep me in a permanent squat. I felt embarrassed. The landing craft was empty except for me and the two sailors who patiently waited for their last passenger to leave before they pulled off the beach. Eventually I rolled over on my side, got onto my hands and knees, and from there I straightened up and walked off.

There is an old Navy expression, "fouled up like a Marine at fire drill." Contrary to plan, Headquarters Company landed first, not last. It didn't matter. Seeing that they were first, the Headquarters Marines scuttled happily into the bush and established the defensive perimeter. I never saw any difference between the members of Headquarters Company and the others.

I had arrived on Choiseul. Where exactly, I did not know. It was dark in front of me and my companions from Headquarters Company were somewhere out in the bush. Turning seaward, I saw other landing craft approaching with the rest of the battalion so I decided that I'd better not remain there as a greeting party, since there could be a misunderstanding. I might not know anything about land fighting but I was an expert on what is likely to happen when a man with a loaded gun sees a blob he can't identify; he will shoot the blob. So I sneaked about ten yards into the bush, found a big banyan tree, and sat down against it, thereby becoming invisible.

I learned to love banyans, big-assed tress with lots of hollows and niches that I could snuggle into and where I could stow my gear out of the rain. On Choiseul I learned to know where the nearest banyan was, just as at sea I always knew where the nearest rainsquall was. On our second day I was wandering along the beach when two Zeros came over the horizon, flying just off the water. I didn't recognize them as Zeros nor did I examine their onrushing silhouettes. Instead I ran for the cover of a big banyan. With my back against the tree, I heard—and almost felt—bullets chunking into its other side while leaves and bits of wood whipped around. Those Zeros were determined little buggers. They went into tight turns and came up the beach toward me again. Why me? Why am I always the primary target? A forty-five–degree shift of position and the big fat banyan again protected me. To this day, whenever I encounter a banyan tree, I pat it on its big behind.

As the Marines moved past me into the bush, I remained quiet as well as invisible. My eyes slowly adjusted to the jungle night so that I could make out the immediate terrain, which was sparser than I expected, with open space between large trees and bushes. The ground sloped upward from the beach at a gentle incline that gradually grew quite steep. During the next week I got to know a little more about our landing area, called Vora Village. Aside from a small shack and the little clearing around it, there was nothing to show that this had ever been a human habitation; this was typical of those islands occupied by the Japanese.

After a quarter hour with my back against the banyan tree, I had become relaxed enough to start dozing. I came instantly awake at the sounds of engines from seaward. Then there came the whispered signal, "Jap landing craft!" The area around me came immediately alive with slithering forms as the Marines prepared to repel what appeared to be an invasion from the sea. I thought, "Brother, you're going to be in the middle of a land battle quicker than you thought." What to do? Staying behind the banyan tree was an option, but if there were Japanese landing on a beach only ten yards away, I decided I might as well try my forty-five—the Army forty-five automatic was not accurate but it always fired and if it succeeded in hitting a bull at ten feet, it would knock him flat. So out it came and I turned and crawled back to the beach on my hands and knees. I had seen infantrymen slithering on their bellies but I wasn't up to that. With one hand gripping my forty-five, I moved forward on one hand and two knees, looking somewhat like a three-legged Saint Bernard. When I got to the edge of the bushes, I stopped, now favoring a Saint Bernard on the point.

"Hey, Mac," came a whisper from directly behind me. I peered back, keeping my pistol trained on the beach. A machine gun pointed right up my rear end. I could just make out the gunner, sitting spraddle-legged behind his weapon with his ammo man squatting alongside. He motioned politely to indicate that I should move to the left. I did. I crawled back to the banyan tree from whence I started.

After a few minutes' silence another command coursed through the bush: "Hold your fire, they're ours." They were LCVPs and their crews, ready to provide us with seaborne transportation. Soon after, word came for Headquarters Company to assemble "over here," so I moved in the direction of the voice. I could make out the battalion doctor sitting at the side of a trail and sat down beside him. The doc wasn't a conversationalist, so I sat back against the hill and slept, something I was good at. Go through enough night patrols and your system acquires an ability to shut down on a moment's notice, and to come alive even more quickly.

The movement of people around me brought me awake. It was beginning to get light. I found myself staring at the very black face of a young native who squatted a yard away on the other side of the trail. I had heard in the briefing that we'd rendezvous with the local coast-watcher and his native helpers, but had no idea that they were already among us. The natives moved so quietly that they were sitting in the middle of us before we realized they were there.

The Solomon Islands' native could see better, hear better, and smell better than I ever thought possible. He could see or somehow sense a Japanese sniper buried in the thick fronds of a coconut palm. He'd point to the tree, whisper to his Marine buddy, " Him Jap," and a burst of fire would bring the sniper tumbling out. He could smell a Japanese soldier (smell us too) at enough of a distance that his Marines could work the problem. He could hear the gentle lapping of water on the beach—I can't say at what distance—but it would take us another ten minutes of walking before we could hear it. This was not his war, so for the most part he did not fight it; he was too smart to struggle against such unequal odds. Fortunately for us, most of the natives supported our side, and they ran great risks acting as guides and advance scouts. Without the coastwatcher and his natives, the Marine parachute battalion could still have completed its mission but the casualties would have been far greater.

Shortly after full daylight, word traveled down the trail that we were to move up about a thousand yards into the hills and establish a base of operations from which raiding parties would help simulate the beginning of an amphibious landing. As I got up to head out, I had my sole disagreement of the expedition. I reached for my helmet but the doctor beat me to it. "That's my helmet, Doc," I said. He sneeringly replied, "What difference does it make?" Little did he know that my head approximated the size of a watermelon, and that I had loosened the adjustable liner on my helmet completely. After a year's steady use, that helmet was big, and all mine. So when the doctor slapped it on his head, it slipped down over his nose. A couple of Marines giggled as he reappeared, glared at me as if it was my fault, and tossed the helmet in my direction. Still sensitive to any signal that these people weren't up to their job, I was worried that the doc's ill humor could mean that he was regretting his assignment to the Marine Corps. I was wrong on this appraisal too. He did a good job.

We trudged up a steep and very narrow path for about an hour, with numerous stops while Marines maneuvered heavy loads of base equipment around tight turns. I thought we had traveled a long way into the hills but the base site was probably somewhat less than a thousand feet up a half-mile of winding trail. The site was ideal: there was sufficient tree cover to conceal us from the air, but among the trees were natural clearings. Not thirty yards from where we bivouacked there was a rushing mountain stream for fresh water and washing, including a pool under a ten-foot waterfall that reminded me of the idyllic spot where Tarzan and Jane cavorted. I found a banyan tree in one of the clearings and settled in—not for long, however. I saw Carden Seton, the coastwatcher, with Colonel Krulak and went over, introduced myself, and explained my mission to find a good base for PT boats and small amphibious craft. I addressed him as Mr. Seton; for some reason we all called him "Mr.," so I will do so here.

If Mr. Seton had had an eye patch he'd have been a dead ringer for Teach in *Treasure Island*. He had a big, curly, black beard, stood a good six feet, three inches, had long arms and big hands, and, in general, looked like a guy I wanted on my side, especially here. Most coastwatchers placed great importance on concealing their locations. Discovery meant moving, giving less time to transmit information, and if caught, they would be summarily executed. Mr. Seton had followed the general policy against waging guerilla warfare during the first year but now that the Japanese, retreating from Bougainville, were landing on the southeast coast of Choiseul and moving along the coast to their base at the northwest end, Mr. Seton couldn't resist the temptation to join the fighting war. He had recently formed his own fifty-man native army to ambush small parties of Japanese moving along the coast. That activity had halted when he got orders to assist the Marine diversionary raid, but it meant that he had already in place a large group of scouts and guides to help. Mr. Seton had traveled across to Vella Lavella to meet with Colonel Krulak, he had selected the landing and base sites, and his fifty-man army had formed a protective perimeter on the night of the landing.

Given his fierce appearance, I was startled by his gentle manner. He sounded somewhat like a school librarian discussing what books were available for a piece of research. "Looking for a small craft anchorage? Well if you had come here a week ago, I could have walked you all over the island. If you want to stay on a few days after these chaps have finished their business, we'll do the same." He didn't tell me anything that I hadn't already guessed: my mission and the Marines' mission were not in sync. It was their job to stir up the Japanese. No way was I going to be looking for future Japanese harbors.

Colonel Krulak asked, "How about today? Is there a site Keresey could look at now?" Mr. Seton said there was a river entrance about five miles down the coast that might be suitable, so the Colonel provided a platoon of paratroopers as an escort and we took off.

Several native scouts led us, single file, down a trail that wandered through the bush and occasionally meandered out onto narrow beaches of fine brown sand. We hurried along these open stretches because they exposed us to anyone down the coast as well as enemy planes.

About a quarter mile from where we figured the river entrance was, the native guides began slowing down. Then they stopped and listened, lifting their faces skyward. Since we were in the jungle, they weren't looking for planes. I realized that they were sniffing the air. We stood completely still and silent. After a few minutes the lieutenant beckoned to me and we moved ahead, passing the natives who remained motionless. I was uneasy.

I followed the lieutenant until we came within a few feet of a river bank. I caught glimpses of the water through the leafy bush. "Go ahead out and look. We'll cover you," said the lieutenant as he turned to me. "With what?" I asked. "What do you mean?" he replied. "Where's the half-inch armor plate?" The lieutenant just smiled appreciatively at my witticism. I thought, oh well, we've come all this way. So I stepped out of the bush onto a narrow sand beach bordering the river. It turned out to be only about fifty yards across at the mouth, with a wide sandbar on the far side that narrowed the channel to about twenty feet. I thought this could serve as a base for a fleet of canoes.

My survey took about thirty seconds and I never ventured more than two feet from the bush. As I turned and walked back into the trees, leaves drifted down in front of my face. Did I think that was odd? No, not at all. I heard cracking sounds from the other side of the river. I was being shot at! I began running, right through the thick bush, leaves coming down around me like October in Vermont. Then as I hurdled a Marine, he made a capital suggestion: "Fall down!" So I did, and just in the nick of time, too, because the Japanese gunners across the river had lowered their aim.

The only possible explanation for why they hadn't terminated me when I'd stood in full view, no more than a pitching wedge away, was that they'd thought I was the pointman for a platoon; and so they had waited for the rest of the men to cross. They'd been surprised when I'd turned and stepped back into the bushes: conforming to my startled-gunner-theory, they had fired high. No doubt they had seen us because the trail we were following had wandered onto the beach for a few yards. The Japanese on the opposite bank no doubt had spotted us earlier and had set up an ambush. Why hadn't the native scouts smelled them or noticed something out of place, which was how they often detected the Japanese? My guess is that they had, but since it was our first day together and they were extremely bashful, they were unsure of how to communicate with us. Once they'd detected the Japanese, they had simply stopped. They hadn't deserted us; they'd thought we'd also sensed the obvious. We were lesser gods to them; and it took them some time to discover that in their world we were nearsighted, hard of hearing, bum smellers, and not too bright.

A firefight developed around me. All I saw was the ground where I'd flattened myself, and I took care not to look up because I could hear the snicks of bullets passing inches overhead. I knew nothing about land fighting but I figured that one principle had to be the same as at sea: never get any higher than you have to. So I honestly cannot describe the battle. Two members of our platoon were wounded. After a time the firing ceased from the other side of the river. The platoon leaders decided there was no point in attacking across the river; they'd accomplished their mission to convince the Japanese that they were the advance force of a major landing. The message to the main Japanese forces would indicate that something big was happening on Choiseul.

The five-mile hike back turned into a tough slog. We had two wounded men to carry, plus the gear of a third Marine who had an attack of stomach cramps. I had to carry my share of a load that I was not remotely conditioned for. Adding to the discomfort was the fact that it was now afternoon and the jungle heat was at its highest. When we arrived back at base, we were all dehydrated. We dumped our gear, took off our shoes, waded out in the mountain stream, and sat down. What a splendid feeling it was to submerge in that coolness! After a good soak, we regretfully climbed out. Within a few minutes the day turned to night and the heat turned to chill. I had no change of clothes—that morning I'd washed my skivvies and socks and they were still soggy— so I had to stay as I was, in soaking-wet clothes.

Compounding the discomfort, all I had for supper were an oversized teabag, some powdered milk, a couple packets of sugar, and a heat tab to bring a canteen cup of water to a boil. I filled my cup from the stream, hunkered down among the roots of my banyan tree, and set the heat tab between two rocks. I lit the heat tab and set my canteen cup on the rocks, over the small fire. Sure enough, the little fellow burned long enough to bring the water to a credible simmer and in went the teabag, the powdered milk, and sugar. I'd never before made a cup of tea, tea hadn't ever been a part of my life; but that was all there was and I was grateful. I let the bag simmer in peace until the mixture took on a strong brown color, then I removed the bag, sat hunched over in my wet clothes, and sipped my tea. It was splendid. What should have been a lonely moment to bring me close to blubbering was quite the contrary: that canteen cup of tea warmed me to a pleasant glow. After finishing my tea, I climbed the hill to my hammock and flopped in. Something dug into my backside.

Aha! I scrounged around, and pulled from my hip pocket a two-ounce bottle of Lejon brandy, a present from a Marine. These bottles were a regular part of their rations but, since most of them did not drink, they gave them to me—I had a mild buzz on almost every night. Gentlemen in their clubs had a brandy nightcap and I was not to be outdone.

This isn't turning out so badly. Here I am, camping in a comfy hammock with four hundred Marines to make my stay as pleasant as possible. And let's not overlook that mountain stream cascading down in little waterfalls. I haven't been this clean in a month. The menu is on the skimpy side but tomorrow I'll get a couple of C rations with some chocolate bars and more of those tea bags. And so to sleep.

There was a warrant gunner in the battalion (called "Gunny," naturally) who'd served in Nicaragua. Gunny was one of the few warriors who really looked the part—that is, he looked like John Wayne. I think Gunny had been a drill instructor for a good many of the Marines in the battalion and he'd decided to find out how well they'd learned their lessons. In their first big action on Choiseul, a surprise dawn attack on a Japanese encampment, his students performed "fire and movement": an intricate and deadly ballet where one or two squad members dart forward while others fire over and around them; then the forward runners drop and start firing while those behind run past them a few yards and drop down; then the first group jumps up and runs again, and so on. Above the noise would be heard the bellow of Gunny: "Fire *and* movement! Move! Move!" Then, "All right, you over there! Are you firing at a Jap or are you just firing?"—in the tone Gunny had used at Parris Island, loud but calm.

Aside from a futile excursion to a small cove five miles to the northwest, I was unable to explore Choiseul. I did find a suitable anchorage for a couple of PT squadrons, right where we had landed, but it had no cover to hide the boats in daylight. I felt pretty useless until the next-to-last day, when I earned my pay.

A couple of platoons had gone ten miles to the northwest, near the end of the island and across the strait from Bougainville. We knew from Mr. Seton that this area held at least three thousand combat-ready

Japanese, far more dangerous than most of those we'd encountered. The mission was to make a big commotion and to draw the attention of the larger forces on Bougainville away from the area where the major landing was planned. Unfortunately, they made so much commotion that the Japanese had gone in hot pursuit and had them trapped. Radio communication was poor but strong enough to alert the Marines at the main base. Their plan was to send up the LCVPs to get them out. Unfortunately, one boat had a bent propeller.

Brute Krulak called me in to ask me if I'd go down to the beach and help out. Two crewmen were sitting at the stern of a landing craft, trying to figure out how to get a bent propeller off and put a new one on. The problem was that, with the stern of the landing craft in the water, the bent propeller was four feet under. I had not the foggiest idea about landing craft or their propellers. For that matter, I didn't know squat about how to change a PT propeller. But, the Marines didn't know that. To them, I was the PT boat lieutenant and knew everything nautical there was to know.

"Fellas," I said, "just take that there wrench and that ball-peen hammer, and take a deep breath and go down and knock that prop the hell off that shaft. Then I'll show you how to get this one on." Instead of asking me to show him how to do the first part, the bigger crewman grabbed the wrench and the hammer, took a deep breath and ducked underwater. He stayed down a full minute, came up gasping, then went down again. On his fifth try, I saw he was bleeding from his nose. "Are you sure they do this on a PT, Sir?" he asked. "Absolutely." I didn't lie. I just didn't explain that it was done with an air helmet. The man went down again, came up grinning, and announced, "It came off!" Without a word, the other man slid over the side and, with a few dives, got the new propeller on. The shaft was a little bent so the craft vibrated, but it ran, and soon the two LCVPs headed north to find the trapped Marines. Each craft had two sailors, and several Marines to provide firepower.

As I watched them go, I thought, "I should go with them. I'm not doing anything here. All they'll do is wander around and if they actually do find the trapped Marines, they won't have enough firepower to get to the beach. Firepower! That's what was missing. Close-in firepower like fifty calibers, a couple of twenties, and how about a forty-millimeter? What am I waiting for? This is a job for PT boats!" I huffed and puffed up the hill to the base camp and proposed to the colonel that we get some PTs from Vella Lavella. He took to the idea immediately and sent a message down the line.

A little after sundown, two PTs arrived and I went out by LCVP to go aboard. I climbed aboard the lead boat, an old PT that had been converted to a gunboat, and was greeted by John F. Kennedy himself. At the time, of course, I did not appreciate the honor. Jack, surprised to see me there, said, "What are you doing here?" "Never mind that, we have to haul ass up the coast. There's a bunch of Marines trapped!"

The reason this exchange has stuck with me over the years is not because it was JFK, future President, who was the butt of my abruptness. I remember stalking impatiently around the cockpit giving course and speed orders as if I was in command; and then I realized that Kennedy, who had two stripes to my one-and-a-half, was the division leader, not me. I stopped, embarrassed, and turned to apologize but Kennedy— and this was typical of him—was following my orders with perfect ease. He wasn't doing this because my competence equaled my arrogance— remember it was Kennedy who'd towed me in after I'd run aground some months back—he knew that at that moment I knew more than he did. I also think he liked me. We liked each other.

We went full-out up the coast for about ten minutes and then slowed to a fast idle. I knew that the trapped Marines could be anywhere in the five miles to the north of us and I didn't want to miss them. I went up on the bow deck where I could hear gunfire better and after a few minutes I did hear something coming from inshore, but not gunfire. It was a breath-catcher: faint shouts, bordering on screams.

I signaled Jack at the wheel to turn in toward the sounds. As the bow swung in I saw the two LCVPs, startlingly close. If we'd continued at our earlier high speed, we'd have gone right by them, for it was the sound not the sight that attracted me. I hailed them and then made one of my dumber greetings: "You're all right, Marines, the Navy's here." Fortunately for me, there was so much noise and confusion that no one heard this bombast. Kennedy drew his boat alongside one LCVP and the second boat captain came expertly alongside the other, and I saw that the two landing craft were jammed with exhausted Marines, some wounded and many with the unfocused stare of men who have met grinning death. It was no time for jokes.

In moments, the two craft were unloaded. I thought briefly about dosing the beach with gunfire, but there were too many passengers who could end up in the line of fire. Besides, our job was to get the wounded back as soon as possible.

One memory remains vivid. One Marine, Corporal Pare, was crying that he wanted to go back. One of the Marines told me that shortly before the LCVPs had arrived, the Marine force had retreated to the northwest side of the Warrior river. Thinking that there was another Marine force somewhere across the river, Lieutenant Johnston, Sergeant Muller, and Corporal Pare had volunteered to swim over to the other side and try to make contact. They had to strip and leave their weapons in order to swim the river. As they'd reached the other side and climbed out of the water, Japanese soldiers had stepped out of the bush and opened fire. Lieutenant Johnston was wounded and was immediately surrounded; the other two had also been hit, but had managed to dive back into the river. Sergeant Muller had swum a few yards and then had disappeared beneath the surface, but Pare had made it back. Two more Marines on the northwest bank had also been hit before the Japanese had retreated, taking Lieutenant Johnston with them. Aboard the PT boat after the rescue, Pare was delirious from his wound and kept crying, "I can't leave them. Let me go back!" He had to be restrained because it was clear he was ready to dive over the side and swim back. I was shaken by this young boy, sobbing over the fact that he had survived when his buddies had not, and also because Lieutenant Johnston had become a good friend in the few days we had served together. He was a genial, handsome young man from a town near my home in New Jersey. I'd enjoyed his company. I took a brief moment and said the Lord's Prayer for him, as I did for any squadron mate killed in action. Johnston had been taken prisoner, but I knew he was either already dead or soon would be.

One badly wounded Marine, Corporal Schnell, was taken down to Kennedy's bunk. The Marine doctor who had lost himself in my helmet was treating Schnell, and asked for whiskey. They scrounged around and found a small bottle of brandy. John Maguire, one of the crew members, later told me, "I thought the booze was for the patient and was shocked when the doctor opened it and drank it. I went topside and told JFK. 'I'll be damned,' he said. We both laughed."

Maguire also told me that after Corporal Schnell died, "a shipmate and I placed the body aft against the smoke-screen generator and covered it with a tarp. A little while later, one of our gunners tried to wake up poor Schnell to relieve him on his gun watch—one of the crew had told the gunner the corpse was his relief." This dark humor helped us get through the war. I'm sure that Corporal Schnell would have laughed the loudest.

I didn't know what had gone on ashore; I'd been intent on getting the Marines back to the base. It was now pitch dark and none of us knew how far we had gone up the coast. One of the Marines who had been with the landing craft that had been sent up earlier told me his story, and it has stayed with me ever since. Contrary to my assessment, the LCVP's crews had found their trapped comrades easily enough, because there was still some light and they had been able to see and hear the firing. When the LCVPs had started into the beach, they'd been taken under fire so heavy that the ensign in charge gave the order to turn away. One of the Marines had placed his carbine against the poor ensign's neck and said, "Go in or you're dead!"

They'd gone in. A ferocious burst of fire drove the Japanese back long enough for the two boats to be loaded, and then they had pulled off the beach. The boat with the bent shaft had conked out when they were less than a hundred yards out. It was now dark, so the Japanese couldn't see well enough to fire effectively, but the boat was drifting back dangerously close to the shore and the enemy fire. Believing this was the end, the command had come: "Fix bayonets!" Those men who could had done so, while others had whipped out their Kaybars: they were going to fight their way out or die. Also in the first craft was a native guide who could have vanished in the bush when the fighting had started, but he had stayed. When he saw the Marines preparing for hand-to-hand combat, he took out his machete, looked around at his Marines, grinned broadly, and ran his thumb down the blade. The second landing craft had turned around and taken the stricken one in tow, and a few minutes later we'd arrived. By then I was a cynical, combat-weary man who was convinced, as I've said before, that this war was simply a conspiracy to kill *me*. But at that moment I glimpsed that rare and beautiful bond that exists between men of courage. When I left that night, because my job was done, and it was time for me to return to my own trade, I felt that I had been given a great privilege to have served with another band of the "happy few."

A MATTER OF
PERSPECTIVE

"Do these people," I said to myself, "really think they can pull this off?" I was looking across the briefing tent at four Marines in baggy camouflage. I knew the one at the left was a lieutenant because the Professor, our base intelligence officer, had addressed him as such. You couldn't tell his rank by his outfit because Marines in combat wore no insignia. The lieutenant appeared chunky, of medium height, and paid polite attention to the Professor (so named because he looked like an English professor, which is what he had been back when all of us had been something else). The other Marines were slightly smaller copies of their leader and were leaving it to him to follow the proceedings while they examined the opposite wall.

I had arrived at the briefing tent, at our brand new base on Torokina Island at Bougainville, knowing that I was to lead the night's mission; but, as was the custom, I didn't have the foggiest as to what was in store. The base command had worked hard all day thinking up things for us to do all night. Usually the division leaders and boat captains who were going to do the dirty were not brought in on the planning sessions. Most of the time our orders were simple: "go patrol from so on to so forth and, if you see anything move, shoot it." I don't think any of us in the operating group yearned to join the planning group. Daytime hours were our time to have an early morning drink or two, alky screamers or raisin jack from the still Joe Roberts had built in his crew's head and which, if discovered, would have sent Joe to someplace worse than Bougainville, a place that Joe said did not exist. After the six A.M. cocktail hour we'd have a good snooze, tend our boats, and then sit around and natter until half of us went on the night's mission and the other half hit the sack. Once in awhile the planned mission got more complicated, like here.

Tacked up on a piece of plywood was a chart of the Bougainville coast and the half-moon shape of Empress Augusta Bay. (Bougainville was a massive island, about 125 miles long and 50 miles wide. I had nominated Guadalcanal as the gloomiest island until I saw Bougainville, where smoke rising from a volcano created a perpetual gray shroud.) The Solomon Islands had been pretty far down on the list of places that our Coast and Geodetic Survey took seriously before 7 December 1941, and the charts were short on detail. Notes on a chart such as, "In April 1857, Captain Bruggemeir of the schooner *Adolphus* sighted reefs," do not inspire confidence. Our ground forces were fighting to extend the beachhead that they'd established near the western end of the bay. The Japanese were being supplied and reinforced from the eastern end of the island, where their forces were concentrated. The Professor explained that our task was to set the Marine scouts down behind Japanese lines. They would proceed about five miles inland to the Japanese supply road, observe the traffic on the road, and then proceed back to the coast where we were to pick them up two days after the dropoff. I was struck by his description of what these Marines were about to attempt at night. It would be all slash-and-stumble with the likely prospect of running into the enemy along the route.

We all liked the Professor—he seldom had any useful information but he was cheery and tried to lighten things up at briefings. He had never really left his schoolroom and become a part of this different life. I never saw him volunteer to ride as an observer like Whizzer White, who'd boosted my spirits back in New Georgia by riding with me on a couple of missions so he could get a better sense of our operations.

(Whizzer had been transferred to cruiser duty, but if he had been there he would have gotten ahold of me early on with a dozen questions.)

The Professor stepped over to the chart and pointed at a spot on the coast about twenty miles from the eastern end of the bay, which put it about sixty miles from our base. The coastline appeared to be straight except for two small and nameless indentations about five miles apart. "These two coves," said the Professor, his pointer bouncing from one indentation to the other, "are barge installations. And this," he pointed to a spot midway between the two, "is our landing spot."

He stared at me over his spectacles. I nodded and looked over at the Marine leader who continued providing the speaker polite attention. What went without saying was that where there are enemy bases for Japanese barges that carry troops and supplies between and along the islands of the Solomons, there are also enemy shore guns to destroy any PT boats that venture within range and enemy jungle-wise infantry able to track down an infiltrating force. When we had no comment, the Professor turned back to the chart and moved his pointer from the coast to a squiggly line about five miles inland, penciled in by someone to indicate the supply road. I wondered how they knew this was a supply road, and why, if they knew so much, they didn't just bomb it to smithereens. The road was probably a native trail, like those on Choiseul, that the Japanese had widened enough for supply vehicles but not enough to be visible from the air. The professor continued, "The Marines and their four native guides"—I looked around and, sure enough, four natives were hunkered down in the back—"will proceed up the road, observe the traffic for two days, and then proceed back to the coast where they will rendezvous with the PT boats at 2400 hours."

The native guides would be able to get the Marines from the coast to the road and back again, but that didn't solve my problems. I stared at the chart. How would I find the same spot twice? First, there was the featureless flat line of the coast to make it hard to tell where I was. Next, the land mass back of the shoreline appeared to climb quite uniformly from sea level to four or five thousand feet, where the chart indicated the supply road, then up to about seven thousand feet; there were no peaks or niches from which I could take bearings—and even if there were, they would be too high for any semblance of accuracy.

Like most of my kind, I'd learned the art of piloting at night without any equipment other than a magnetic compass. We had a handheld

Polaris for taking bearings, but its built-in magnetic compass could be off by over five degrees. Over time I'd learned to use the outlines of land features—mostly peaks and notches and sometimes a palm or clump of palms that stood out. This only worked when I'd been someplace and was trying to get back again. When I left a harbor, for instance, I'd turn, look directly astern and memorize the skyline. Every skyline is different, like every fingerprint. Sometimes two objects line up. More often there's a shape that's only that shape at that bearing. Every time I left someplace I tried to memorize its silhouette. Then if I had to return in the dark, I'd fuss around outside the harbor until I found that same silhouette—and if I couldn't find it, I'd wait for daylight. The daylight option was not going to be available this time. But maybe, just maybe, I would get an outline to help me return to the same place. The chart, however, was telling me that there would be only a shapeless blob. Radar? Yes, we had all been equipped with radar for a couple of months. Our set was good on ranges but not so good on bearings, because a PT underway was not a very stable platform. The problem was that I could see nothing on that massive coast that would stand out to plot a fix. With radar I'd know how far I was from the coast—plus or minus a hundred yards—but this time I could be off by a mile on where I was along that coast and end up too close to one of the barge bases.

I was also worried about the usefulness of radar after hearing Charlie Bernier describe his horrifying experience from the night before. "I was just moseying along keeping station on the lead boat," Charlie had said, "when I heard my radar man say 'I got something dead ahead and closing fast!' I pick up my binoculars and look ahead. Nothing. I look at the lead boat but it's just idling along. I look ahead. It's just dark, nothing. So I stick my head down in the charthouse to take a look at the screen. The radarman is up close to it and I can't see, so I tell him to move aside and there's a blip that can't be more than five hundred yards away. Just then I hear my exec yell, 'Holy shit!' I pull back up to see what the hell's coming at us and, I swear, one second there's this big bow wave and, the next second, a big Jap destroyer or cruiser or whatever-the-hell-it-is comes charging past, no more than ten feet away. No gunfire, just this big woosh of sound. Then the stern wave hits us broadside and we keel over, I swear, fifty degrees to port and then the same to starboard, and I damn near went overboard."

Charlie had paused, looked at the ground between his knees, and muttered, more to himself than to us, "God almighty, that was a big ship. Why he didn't run right over me I don't know." "How come the radar didn't pick it up earlier?" I had asked. Charlie had shrugged. "How about the lead boat?" I had wanted to know. Charlie had replied, "They had just got a blip on the scope. They said they called me or maybe they said they were about to call me. Anyway it doesn't matter."

No damage had been done except to Charlie's nerves but none of us had yet forgotten the 109: without radar, Kennedy never had a chance of seeing the destroyer heading right for him with the mass of Kolombangara blotting out any silhouette until at maybe a thousand yards, more likely less than that. With this great new invention, we thought the risk of being run down or blown out of the water before we could react was a thing of the past. But Charlie's story had made it clear that the great new invention had flunked. Charlie had simply had ten more feet of luck than Jack Kennedy.

The Professor brought me out of my reverie with, "Any questions?" I was tempted to ask "How in hell do you think I can put these poor bastards down on that coast on a moonless night and not get them stuck in a mangrove swamp and then find that same spot two nights later, and get close enough so I can see that tiny little light they're going to blink from their tiny little raft two feet off the water?" I said nothing, partly out of arrogance (of which I had a full tank), and partly because of the presence of my CO and the COs of two other squadrons. None of these guys knew anything about the area and not much about night operations, but they were likely to say something that would limit my options. Another reason I kept my mouth shut was that one of the COs might decide that I lacked the necessary 'can-do spirit,' and some other guy would get the job. My CO was a nice guy. I liked him and, in his aloof, withdrawn way, I think he liked me. If the job were given to another squadron, he'd be embarrassed.

No questions were forthcoming from the Marine lieutenant, either, so we filed out, walked the few yards to our makeshift dock and boarded an LCVP that ferried us to our boats. I had the 105 with John Iles as skipper. Jack Weeks, in an old seventy-seven footer, had the job of second boat.

Weeks and I had been in the same class at Melville and he should have been a division leader by then, but he had no combat experience. His first assignment had been with Squadron One in Hawaii and then he'd gone to Funa Futi, home of carefree Polynesian girls, far from the war zone, where he had spent six glorious months. While Jack was sunning himself and gathering stories to entertain me, I was having a miserable time advancing my career in PT boats. Which meant, however, that he had to pay for his good time by riding second to the likes of me. This was painful for both of us. Jack knew me too well, and wanted to do more than just stay a boat length on my starboard quarter; he wanted to keep me from grievous error. He was a good man and on this mission he provided (in a bizarre fashion) the clue to my piloting problem, and pulled off a bit of great seamanship and boat handling that turned into high comedy.

When the LCVP pulled alongside the 105 it was already dark. I had thought about arrangements on the ride out and said to the Marine leader, "I want all your people and gear on this boat, Lieutenant." Jack was standing next to me and said, "Hey, that's a lot of people, how's about my taking half?" I knew why he wanted some of the scout party. Jack was extraordinarily interested in everything that went on around him. I knew that, if Weeks had Marines with him, he'd be thrilled at the opportunity to quiz them about what they did and how they did it. But suppose his rotten old 77 broke down or sprung a leak? Or, worse, suppose he lost me. But I didn't give him my reasons—give Weeks a reason for anything and he'd offer a better counter reason. I could see Weeks was waiting for my explanation, so I gave it to him. "No," I said.

The four Marines and their native guides clambered aboard and the 105's crew manhandled their raft up and onto the ready-room canopy. A disgruntled Weeks rode on in solitary gloom to his old tub, no doubt thinking dark thoughts about me, his old Melville buddy.

We picked our way through the assortment of PTs and small amphibious vessels that crowded the little harbor between Torokina and the Bougainville mainland. When we cleared the entrance we revved up to a cruising speed of seventeen hundred rpms, about twenty-five-plus knots, and headed east. I saw that Weeks was tucked in about a boat length off my starboard quarter. I was glad that I didn't have to tell him to close up. Back in training school we were taught that distances between boats should be three lengths—so on their first missions new boat captains could get lost, which was unhealthy. It was better to risk running into the lead boat if she suddenly went hard to starboard than to lose the lead boat if she suddenly turned to port or abruptly increased speed. Lose the lead boat and you become part of the Japanese navy.

Satisfied with my wing boat, I checked to see that my passengers were safely hunkered down, and then I turned to the lieutenant, who was standing next to me in the cockpit. I noticed that he stood almost at my eye level. He had looked on the short side in the briefing tent. I checked to see if he was standing on the two-inch-high box that Mechin, who was quite short, used when he had the wheel. No box. The lieutenant was not short and chunky, he was tall and chunky. "Lieutenant, how much do you weigh?" I asked. "Oh, last time I got weighed about two-thirty," he said, smiling, as if it were perfectly all right that my first words to him were not, "welcome aboard," or, "pleased to meet you," but an irrelevancy. I stared ahead, over Iles's shoulder as he stood at the wheel, wondering how a guy built like a Chicago Bears' guard could ever manage to tiptoe through the bush and spy on stealthy and highly trained Japanese moving along a jungle trail. Conversely, I tried to imagine a Japanese soldier rounding a bend in a trail, only to come face-to-face with this Marine King Kong!

"It's a long way from Columbia Law School," said a voice next to me. I turned my head and realized the voice had issued from the Marine lieutenant. "What?" I asked. "Columbia Law School." I looked at him and his smile turned to a broad grin. Then he said, "Dick, I'm Larry Bangser." Larry Bangser had been a cheery guy a class behind me, kind of short and stout—or was he? I guess I'd seen him mostly sitting, across a table in the library. We used to natter about this and that. He was clearly not short and stout, although still cheery, and now I recognized his grin, which looked out of place in a face covered with streaks of camouflage grease. "Good grief Larry, you look kinda different." "I know," he said, "I couldn't place you at first either. But when you talked to the other fellows, I recognized your voice." He grinned at me again. "I thought you'd be doing intelligence work, or something. Never pictured you driving a PT boat." I responded wryly, "Yeah, well, the Navy has its little jokes."

I didn't ask Larry what twist of fate had brought him here or how the Marines had changed my stoutish little law school chum into this fearsome character. I realized that now I had a personal interest in this operation: it's one thing when you wave good-bye to a guy in a rubber raft whom you have never seen before and, frankly, never expect to see again; it's quite another thing when that guy is a warm human being you laughed with in a library three years earlier. An inner voice said, "Crank yourself up, boy. You're going to put your friend down on a nice beach, and you're going to come back to that same beach and pick him up."

I admit that another human could be just a cipher and that the level of risk I'd take could be considerably higher when there was a bond. So now I had to do my best for Larry, Columbia class of '42.

"Okay, Larry," I said, "we got a few problems here. Number one: You ever been in a mangrove swamp?"

"Yeah. If that happens, we'll backpedal and look for a beach. There are some?"

"There should be. I'll set you down on one, can't have you wallowing around in that raft." I felt that at about a quarter mile from shore I could probably distinguish a beach from a mangrove swamp by the slight difference in their dark shades. I couldn't go any closer than a quarter mile because there might be outlying coral reefs. Rocks or coral reefs a short distance offshore would not appear on our charts, which were only good enough for vessels that never ran close to shore. Joe Burk always liked to get within a few yards of the beach and lie in wait for barges running further offshore. As the barge pilots scanned the horizon for PT boats, they'd get a terminal blast from Burk. Joe ran aground on several occasions, a condition scary beyond contemplation. I reached my fright level at four hundred yards—and only someone like Larry could get me that close. I was terrified of grounding, of that sudden stop that would ram me against the cockpit bulkhead, and of the disgusting grinding of propellers embedding themselves in coral.

"Do your native guides have any knowledge of the trails up from the coast?" I had in mind that maybe I could get him on a beach with a trail leading down, but Larry answered, "These guides are from New Guinea." "They're *what?*" I asked incredulously. "Yop. First time here for them, too." This was ridiculous. The terrain was all uphill through thick jungle, at least for the first couple of miles; at higher altitudes there might be more open forest. Having spent time in the jungles of Choiseul—an island with similar terrain—I knew firsthand that any traveling off the trails would be all slash-and-stumble. And worse, gone was my forlorn hope that the natives might know enough of the coast to keep me away from dangerous coves. Well, there was no use in getting into that. The Marines must know what they're doing—or do they?

By this time we'd passed the eastern end of Empress Augusta Bay and it was time for me to do some charthouse work, so I swung down below while Iles came down to idling speed. We had plenty of time and would travel from here on at a speed to minimize our wake, which might be seen by Japanese spotters in the hills as well as the ever dangerous night-bombers.

Mechin had already started a dead-reckoning plot to bring us to a point three miles off the coast and, hopefully, halfway between the two barge installations. The only bearing he had was on the fuzzy shape of the eastern end of Empress Augusta Bay. Other than that, the radar of the coastline was, as I had thought, a straight line. I tried to pick out the indentations of the two coves but there was too much clutter close to shore. "Johnny," I called up through the charthouse door to Iles at the wheel, "keep you rpms steady so you can run at the same speed on the way back." John already knew this but he was used to me telling him to do the obvious. We pooped along for half an hour while I alternated between the chart and the radar screen. We were coming up on what I guessed was the right place to turn into the shore when our VHF came alive.

"Baker One, from Baker Two. Over," Weeks called from the 77 in a hushed voice, as if someone might hear him. I responded with, "This is Baker One. Hear you five-by-five. Go ahead." Old hands like Weeks and I couldn't break the habit of testing reception, born from the TBS sets we had had back when the 109 was run down. Back then, sets drifted off frequency, so the first transmission might be nothing but static until the operators could match up frequencies. The TBS sets had sometimes gotten so jarred from the bouncing they took that their messages just spun off into space, or were heard by some boats but not by others—that's why Kennedy hadn't known about the approaching ship that ran him over. With these VHF crystal sets that problem was gone, but not the old habit. "I have a target," Weeks came over in an excited, hoarse whisper. Good grief! I didn't need that. "Ellis," I turned to the radar/radioman. "Do you see anything?"

"Nossir, Nossir. Nothing."

"Where is it?" I asked Weeks.

"Bearing ninety degrees relative, range five thousand yards. Speed dead slow. Looks like a Jap destroyer. Wait. We've picked up a second, I think." I bolted out of the charthouse, raised my binoculars, and looked in that general direction. At five thousand yards I should be able to see it, but my night vision was gone. "John, take a look." I handed the glasses to John Iles. "I see something there," John said. "Just a blob.

I think I see a bow wave, pretty big." For the next few seconds, I stood stunned.

"Baker One, lemme attack. Over," from Weeks. That was a possible: Weeks attack while I landed our party. That was not a possible. Finally, here was a third chance for me: my first two chances had been the night the 109 had been sunk, when I'd fired twice. Here was an enemy ship—probably a destroyer, maybe a cruiser—unaware of our presence, sneaking along with some nefarious purpose. If we launched eight torpedoes from our two boats, we couldn't miss. The last time, it had been every boat for itself; this time I'd conduct the first coordinated attack. I'd get a medal and all sorts of good things. But first I needed to call in a contact report. No, first I needed to get the passengers belowdecks and out of the way. I had just thumbed the mike to call Weeks when Mechin called up from the charthouse, "Skipper, come look at this."

I slung myself down and Mechin pointed to a tiny dot on the chart in the same spot where Weeks had picked up the blip on his screen. I looked at our screen. There it was. Jack, bless his heart, had mistaken a coral islet lying five miles offshore for a ship, and had even gotten a course and speed. We had nearly won ourselves the Dingleberry medal with oak leaf cluster, awarded to all boat captains who torpedo coral islets; along with this medal went command of the officers' laundry.

I had already received the Vasco da Gama award for running aground in Tulagi and this near-miss caused me to shudder and grasp Mechin so hard that he whined and dropped his "gotcha" leer. I hollered, "Goldarnit Mechin, I knew it was a goldarn coral islet." Then, as calmly as I could, I called over the radio, "Baker Two, that is an island and so is the other. Over and out."

Mechin had his dividers on the chart. I took them and, while Mechin called off the ranges from our boat to the two islands, I drew the two ranges, and where the lines crossed was our position. This showed me two things: missed by two miles through dead reckoning; and if we'd turned when I thought we should, we would have run right into the entrance of the first cove. That would have been the finish of the landing party, and probably us as well. But now I knew how to get in at a safer place and find it two nights later.

I looked at Mechin, "Hot damn, Tommy!" I only called him Tommy when he'd done something wonderful like this. "Yeah!" he said happily. "We got it now Skipper." "OK," I said, "Keep plotting ranges, let me know when we turn in, and then keep plotting ranges all the way in. Don't let anybody touch the chart."

Then I hurried back to the cockpit where John Iles was at the wheel carefully holding course and my law school chum still watched the proceedings with the calm detachment of a man commuting to work on the eight-oh-five from Montclair. Good Marine that he was, he was undisturbed by all our frantic activity. Every man to his own trade. It was up to me, the tall, skinny, fidgety guy with the thousand-yard stare, to deliver him to his place of business and come back in forty-eight hours to take him home.

After a quarter hour, Mechin called, "Turn!" John Iles cranked the wheel and we began idling directly in toward the massive hulk of Bougainville. I watched Weeks' 77 swing across our wake and settle down again close on our starboard bow. I was glad that Weeks was there, notwithstanding his recent interest in blowing up an inoffensive coral islet. That wasn't as dumb as it may seem. Weeks had settled himself at the radar scope, leaving it to me to handle the piloting. His main concern was the real possibility of another foray by Jap surface ships from Rabaul. After Bernier's horror the night before, Weeks wasn't going to rely on my radar watch. Besides, I still didn't trust radar. I still argued that I could pick up a target just as quickly with my trusty binoculars, which he thought was absurd. So he had overlooked the two specks on the chart and was tricked by relative movement, which on a radar screen makes a stationary object look as if it's moving. What was important to me about Jack Weeks was that, if I misjudged my approach to this dark coast or was just plain unlucky (if my boat was ambushed or if I ran aground), he would stay and help with firepower, smoke screens, or towlines as called for. I couldn't be as sure of all boat captains. Weeks wouldn't go home.

My night vision was now pretty much restored and I concentrated on the water ahead, straining to pick up any flickers that might show water breaking on reefs. The young gunner in the forward turret was standing as high up as he could, doing the same thing. The gunner for the bow fifty was lying on the bow and watching the water for any sign of a reef; by the time he could spot one, probably it would be too late but we could at least have our props stationary before they hit coral. Mainly, I just had to hope for the best as Ellis called off ranges both from the two islands astern of us and from the shore. When we were four hundred yards offshore, John Iles threw the engines to neutral and we coasted to a stop two hundred yards out. Weeks now had his boat directly astern, following in my wake to lessen his chance of running aground. I now had a fair chance of discerning beach, mangrove swamp, or sheer cliff. "Looks like beach," I said. John Iles was staring through his glasses. "Beach," he agreed. The young gunner said, "Beach."

I turned to my law school chum and nodded.

"OK, Larry. I'll wait ten minutes. Flash your light if it's no good and come on back. Otherwise, I'll see you here night after next at 2400." He and his men were already at work and the raft was in the water in something like ten seconds. The four natives and the four Marines slid in and, with the four Marines paddling, they took off for the shore without any farewell chatter. Once in their raft, they were in their trade. The thought of what lay ahead of them chilled me, but they seemed quite content. They paddled off in such a synchronous rhythm that I hummed the old ditty, " Row, row, row your boat, gently down the stream." John Iles mimed along with my attempt at humor.

Ten minutes was a long time. If a barge happened along, the resulting gun battle could louse up the security of the shore party; but Larry and I figured that ten minutes would get him to the beach and if enemy craft showed up before that, it would be better for the landing party if we opened fire.

After those ten minutes, we carefully turned around, idled out to about two miles from the coast, and began an anti-barge patrol, moving slowly eastward. At dawn, having found nothing, we turned around to head back to Torokina. It was then that my decision not to trust any of the landing party to the old 77 proved out. One of her two rudders dropped out, leaving a hole in her bottom about the size of a golf cup.

I saw that something was wrong before Weeks came up on the radio because as I happened to look over at her, now plainly visible, I thought that she looked peculiar, down by the stern. We were now doing about twenty-five knots, and I thought that maybe that was how those boats looked at that speed, when Weeks came up on the VHF, "Baker One from Baker Two. Over." I responded, "Go ahead Baker Two." "I've dropped a rudder," Weeks reported, "Sinking by the stern. Request permission to jettison torpedoes." Weeks wanted to lighten his boat. He was asking permission to deep-six four umpteen-thousand-dollar naval ordnance torpedoes. No one let go of that much naval ordnance without filing many forms and answering many questions. It would have been better for all concerned if he'd fired them at the coral islet. I looked over at the rotten old lady with her stern down. On the other hand, if his boat sank, particularly *that* boat, no one would care. PT boats sank. Torpedoes were fired at the enemy.

"Baker Two, negative, I repeat negative." I got no reply. I thought for a moment Weeks might pretend that he hadn't heard me. But the torpedoes stayed put. Jack let loose one "Sumbitch!", went down into the engine room, grabbed an ax, waded into the flooded lazarette, and chopped a hole in the stern. The seawater rushing through the hole in the bottom then rushed out through a hole in the stern—as long, that is, as the boat proceeded at twenty-five knots so as to create a hole in the water abaft the stern. If Weeks slowed down, the boat would sink for sure. The lazarette is the last watertight compartment in the boat but it wasn't watertight enough; there was already water in the engine room. Having taken his desperate measure, Weeks came back on the airwaves and said, without further introductory Baker Ones and Twos, "Let's go someplace where there's a pump."

I checked the chart. We'd gone so far east that we were closer to the PT base at Treasury Island than at Torokina. It was a more established base with a better chance of having a good pump. Bob Kelly was base commander there and I felt his base would have a good setup. I liked and respected Kelly, one of the heroes of *They Were Expendable* (William Lindsay White, 1942). He had a quick and roaring temper, but he was a first rate seaman. I said, "We'll go to Treasury," and we reversed course for what looked like an hour's run. I radioed our home base of our detour and then spent the rest of my time on the radio convincing the Treasury Island people that we needed the biggest water pump they had on the dock ready to go.

As we approached Treasury, we had a tricky entrance to take into account. The Treasury Island base was on a broad lagoon, protected by a series of coral reefs. To get into it required three serpentine turns, and any boat captain in his right mind took these turns at idling speed. So when we came to the first turn, John Iles naturally slowed abruptly from twenty-five knots to ten. Weeks suddenly came flying by, his grommetless cap—which he affected while the rest of us prudently wore helmets—scrunched down around his ears. He stared straight ahead at the first turn, knowing that if he reduced speed his boat would sink and thereby close the harbor entrance, and wishing, he told me later, that he had thought of this while still out in open water. All of us on deck watched as, with only the one rudder, he skidded around the first turn heeled over like a speedboat around a pylon, raced past us in the opposite direction into another skidding turn, then another, and then disappeared from view. It was all class and panache. But it did him no good. Commander Kelly viewed all reserve officers with suspicion. Plus, on the opening of the New Georgia campaign Kelly's squadron had torpedoed and sunk the USS *Macauley,* so he did not need any other mishaps.

Bob Kelly had sprung into action when our call had come in for a pump, and the pump was sitting on the dock, ready to go, when Jack Weeks roared into view, a half-mile away and headed directly for the dock at twenty-five-plus knots. Kelly and his emergency pump crew stood on the dock three feet off the water and watched, with growing unease, the approach of the 77. At a hundred yards it suddenly came to them that the dock was an unsafe place, and they all took off for shore. Weeks, superb boat-handler that he was, went all engines astern, cranked the wheel hard over, and the boat slid into the dock with a modest jolt. There sat the pump, but no pumpers, and before the base force crew could get back to the pump, Weeks' boat began settling by the stern. She continued to do so until she hit bottom, leaving Weeks and his crew in water up to their navels. The base dock was out of commission. Kelly was out of his mind. I tried explaining several times to Weeks (but never once to Kelly) that he'd saved four torpedoes which were worth far more than his cruddy boat. He never bought it.

Two nights later, I went back with the 105 to find Bangser and his party, accompanied by another boat and boat captain of whom I had some doubt. At the briefing I thought of suggesting that Weeks ride on the second boat but gave up on this after I'd used up my ration of goodwill by insisting that I ride on the 105. I tried to explain to base command that I could only get back to the same place by using the chart on the 105. They didn't understand what difference this would make and told me to take the chart with me on another boat. They never understood me and maybe it didn't matter what boat I took, but they finally relented. With John Iles holding course and speed exactly as before, we reached the point where our first ranges had crossed and we turned into the coast. I know you will think I'm making this up, but as we were idling in with Ellis calling the ranges on the two coral islets, the new boat captain came up on the VHF, "Baker One, I have a target-no-wait-I have two-er," he paused, the VHF humming as it does when the mike is pressed while the sender listens to someone, then continued, "Oh. Baker One, cancel that last. No target, no target. Over and out." Iles and I smirked at each other. Those islands had once again escaped attack.

We were about five hundred yards from the beach when what do I see through my binoculars—broad on the starboard bow, somewhere between fifty and a hundred yards—but two Japanese barges in column on a course ninety degrees relative to our own. "Stop," I said and John went to neutral and gave a reverse on the center engine to check any forward motion. I kept them in my binoculars. They held to their course and speed. What now? Here were some real targets. Should I turn to port, parallel their course, and open fire? It was now a couple of minutes before 2400 hours.

The chances that the Marines were somewhere back of these barges seemed remote. Assuming that they hadn't been detected and terminated, I'd never believed that they'd get back to the same place on the beach at the estimated time. They were at best probably still fumbling around, trying to locate where they'd hidden the raft. My second boat was a good hundred yards to my rear and I did a quick check to make sure he had stopped. He had. On his own, he had dropped behind as we got close to the beach so that only one of us would risk running aground or getting blown out of the water—very prudent. I preferred Weeks, who would have been practically up on my fantail, but this was probably better. My substitute second boat would stay put. He was far enough back that he couldn't spot the intruding barges and no doubt he assumed that I'd simply stopped to wait for the Marines. John Iles was acting like he needed to visit the head, but he said nothing.

"We let them go, John," I said. My job was to pick up four Marines and four native guides in a raft which could be directly behind the two barges. If the 105 opened fire, several thousand rounds would pour into the barges but also over them. I didn't know for sure that a raft filled with eight people wasn't in the line of fire. So I stood, my elbows propped on the cockpit steadying the binoculars which were filled with the image of the lead barge. I could see one Japanese, the coxswain, standing at the stern staring straight ahead in a pose so stiff that it was obvious to me that he knew we were there. Whatever you may read about PT boats, they terrified the Japanese barge crews. I watched this fellow as he steered past and then I watched the other barge pass. He, too, went by as if the PT boat glowering at him did not exist.

We stayed still in the water for a few minutes and then my starboard gunner said, "Light on the water, dead ahead." I turned and saw a light blinking low on the water. John put his engines in gear and we idled toward shore. The raft, the four Marines paddling and the natives sitting in the middle, came out of the dark and they all climbed aboard. Larry Bangser came up to the cockpit. Again I was impressed by his massive bulk and streaked face that made me wonder where my law school chum had gone. "Did you—" I started. "We sure did," Larry answered my incomplete question, "We had just shoved off from the beach when our guides said 'Stop.' They said they heard boats coming up the shore and they didn't mean you. We couldn't hear anything for awhile, then we did. We saw those barges and you coming in at the same time." "Lotta traffic out here," John observed.

On the way back Larry Bangser told us about their mission in terms that made it seem like a stroll in the park. The native guides had found a trail near the landing spot (which, he said appreciatively, was a nice sandy beach). They climbed most of the night until they reached the supply road, where they sat in the bushes, watching the traffic and taking notes. They left after dark on the second day, after planting a little American flag in the middle of the road. Larry seemed oblivious to the fact that the Japanese might find the flag in the dark and start a search party. Marines just did these things.

On our way back to Torokina, I had a chance to get a better look at Larry Bangser. Two days ago I'd been preoccupied with setting his group down. Since then, thinking back on our days at Columbia, I'd decided that my estimate of his size and demeanor as a Marine had to be wrong, that he must still be the same cheery little guy I remembered. Now, while we talked about the mission, I discreetly looked him over. If it hadn't been for his smile through the camouflage grease and streaks of mud, I'd have said that this massive and ferocious-looking Marine standing next to me was some other guy named Larry Bangser. It must have been a matter of perspective.

COAST-
WATCHERS,
MELANESIANS,
AND RESCUES

I took the coastwatcher Henry Josselyn off Vella Lavella one night in September 1943. He was a soft-spoken man who showed a near court-liness to the natives who paddled him out to the 105. I took another coastwatcher off New Ireland around the same time who treated his natives like serfs. I also lived with Carden Seton, coastwatcher on Choiseul, for almost a week. The standard procedure for coastwatch-ers (issued from Australian headquarters on Malaita) was to avoid com-bat, but after his first year Seton had an active force of natives that reg-ularly ambushed small groups of Japanese. From these and other contacts with coastwatchers I developed the impression that among these extraordinary men, each did what he thought best to carry out his mission to provide the Allied forces with intelligence from behind enemy lines.

The Australians had formed a coastwatching service in the middle 1930s on their desolate north coast and the rim of islands to their north, but it had been based on a peacetime premise. The service recruited its members from local Australians and British who were equipped with radio transmitters. Their mission was to report unidentified ships and airplanes. They assumed they'd be doing this from coasts controlled by Australia or it allies, not as spies hiding out in enemy occupied territory. But after the Japanese moved quickly through the islands, the original organization fell apart. It had to be rethought and adjusted in order to accommodate the fact that coastwatchers were becoming men who operated behind enemy lines in one of the most dangerous operations of the war.

I became quite familiar with the unenviable business of coastwatching. If I'd been asked to choose between bomb disposal and coastwatching I'd have said, "Hand me a wrench, show me the bomb, and stand back." Only a small percentage of coastwatchers were actually caught and then promptly executed, but that statistic is meaningless. The coastwatchers' working conditions were spooky, lonely, and dreadful to use unmilitary terms. The coastwatcher hid in the hills at a spot with a broad view of the waters of the slot where enemy ships could be seen. Except for the Melanesians, in whose friendship his life depended, he was there alone. He survived mainly on the meager fare of the island. Since their observation posts were seldom near prewar buildings, the coastwatchers often lived in hastily built shacks overrun with rats and they suffered inadequate netting in their battles with mosquitoes and flies.

I think most of the original coastwatchers left before the Japanese invasions because they were not emotionally equipped or well-enough trained to do the job. The incredibly brave men who became the real coastwatchers were from many different backgrounds. Most had lived in the islands and were familiar with the Melanesian natives, but a few had never seen the Solomons or any place like them. One coastwatcher, Franklin Nash, was an American Army enlisted man who volunteered for the job and was somehow transferred to the Coastwatching Service.

One or two were missionaries. In the beginning of the war, most missionaries believed they should and could be neutral. As men and women of God, they thought the Japanese would allow them to continue their work. In the first few months of Japanese occupation, several missionaries were summarily executed. No one knew why but after the tragic news was delivered by the natives who traveled from island to island, the missionaries realized that their only friends were the

Allies. Most missionaries left, although some disappeared into the hills with their native flocks. A few brave souls took active roles as coastwatchers, or rescued and hid Allied airmen and sailors. A Father de Clerk who lived on the southwest coast of Guadalcanal went from pacifist neutral to the leader of a native guerilla force.

Most coastwatchers moved if they got news that the Japanese were getting close to them. This was difficult because their radio transmitters and receiving equipment were bulky and heavy. One coastwatcher on New Georgia approached the problem differently: The Japanese sent small groups of soldiers to reconnoiter an area—they might be looking for good base sites or for coastwatchers; when a group came too close to this man's hideout, they were ambushed and all were killed by him and his native commandos. The secret was to kill *all* of them. The enemy command then knew only that their scouting force had disappeared. In this way he survived, sending extremely important information about enemy ship movements, for nearly a year before the American forces arrived.

It seemed incredible to me that men could sit on an enemy-occupied island and send reports by radio without being caught. The Japanese monitored these broadcasts and were very adept at locating the source of the transmissions. PT boats adhered to radio silence to a fault for fear that their location and intent would be discovered, so it always amazed me that men would sit on enemy islands and calmly detail ship movements over the air. The Japanese did catch and execute two coastwatchers on Bougainville, but they never came close to shutting off the stream of intelligence flowing down the slot.

How could the Japanese have failed at a job that, next to their other military feats, seemed easy? First, these islands were very big—from sixty to over a hundred miles long by twenty to thirty miles wide with no roads except for those on a few plantations. They were ruggedly mountainous and cut with ravines so deep that travel was an exhausting up-and-down, slash-and-stumble process. Heavy tree cover made spotting from the air impossible. The brush beneath the trees was often so thick with massive palmettos and bushes that a man could push his way ten feet off a trail and disappear. Native trails usually led from small villages in the hills down to the coast. Even along the coast traveling any distance was difficult; there were beaches, but they seemed to peter out after a mile or two and became either cliffs or mangrove swamps. I found myself in a mangrove swamp just once, and after ten minutes of straddling knobby, knee-like roots, sinking up to my armpits in water, and being the subject of a mosquito feeding-frenzy, I retreated to the beach from whence I'd come. What I did after that I forget.

The other reason that the Japanese failed to search out and destroy the coastwatchers was their astounding inability to cultivate friendships in the areas of the South Pacific that they conquered and occupied. I think this was the only pleasant surprise for the Allies in the first year of the war. We all assumed that the Japanese would know better how to deal with the native peoples of the Far East than we would. They had everything going for them when they invaded the Solomons.

The Melanesians had little or no affection for the Europeans who inhabited their islands and who, in the main, treated them as inferiors. Reading Conrad and Maugham gives a pretty full picture: Their main characters are usually whites; natives are faded into the background with the rest of the flora and fauna, but when a native is made a main character, he is usually quite bizarre. All the Japanese needed to do was to exercise a little patience and tact when dealing with the local populations to win them over. Instead, the typical scenario started when a Japanese force would land and establish a base at a native village. For the first week or so, relations would be good. (This was the most dangerous period for any coastwatcher.) Then an issue would arise, the kind of problem that the native elders were used to taking up with the Australian or British district officer who would deal out some kind of rough justice acceptable to the natives. Not so with the Japanese, where the meeting often turned into a confrontation in which the local chief got his face slapped. The Japanese military seemed to think that face-slapping was a good way to end negotiations.

The following morning, the Japanese would wake up to find themselves alone. Entire native villages could disappear in a single night, fleeing into the hills. Some Melanesians isolated themselves for the balance of the Japanese occupation but others, I think the great majority, allied themselves with the local coastwatcher. I knew of no exceptions to this except on Bougainville, which was occupied by the Japanese for so long that many of the natives must have concluded it would never change, and they submitted to Japanese rule. This meant the end for the coastwatchers there.

The Melanesians did much more than act as auxiliaries for the coastwatchers; in isolated, unreported skirmishes I know they fought the

Japanese themselves. In my early days at Rendova, some natives came by the 105 in a canoe, holding up the severed head of a Japanese soldier. I thought they were coming to trade but they paddled by where we were moored, just to show us whose side they were on.

The main missions of the coastwatchers were, of course, intelligence gathering and transmission, but they also functioned as rescuers. Jack Kennedy was rescued by a local coastwatcher, Evans, and his Melanesian force. The Melanesians—on their own turf much smarter than their civilized invaders—rescued hundreds of American and Allied fliers and sailors, most often bringing them to the local coastwatcher, who arranged for evacuation. It was in this rescue function that PT boats filled a critical role.

For example, there was a small island named, I believe, Mono, one of the Treasury Islands not far from the southern end of Bougainville. In June 1943 the crew of an American dive-bomber that had been shot down took refuge with the natives of this island. Mono was the cone-shaped tip of a submerged volcano and about five miles in diameter; hiding out there was not as easy as on one of the major islands. There was no radio transmitter there, so the fliers just stayed put. Eventually, the Japanese sent a large search-and-destroy team. A coastwatcher on one of the main islands had heard that the fliers were now the objects of a determined search and he radioed to Guadalcanal, where a rescue mission was ordered using the PT boats at Rendova.

I was assigned the mission. The intelligence officer showed me a small stretch of land between two promontories where the fliers would be waiting for me around midnight. Base command asked me how many boats I wanted. "Two." I said. A normal patrol was three or four. "Why only two?" "Any more just increases the chance of detection, and if we're detected that's the end of the rescue. I'd go alone but I want a boat along to pull me off a reef." The intelligence officer looked at the chart and replied, "There are no reefs." I shrugged, saying, "So it says. That's what some guy reported a hundred years ago. There could be some now." There was a moment of silence while the staff digested the fact that I didn't trust the U.S. Coast and Geodetic Survey. The silence was broken by a wise-ass boat captain's remark: "And if there is a reef you'll find it, Gunga." I was maniacally fearful of running aground ever since I ran aground but this mission really did have a built-in reef problem. I wanted to go very close to shore. The closer I got, the smaller the chance that I'd be detected. The shorelines of these islands were thickly covered by heavy bushes. Sand beaches were rare and narrow. Therefore a man standing on the shore had a restricted cone of vision to his right and left. Retrievals take a long time when there are as many as seven men, as there were in this case, because most native canoes can only hold two men at a time. If I stayed a quarter mile offshore, I could easily be seen by a Japanese sentry from a mile or more away, but not so if I were a hundred yards or less from shore. But that meant risking reefs, so I wanted a boat a hundred yards behind me that could pull me off. I also needed a captain I could count on.

The boat captain who was going to follow me was a new guy. On the way down to the dock I collared him and whispered in his ear, "Listen close, old buddy"—he was not an old buddy and that is why I was making myself clear—"When we start in I want you to drop back to four boat lengths, as far back as you can without losing me. Keep that distance. When I stop, you stop. If I come up and start singing, 'How Dry I am,' that means I've run aground, so come in and get me off. Have a towline on your sampson post and another at the stern so you can pull either way. If we get caught under fire, push up against the stern so we can climb aboard, OK?"

This new guy was all bright-eyed and bushy-tailed. He was so excited he might not understand that he had only one job, to get us off. I could see that if I sang, "How Dry I am" he might just join me in the second chorus. I decided not to try to fool any Japanese listeners. I'd just holler for all the world to hear, "I'm hard aground! Get your ass in here and haul me off!"

We proceeded to Mono. At rendezvous time I was so close to the beach that I could make out the outlines of trees and slight glimmers of white from the small waves breaking on the shore. Two crewmen had alternated throwing lead lines and another had his head over the bow looking for changing shades of color in the water that would indicate coral. We waited for a light. Nothing. I rechecked the bearings we'd been given. I was certain we were in the right place but, even if we weren't, wandering up and down the coastline would do no good—the chance was too great that I'd leave a location just before they showed up. I believed firmly in staying in one place and letting people find me. I'd heard of parties arriving on the beach only to watch their rescue boat disappear down the shore, looking for them.

I waited for four hours and then went back to Rendova intensely disappointed. All the next day I kept thinking that maybe I'd picked the wrong location or maybe I should've waited another ten minutes. I'd just decided that I'd make a career of sitting off that damn island every night when a cheery-faced stranger walked into my tent and sat on the cot with me. He introduced himself as a pilot who'd been taken off that island a week earlier. He'd been the source of the coastwatcher message.

"Not to worry," he said. "You were at the right spot, but the right spot became the wrong spot. A Jap patrol was probably sitting down there, waiting for our guys to show up, and our guys knew it. They'll be OK."

His description of the situation on Mono helps to explain the tremendous advantage we had with the Melanesians on our side. The Solomon Islanders I'd met were shy but far from subservient. When the Japanese search-and-destroy party had arrived, they'd been greeted by one of the elders who, my informant claimed, had practiced groveling. This had impressed the officer in charge that these were indeed people who'd seen the light, and the light was the Rising Sun. Without being asked, the elder had volunteered that there were American fliers on the island and that, although he didn't know where they were hiding, he'd help to find them. The party took off on one trail wandering aimlessly through the bush and gradually up the mountain. As the search party had worked its way up that trail, another group of natives had led the fliers down another trail several miles away. My visitor then took a stick and traced trails in the dirt to show how the search party and the fliers had gone in opposite directions. They'd been close enough at one point for the natives with the Japanese to warn the natives with the fliers—while seeming to talk among themselves, they were, in fact, telling their buddies on the nearby trail where they were going and how far.

I felt better at hearing this. I even felt better about the base command, because someone must have seen how shook up I was and had managed to bring this fellow over to talk to me. I'd like to claim that I finally rescued them but I didn't. Another PT group was successful several nights later.

Coastwatchers tallied over a hundred airmen rescued and returned to their units. About 165 men from the cruiser *Helena*, sunk in a battle off Kolombangara Island, managed to go ashore at Japanese-occupied Vella Lavella. They arrived in clumps over a ten-mile stretch of shoreline. The local Melanesians gathered them in and held them safely until they were evacuated ten days later by a force of destroyers. Without the Melanesians and, of course, the local coastwatchers, these men would not have survived.

PTs excelled in search-and-rescue and, in the Solomons, PTs were not just the better alternative, they were often the only alternative. PBYs did a good job of locating and rescuing downed fliers, but couldn't cope with a large group. Submarines performed wonders rescuing people trapped in the islands during the early stages of the war, but they were seldom available later on and couldn't run search patterns. PTs had the unique advantage of speed and toughness. They could bull their way into enemy waters with a fair chance of success, even when under attack from aircraft or shore guns. Murray Preston proved this to the extreme and got the Medal of Honor for it. A Navy pilot had been shot down in Japanese-held Wasile Bay on Halmahera Island off New Guinea. He was about two hundred yards from the docks of a large Japanese base, staying as low in the water as possible while his squadron mates kept enemy boats at bay with repeated strafing attacks. A PBY attempted to rescue him behind a smoke screen but was driven off by heavy shore-gun fire. Preston volunteered to give it a try with two PT boats. In order to reach the Japanese harbor and the pilot, he first had to take his two boats through an eleven-mile-long strait protected by shore guns. Under a covering smoke screen, but still under vicious point-blank fire, he retrieved the pilot and left, slowing on his way out to destroy an enemy boat trying to intercept him. All told, he was under fire for two and a half hours.

The action report termed the mission suicidal. Preston did not see it that way. He knew his boats had a reasonable chance of evading the shell fire with their speed and agility, although he hadn't figured on two and a half hours of shelling. He also knew that when he stopped to pick up the pilot his own boats would lay down fire so intense that, at that short range, nobody would care to be an enemy gunner standing on that dock. Only PT boats could pull off that sort of Wyatt Earp routine—it also took a Murray Preston and a couple of dozen PT sailors, all willing to put their lives on the line for the sake of one downed American flier.

Walter Lord's fine book, *Lonely Vigil* (Viking Press), is a splendid account of the work of the coastwatchers. Lord quotes Admiral Kelly Turner saying, "It means a lot to know that if the worst happens and you get blown off your ship and washed ashore somewhere, the Navy isn't going to forget you." I read that ruefully; that rule did not seem to apply to the "expendables" in PT boats. Jack Kennedy and his crew had to find their own way home after a week of hiding out on a tiny island deep within enemy-controlled territory. It had been even worse for my friend Henry Cutter and his crew.

I first met Henry at the Melville PT Training Center in the spring of 1944 after I'd returned from the Pacific and was teaching gunboat tactics and torpedo fire-control. He had permanent duty orders, which puzzled me because he was clearly a qualified PT officer. After we became friends and he recounted what had happened to him, I understood.

Henry's boat and another were attacking two barges in Hansa Bay, a Japanese stronghold in New Guinea, when shore guns hit Henry's boat, setting her on fire. After a futile effort to douse the flames, they put the balsa life raft over the side and everyone took to the water. Henry expected the other boat to pick him up but she too was under fire and sped away under a smoke screen. She returned to base, her captain reporting that heavy shore-gun fire had prevented him from returning to look for survivors.

The life raft on a PT boat was a joke, nothing but an oval balsa ring, seven feet long by three feet wide, with wooden slats on the bottom, so if you sat in it you sat in water. It was designed as something to hold on to, not to sit in. It had a box of skimpy survival rations and a small, wooden water keg that might keep a crew alive for a couple of days. Since Henry's boat had a crew of twelve, men had to take turns in the raft, with most of them in the water, holding to the sides. During the night, they managed to swim and paddle the raft out of the bay and a couple of miles farther offshore. By the fourth day, they were only five: one man died of wounds the first night; the others were never found after the war, having either swum ashore, or slipped beneath the surface.

An account of their ordeal appears in *At Close Quarters*. My account, which doesn't differ in substance, came straight from Henry. I felt a chill of fear just listening to his story and wondered whether I could have survived his ordeal. By the third day, Henry and his remaining crew were delirious from the heat, thirst, and the painful sores that covered their bodies. Henry, in telling me his story, could not place things in a time sequence. He remembered the events as if they were dreams.

They had heard the sounds of PT boats a few times during the nights. Sometimes they saw planes high overhead, probably our own, going to or returning from a mission. No one seemed to be looking for them. He told me that he thought it was on the third night that a boat seemed to approach them. When he saw the boat he first thought she was a rescuing PT boat but as it came closer it appeared too small, so he thought she was an enemy boat and prepared himself for death or capture. The boat stopped a short distance away, stayed for a long time as if her crew was watching them, and then disappeared. The next morning as it grew light, they saw an overturned boat drifting only a few yards away. The five remaining survivors pulled their raft alongside and managed to right the boat, which turned out to be a light, flat-bottomed rowboat made of plywood. They climbed out of the sea for the first time in four days. In spite of their thirst and the pain of saltwater sores, Henry told me that he had a sense that this boat was a good sign. They had no water left, were floating only a few miles from enemy shores, and their newly acquired boat made them more visible to people on that shore than when only their heads were showing; nevertheless, Henry felt that the boat would be their salvation because they were now visible from the air. He was right. A group of B-25s returning from a mission spotted them and circled to take a look. Henry frantically semaphored his name and boat number. The planes circled again, flew low over them, and dropped packages of water, food, medicines, and cigarettes, along with the message that a PBY would come to pick them up at noon the next day. They endured another night, fearful that the air activity might have attracted the Japanese, but their newfound luck held and the PBY successfully retrieved them.

Henry's account gripped me so that I even remember where we were when he related it. It wasn't over a drink at the Reading Room where stories like this were usually told. We were simply standing outside one of the classrooms at the training base. I don't know what triggered his need to talk but once he started, I was rooted to the spot. The grim fact that only five out of the twelve survived is enough to gauge the suffering that those men endured. What seemed to matter the most to Henry was that he felt that he'd been abandoned: the days drifting in the sea were empty of signs that anyone was searching for him. Clearly the planes he did see weren't looking for him, and with only their heads above water, they had no chance of being spotted. He kept repeating "If that boat hadn't drifted by—" he did not finish the sentence, and looked away. Like Cutter, Kennedy also had felt that he'd been abandoned.

I don't believe either one was abandoned. They were the victims of a mind-set that saw them as lost, that could not believe that men could survive such disasters. Kennedy's 109 had looked as if it had gone up in a ball of flame to boats little more than a hundred yards away. Cutter's boat had seemed to vanish in a storm of shore-gun fire. I'm sure, as reports in both cases say, that PBYs went to search for them—but without the hope of finding anyone. I contrast this with the attitude of Pappy Boyington's squadron mates after he was shot down. They flew relentlessly for more than a week along the coast where Pappy had gone down. When senior officers told them they were on a hopeless quest, the fliers replied, "He's too mean to die." And they were right—Pappy returned from a Japanese prison camp.

I rescued a flier from Pappy's squadron who was in the water about twenty miles from our Bougainville base. It was an easy mission. I had his exact position and went after him in broad daylight. At least five miles away from where I was told I would find him I spotted his circling squadron mates. When they saw me, one of them detached and flew low across the water, directly at me. As I've said elsewhere, I didn't like planes flying right at me and, even though he was clearly trying to help by leading me to his friend, he scared the wits out of me. He zoomed overhead about a foot above the radar mast, made a tight turn, and sped back, waggling his wings. Then another plane did the same thing, scaring me all over again. In their anxiety over the flier in the water, these pilots didn't understand that their buzzing around could attract more of the Zeros that had shot the fellow down in the first place. We picked the kid up out of his raft. When I learned that he was a seminary student at Drew University, I wondered how he dealt with Boyington's profanity. I admired the way his buddies had stuck around and hoped that if the 105 were ever lost, PT boats would keep looking for us beyond reason. I knew some would, like Payne, Shearer, Iles, Battle, Kennedy, Webb, and other members of "the happy few"—but would they be allowed to waste time over an "expendable?"

15

I GO HOME

My long voyage home started in Bougainville in December 1943, a journey that took until February of 1944. In fact, I was not entirely aware of anything, since I had a fever that reached over 103 degrees.

Torokina, our Bougainville base, plumbed a new depth in grim. While the actual patrols weren't as bad as in New Georgia, the time between patrols was a real problem. Torokina was less than an hour's flight from the big Japanese base at Rabaul and our base force was taking a pasting from the air. My crewman, who'd been transferred off the 105 to the base force after suffering combat fatigue, now had to be carried off base in the company of half a dozen men who could not bear up under the relentless bombing.

Boat crews that had the night off often wished they were out on patrol. Somewhere up in the hills of Bougainville was a large howitzer that seemed intent on hitting things in the harbor. We figured that the enemy was probably rationing shells, since the gun only fired three or four times an hour. First there would be a far-off "pop," followed by five seconds of silence; then a faint flutter high in the air that increased in volume until, in the final rush to the water, it sounded like a demented ashcan rolling end over end. The blast of the exploding shell was a relief because if you heard it, it had missed, obviously. After my first night ashore, the night that I spent in a foxhole with my steward's mate Essex, I usually slept aboard the 105 when not on patrol. I liked the company of John Iles, Mechin, and the rest of my old crew, and besides, the moored boats seemed safer than the base, in spite of the howitzer.

I'd recovered from both malaria and dysentery. My stay on Choiseul with the Marines had been an odd health cure of sorts. I'd done a lot of walking, some good wind sprints under fire, and by the time I got to Bougainville I was in as good shape as I'd been since the Galapagos. So I was annoyed and puzzled when, after a couple of weeks, I began aching in my joints. Medical malingering was a curse. I was convinced that my aches were caused by my fervent wish to get out of patrols. One early evening on the beach, I was sitting at the supper table but not eating. The base doctor was sitting next to me when I aimlessly complained that I felt rotten and he whipped out a thermometer, stuck it in my mouth with a flourish, and resumed his meal. A few moments later he pulled it out, looked at it, and said, "Holy Smoke!" He shook it down and stuck it back in my mouth. He watched me carefully. When he read it the second time, he said accusingly, "You have a 103-degree temperature!"

Now I really felt awful. If he hadn't said that I might have walked through whatever I had with some aspirin and Atabrine. He helped me up, held me by the elbow, walked me down to a cot in the sick-bay dugout, laid me down on a cot and told the pharmacist's mate on duty to do various things to me. I felt relieved, I must admit, that I was off the night's patrol and I had only a twinge of guilt that somebody else would have to take my place. A new squadron had arrived and some extra work would do them good. It was not the same as in New Georgia where, if someone dropped out, an already tired man had to do extra duty.

I started to doze off contentedly when that "strumpet, Fortune," noticed. Our base force boatswain's mate, a very large, tough man—as befitted his rating—went berserk. Since I was mentally whirly myself at the time, I never found out why he went berserk or how much damage he did. The doctor who'd put me in semi-intensive care appeared alongside my cot, shook me awake, and said, "The bosun has gone nutty and wants to talk to you." I did not understand. Did he mean that because the man wanted to talk to me, it proved that he was insane? The doctor impatiently explained that the man wanted to talk to me, that he agreed to stop bashing people if he could tell me his troubles. I felt awful again but then I realized that the man was our own Squadron Five boatswain's mate. He'd ridden as a volunteer on patrols with me, had been aboard the night I ran aground, and had suggested at least one of the five methods I tried to get unstuck.

He was brought down into the sick-bay dugout, with his arms secured by rope like a straitjacket, and seated beside my cot. He looked all right to me except that his eyes rolled around in his head once in awhile. We talked for a couple of hours before we both dropped off to sleep. The next morning I couldn't remember anything that we'd talked about. I think the doctor suspected that I was withholding information, and he would have been correct, except I really could not remember anything. The pharmacist's mates who'd listened in said they hadn't followed the conversation or even understood most of it because the boatswain had spoken in sailors' jargon laced with expletives and I'd responded by informing the boatswain that I'd met a peach in Orange, New Jersey. By morning my fever was down and the boatswain seemed fine, if bleary eyed. Ignoring the doctor, who seemed confused, I ordered the boatswain to go back to work and stop bitching. I may not have remembered our conversation, but I did know the boatswain—he'd probably gotten into some bum raisin jack.

My quick and inexplicable fever coincided with another problem, concerning friendly destroyers. Now that all boats were equipped with radar and IFF (Identify Friend or Foe, a device by which radar could detect whether a blip was friend or foe, hence the initials), I argued that PT boats should not be kept at home just because friendly destroyers were in the area. On the contrary, it was time for the two weapons to be used together in the war against enemy barges. Destroyers were highly effective against barges with their rapid-firing five-inch guns, but they were not good at finding them. The barges would run so close to the beach that destroyer radar could not pick them up. PTs could run much closer inshore to locate suitable targets, but were sometimes out-gunned (this was before we used forty-millimeter guns). The problem was, no one wanted to chance another foul-up where we might end up fighting each other. Admiral Halsey himself had been furious over the last friendly-fire incident largely because we'd both made completely spurious claims of hits. The base command decided that since I was the most vocal proponent of coordinated destroyer-PT attacks, and since my temporary bout with fever had left me an uncertain division leader, I should go down to Tulagi and try to work something out. I left Bougainville in the middle of December, expecting to be back in ten days at the most, and never saw it again—and never want to. Leaving the 105 that way was another matter.

Working my way back to Tulagi was not quick. The boat I took from Bougainville stopped for good in the Treasury Islands and I was there for three days before I could find a boat to Tulagi. While there a surprise followed by an untoward event occurred.

As a transient, I had no duties. I spent most of my time reading or gabbing with anyone available. One of those happened to be a chief yeoman who, like all chief yeomen, knew everything before it happened—including the splendid news that my name was on the list of those about to get orders home. That was the surprise. Then came the untoward event.

In the absence of an officers club in which to celebrate properly, I accompanied the officers down to the briefing for that night's patrol, figuring that Bob Kelly was bound to provide some entertainment. I was right, Kelly was in great form. The previous night, PTs had found a group of barges and had tried to engage them at a safe distance which, Kelly explained in carefully chosen invective, was not the way to fight barges. All the barges had escaped and the only things the PTs collected were some bullet holes. I was listening to Kelly's amazing vocabulary and not paying attention to what, exactly, he was saying. I put my arms up to stretch at the precise instant that Kelly roared, "I wish I had one of the old division leaders to take you guys out and show—" Kelly saw my hands in the air and did not complete his sentence. He didn't have to complete it, the dreadful ending hung there, unspoken. He thought I was volunteering to go out and show these men how to fight barges!

Volunteering was a sure way to tempt luck; volunteering to go out and teach men barge-fighting was about the dumbest way to tempt luck; volunteering to go out when you had orders home was insane. I knew all this; the men standing in the back with me also knew this. I could see my epitaph dancing in step with the strumpet Fortune: *He volunteered to teach people how to fight barges* or *He had orders home.* I was paralyzed, my arms still stuck up in the air, while Kelly fixed his gaze upon me. Silence pervaded the briefing room. He was thinking upon what he took to be my act of volunteering. I was thinking of what I'd say if he accepted. I could say it was a mistake, I could suddenly remember that the doctor had told me not to go out on any patrols, or I could simply bolt out of the door. Then Kelly spoke, "Keresey,"—I thought, "It's coming, here goes my career, my life, I will be handed a white feather, branded a coward."—Then he said, "No." He glared at those who had perpetrated last night's fiasco and pointed dramatically at me. "There's an old-timer willing to go out and show you how it's done but I won't allow it. It's too simple. All you have to do is close with them. The closer you get . . . " Kelly went on to describe how to get in close, use the shore as a backdrop, and so forth. I felt blessed relief flood through me. My arms collapsed to my sides and, along with my dumfounded friends, I left the briefing. When we got outside, one of them turned to me and asked, "Have you lost your mind?"

None of these veterans could believe that I'd done such an idiotic thing. I decided that it was too complicated to explain so I just kept silent. Eventually the conversation moved to safer ground. I left the next day for Tulagi.

The best-known of the World War II destroyer men, Arleigh Burke, was stationed at Tulagi, in Purvis Bay. Our flotilla commander, Commodore Moran, arranged for me to meet with Captain Burke on his destroyer flagship. I could not foresee that he would later be chief of naval operations, but I was nonetheless impressed by Burke. He greeted me cordially and with respect rather than with the amused, close to disdainful attitude of some of the other regular Navy big ship officers. I've always felt that the more actual combat an officer saw, and the better he was at it, the easier he was to meet and talk with. It did not bother Burke that I was only a lieutenant (jg) off a torpedo boat. He wanted to know what I had learned in combat and what ideas I might offer in coordinating joint attacks. I struck a chord in him when I said that no matter how I tried to plan out an operation, things never seemed to go the way I thought they would. Burke laughed when I recounted the barge attack where my boats had ended up firing at each other. He said, "My destroyer captains and I have thirty different plans of maneuver, depending on the actual situation. We have them so well worked-out that all I have to do is come up with a code number and every ship knows exactly what to do. I have yet to run into a situation where one of those plans actually fit. But you know what I do? I take the closest one. I don't improvise. You know why?"

He leaned forward and it occurred to me that, with his high, balding forehead, he looked like a professor. When I shook my head, he continued, "Because then everyone knows where his friends are. We cut the risk of firing on each other. If we see a ship someplace other than where one of ours is supposed to be, we can open fire with less risk that we are firing on one of ours."

Captain Burke invited me to lunch. I spent four years in the Navy and this was the only time I had a meal on a combat ship larger than a PT. I was impressed. I was a country bumpkin sitting down at Lutece. We sat at a table big enough for a dozen officers, covered with a spotless white tablecloth, and sporting place settings. There were eight or so officers standing around who took their seats after the captain sat down. I was suddenly conscious that my appearance was substandard. While all of these officers wore khakis that someone had pressed, my pants hadn't seen a crease in a year; the tips of my shirtcollar turned up; I was badly in need of a haircut. None of these had been deficiencies in my usual surroundings, but now I felt as if everyone was barely suppressing laughter at the sight of me. I seated myself where one of the officers politely indicated, near the middle of one of the table's long sides, and was served a plate of Eggs Benedict. I stared down at that marvelous creation, astonished. I hadn't seen an egg of any sort since I'd left Noumea. Underneath those glorious eggs was a thick slice of real ham, sitting on a real toasted English muffin. Realizing that I should do something or say something, I looked up to see everyone at the table grinning broadly. One of them, the exec I think, said, "We decided to make this an occasion. Those are the last eggs we've got." I was embarrassed but very pleased that these people had made an effort to give me a treat. It was a splendid treat!

Captain Burke agreed that a combined destroyer-PT operation was worth a try. He thought that our first exercise should be as simple as possible: maybe just his division running at night off Guadalcanal along with half a dozen PT boats, to see how we showed up on each other's radar. Then we could have a couple of PTs act like barges while other PTs vectored in the destroyers for an attack. That first simple exercise was all we ever got, and it was surprisingly difficult. I made the rendezvous all right but had a tough time keeping station on the de-

stroyers. I realized when I got in that it would take a good deal of practice for us, with our primitive radar and limited skill at station-keeping, to actually carry out a coordinated attack. Unfortunately there
wasn't time for additional maneuvers. A month later at Bougainville a
coordinated barge hunt was attempted and the worst happened: one of
our destroyers mistook a PT-blip for an enemy barge and the PT took
a direct hit from a five-inch gun. That put an end to coordination; PTs
went back to operating alone.

December turned into January, then February, before my orders
came through. I think I got them through a mistake by the flotilla personnel officer, because my squadron CO was furious when he found
out that I had received them and heatedly dressed down the personnel
officer for putting my name in without permission. I was mystified
about why there was such a fuss until I found out, again from a chief
yeoman, that the CO wanted me for his replacement. If I'd been selected, I'd have taken the job without protest, in spite of my intense
dislike for where I was and my longing to go home. Jack Searles stayed
on as a squadron commander when all the others had gone home.

With the memory of all the missed torpedoes still alive, I spent my
long, idle hours designing a torpedo attack-trainer I called *Fantasia*
after the Disney cartoon movie. Students would see a blip move across
a mock up radar screen. They would plot the blips on a manuevering
board, estimate the target's course and speed, then "fire." The train-
ers, a small group of quartermasters, would work the problem to see
whether or not the students had scored hits. It was a simple device but
replacement officers coming through Tulagi found it entertaining and
it attracted a big audience.

My voyage home started with a plane ride to Espiritu Santo. I
stopped there for a long week after which I had an excruciatingly boring ride on a four-engine amphibious plane to Midway, where I spent
my first night in ages sleeping on a real mattress. It was only the in-
nerspring, since the top mattress had long since been appropriated by
the base officers, but I still thought it was marvelous. From Midway I
took another long trip to Hawaii and civilization. I even spent a day on
the beach of Waikiki. From there it was ten days on a Liberty ship to
San Francisco.

San Francisco was made for welcoming back people like me. I walked
off the ship and was promptly greeted by ladies who devoted themselves to welcoming men home from the war. They were middle-aged

society ladies, so the welcome was limited to driving us to our hotels, but they were gracious and enthusiastic and made us all feel like heroes. Two days later I was home and into the arms of my mother— and the arms of that peach I'd met in Orange, New Jersey. We were married two months later.

The 105 continued bouncing up, down, and sideways throughout the war, all the way to the Philippines. I have a blurry snapshot of her taking her ease in port somewhere in the spring of 1945, snuggling her crew on her forecastle. When the war ended, the Navy rightly decided that bringing home the PT boats wasn't worth the expense. The 105, along with her sisters, was towed out to sea and set afire. When I first heard how she ended, I felt some resentment but, come to think of it, that was a good way for her to go.

I wasn't sent overseas again, and spent the balance of the war teaching and hoping for a squadron command. I thought I'd put my days with PT 105 behind me but, almost fifty years later, she and the days in the Solomon Islands came vividly alive.

A DIFFERENT
KIND OF
RESCUE

November 22, 1990. I could not place him. He had taken the last avail-able seat at the round breakfast table, after seven of us from Squadron Five had taken all the rest. It was 22 November 1990 and the occasion was a reunion of the PT officers who'd served with Jack Kennedy. Al-though the purpose was to remember Jack, the seven of us had also come to see one other again and tell sea stories.

We had been doing just that, with a few hours off for sleep, since noon the day before. It had been splendid. While PT people hold more reunions than Princeton alumni, our small group had never been much for reunions, so we'd seen each other only rarely since the war. We mar-veled at how little we'd changed: a little bent over and paunchy but to each other we were the same "swave" and "grommetless" veterans of the Solomons. ("Swave" is a guy who is in fact gross, trying to act suave. "Grommetless" you can look up.)

The stranger at the table seemed to know all of us. He smiled at the disjointed, laughing gabble that passed for conversation, but he didn't join in. "Who's the guy across from us?" I muttered to Al Webb, who was sitting next to me. "Don't know," he replied. Gene Foncannon said, "Remember when we picked up all those Japanese? I damned near blew it. We had a dozen on deck and I'm in the crew's quarters where we're divvying-up souvenirs. I look around and realize we're *all* below. I rush up on deck, expecting to find them getting underway for Rabaul. They're all sitting exactly where we left them."

Through the laughter, John Iles said to me, "You led that one, didn't you?" I nodded, "That I did." I was about to go on when the stranger across the table broke in: "They were Imperial Army troops." He looked across the table at me. "We sent another group of boats up there to finish off the ones you left behind." He said this in a very pleasant way, just adding a detail, just being part of the conversation. I felt as if he'd reached across the table and pushed my face into the scrambled eggs. I thought, "Dammit, how can he say they were soldiers? They were not. They were sailors off a sunken ship."

I knew who he was now: the base staff officer who had chewed me out for not disposing of the Japanese left in the water. I said nothing for fear that my rising anger would spoil the show for the rest of the group. Everyone was having such a good time. No one here but me and this other guy gave a damn whether they were soldiers or sailors or cowboys or Indians. So I shut up. When the breakfast ended, the stranger came around the table to me. I thought he was going to renew the argument. Instead, he held out his hand, smiled at me, and said, "Dick, I want you to know that it was a pleasure serving with you." What the hell, I thought, why argue about something that happened fifty years ago? I smiled back at him, shook his hand, and so ended the matter.

It did not, however, end the memory; his comment shot me back in time:

October 7, 1943, noon. My briefing for the mission was, as usual, truly brief: take a division of four PTs up to an area five miles west of Vella Lavella, roughly eighty miles from our base at Rendova, and search for any survivors of the destroyer *Chevalier*, sunk in a battle with Japanese destroyers the night before. I did not know that a Japanese destroyer had also been sunk, or why we were ordered out so late, or (most importantly) that the *O'Bannon* had picked up the *Chevalier*'s survivors the night before. Maybe it took a while for the thought of sending up

PTs to occur to anyone. Maybe my mission was in the just-in-case, might-as-well category.

Regardless of what I did or didn't know, I was glad to get the assignment. It had been quiet lately. I hadn't done anything for a week and my life was pushing the limits of the boredom scale. This was a daylight mission and, while that greatly increased the risk of air attack, particularly where we were going, it was a welcome change from the spooky nature of night missions. Search-and-rescue work itself was a nice change. But I had a couple of problems.

One, we had to hustle to get up there and still have enough daylight left for a search. Once it got dark, searching for men in the water was fruitless. When Jack Kennedy and his crew were hiding from the enemy, Jack swam out into Ferguson Passage, hoping to attract our attention when we came through on night patrols. We wouldn't have seen him without practically running him down.

Two, we were going to an area that enemy fighter planes could reach quickly and we had no air cover. It was "no-man's water." Ships on either side stayed away from it in daylight. I therefore told my boat captains that there was to be no radio chatter and I also told the base duty officer that if he heard us at all, it meant we were under air attack and to send us some Corsairs or something, as I would be too busy to make a formal request. My boat captains laughed appreciatively and we left for our boats. Rousing the crews from their noon lethargy, making sure everyone had full fuel tanks, and doing the odds and ends necessary to get four boats up and running meant that we didn't get underway until after 1300 hours.

About two hours out, we came upon the bow of a ship sticking out of the sea, an eerie sight, about twenty feet of it bobbing along all by itself. The way it swayed back and forth told me it was only the bow. The location puzzled me since we were still ten miles from the designated battle site and what little current there was couldn't have carried it there. We slowed to idling speed and searched the area but there was nothing else: no debris and certainly no people. We took off again for the northwest. Now I was concerned that we might miss someone, so I signaled my boats to spread out. We traveled line abreast, three hundred yards apart at a fast idling speed of fifteen knots. My plan was to go on a northwest course to where I thought the battle site might be, then move the line south and double back. We saw nothing.

When we were about five miles west of Vella Lavella, two PBYs appeared astern, flying low and heading straight for us. I hadn't been told that there would be any friendly aircraft. Bob Shearer, captain of the 104, the boat I was riding on, looked at me and grinned, "Good thing they're PBYs." What he meant was that we could at least identify PBYs: big, slow, flying boats that looked like nothing else. If someone had decided, without telling us, to send up fighters to help in the search and to provide cover, there might have been a disaster. Our gunners were extremely distrustful of any fighter plane flying at us. PTs had been strafed twice by friendly aircraft. PT men had been killed and, in each case, one of our planes had been shot down by enraged PT gunners. Both action reports stated that our gunners had fired "without permission."

I doubted that. I had my own recognition system. If fighters headed directly at my boats, as they did once, I opened fire without trying to figure out which side they were on. If they turned away from the heavy stuff we put up in the air, they were friendly. If they continued flying in on us, they were enemy. Whizzer White, our base intelligence officer, had sent a description of this recognition system down to the fighter strips, with the caution to avoid any craft that resembled a PT boat, "because they fire at anything and their gunners are accurate."

I was delighted to see the PBYs. They were far better at searching than we were. They could see a head bobbing in the water that we'd miss from more than a couple hundred yards away. I dismissed the idea of contacting the pilots by radio; the enemy always monitored aircraft frequencies and would certainly scramble Zeros, and that would be the end of the PBYs. I thought, "If they are nutty enough to contact us by radio, we'll talk. Otherwise I wait for a visual signal." For some minutes they circled the area around us while we kept idling ahead. Then one dropped a smoke pot, and then two more, about a mile away. My four boats, without any signal from me, turned and converged on the smoke pots, helter-skelter. As my own boat approached, I went from the cockpit to the forecastle deck to get a good look at what I assumed would be the survivors of the *Chevalier*. At first I thought I saw disorderly pods of drifting coconuts. I thought, "Good grief, those PBYs have to do better than this!" As we drew closer one of the coconuts turned and looked at me. It was a Japanese! All the coconuts were Japanese!

I turned to tell Bob Shearer but he had his back to me and was looking to the southeast. He was looking at the rear ends of the two PBYs heading home. My first thought was, "Shit! Zeros! They've seen Zeros!" The PBYs would see them before we did and then they'd make a run for home. I crouched and whirled around like a gunslinger in a western. The horizon toward Rabaul and Buca was without blemish. No Zeros.

"Where the hell are they going?" I yelled in exasperation. Bob shrugged and looked at me in his calm, deadpan way, waiting for orders. I got the boats moving northwest again, in something approaching a search line, but I knew it was useless. American sailors would not be northwest of the Japanese floating in the water unless the ships had whirled around each other, which didn't seem likely. After ten minutes I came to a decision. We had about twenty minutes left until dark. I went back to the cockpit and said to Bob, "Let's go back and pick up Japs." I did not ask. This had to be my decision. If there were still American boys out there somewhere, then I was to blame.

"Sure, let's do that," Bob replied. He cranked the wheel hard to port and headed back at a fast idling speed. The other boats turned with him and then closed for instructions. I stepped up on the dayroom canopy and hand signaled them to pick up the Japanese. We were adept at this kind of signaling, which was standard semaphore without flags. Dave Payne and I even played boat-to-boat chess by hand signals for a few moves, until one of us misplaced a piece and we started arguing.

As we approached the floating heads, a sailor on one of the other boats ran up on the bow and started firing at a clump of Japanese standing waist-high in the water on a submerged raft and waving clenched fists defiantly at him. It did not occur to me that one of my other boat crews would think differently than I did; when I saw those heads in the water I'd thought, "Well, the war is over for these guys."

Those heads that I had mistaken for coconuts belonged to men who were only trying to stay afloat. I'd have left them there if there'd been something better to do, but I was not about to shoot them or allow anyone in my command to shoot them. This may seem like a simple decision today. It was not, then. The war in the Pacific was *une guerre à l'outrance*, a fight to the finish. The Japanese had let it be known from the beginning that they did not believe in surrendering. As far as we knew then, they never took prisoners or, if they did, they shot them. Only after the war did I learn that some captured Americans, like Pappy Boyington, survived.

I did not know that a situation somewhat similar to the one I was facing happened in New Guinea at about the same time. A Japanese troop transport had been sunk, PTs went out and dropped depth charges on the men in the water. They were Imperial Army soldiers who, if they got ashore, might be effective militarily—whereas these men looked like sailors. Whatever the differences or similarities between my situation and that one, I had made the decision and was certain of one thing: no one on these four boats was going to do something else.

I scrambled out of the cockpit and up on the bow. "Cease firing!" I hollered at the sailor with the tommy gun. He had already stopped and he turned around and went aft. That seemed to be the end of the matter, until an engineer on the same boat appeared in the sailor's place and blustered, "What's the matter! Let's kill these bastards!" There was now little more than a boat length between us and I could hear him clearly. This man was arguing with me, the arrogant son of a bitch!

I'd known him since I'd joined the squadron fresh out of training school. He was part of the small nucleus of regular Navy sailors upon whom the rest of us depended while we learned our jobs. He was the only one of that group who annoyed me, right from the start. I'd hear his loud, honking voice intermittently issuing comments on the ineptness of reserve ensigns like myself ("seagulls" was what he called us because, he said, all we could do "was shit, eat, and squawk."). He'd never said this directly to any of us but just near enough and loudly enough that we could hear. We'd all ignored this then, but that was fifteen months earlier. I was momentarily speechless with rage.

I doubt that in today's Navy the art of the " chewing-out" is anything like it was then—it may even be illegal. It was a grand experience to listen to a master of the " chew-out" describe, nonstop for several stanzas, the total inadequacy of the miscreant standing at attention before him. I had neither the experience or the practice in this art, so I simply said, " Shut up. Turn around. Go back in the engine room. Stay there." He did.

The boat captain told me later that the sailor was just firing over the heads of the men in the raft to take the fight out of them. The engineer had just come out of the engine room and, like all engineers, didn't know what was going on. The boat captain grinned and said, "He thought he had a vote, Gunga."

I got down to the business of picking up the men in the water. We had no training in prisoner-taking, so I made up my own procedure on the spot. In light of what later happened on one of the boats, I wish I'd told them how I was going to handle it, but division leaders didn't tell boat captains how to run their boats.

I decided that I would be the only one within possible reach of any prisoner. I took off my forty-five and left it in the cockpit because, if I had to draw and shoot, I'd probably either forget to thumb-off the safety or else shoot myself in the foot. I told two experienced gunners to stay several paces to my rear and on each side so that they'd each have a clear shot, one with a tommy gun and the other with a drawn forty-five. The three of us went up on the forecastle deck. Two seamen draped a landing net over the port bow and retreated. A cluster of three dozen Japanese floated twenty feet from the boat, staring at us impassively. I motioned to them to climb aboard one at a time. No one moved. One or two began swimming away. I yelled at those who stayed where they were, "Come on aboard, the war's over for you," not expecting anyone to understand my English but hoping that my tone might convey the message. After a minute of reciprocal looking, one man who appeared to be older than the rest swam to the net and laboriously climbed aboard. These men had been in the water for sixteen hours. They did not appear to have life jackets but had stayed afloat by holding to debris. Yet this exhausted, middle-aged man climbed up that net all by himself. I was not about to help him, for fear that I would join those in the water.

The first man slumped on the deck for a moment, catching his breath. Then he slowly got to his feet, bowed to me, turned to the men in the water, and waved for them to follow. They all approached the net except for one, middle-aged like the man already aboard. The one holdout turned contemptuously, swam away with a few tired overhand strokes, and remained with his back to us to show that he had no intention of surrendering. I had no intention of persuading him or anyone of like mind. There was no time and, besides, I wanted no one who had any fight left in him.

Before the next man could come up the net, I raised my arm signaling "stop" to the man already aboard, and he repeated it to those in the water. An amendment to my prisoner taking routine had just occurred to me: a man who is naked has less fight in him than when he has clothes on, whether American or Japanese. I told the lone prisoner to take his clothes off. When he didn't understand, I began acting it out. He watched respectfully as I went through the motions of taking off my shoes, pants, and shirt. He managed a tentative smile, but did nothing. I went through my act again. He watched with interest but still didn't get my point. Presumably in order to help, the crew started singing that old burlesque striptease ditty, "Take it off, take it off . . . "

I was astounded. They had no sooner completed the first line than the man began taking off his clothes, stripping to the buff. I motioned him to the bow where he sat facing forward. As each man climbed aboard, he took off his clothes and went forward. They arranged themselves together like bowling pins. I did have one momentary fright: one man, again one of the few middle-aged ones, crawled aboard and, when he stood up, he reached a hand into his jacket. "God! He's got a grenade!" I thought, recalling how Marines had been killed at Guadalcanal when a surrendering Japanese had pulled the pin on a grenade hidden in his jacket. I leaped forward to clutch his hand, whereupon he leaped back, raising both hands over his head. "God! He's a judo expert!" I thought, and leaped back. His hand went back in his jacket and I "re-leaped" forward and pinned both his hands. We stood in this position and stared at each other. I suppose it was a ludicrous sight because the prisoner was short and squat and I was tall and skinny, so my butt stuck up in the air. My two guards started to giggle, which I found very disturbing considering that I was keeping this man from pulling the pin on a grenade. I made a mental note to talk to Bob Shearer about this.

Very slowly, I pulled his hands out of his jacket. They came out holding his wallet. He was offering me his money! "He wants to bribe you, Gunga," Shearer commented from the cockpit. I shook my head, put the wallet back in the man's jacket, and tossed the jacket along with the rest of his clothes on the growing pile. I signed that he'd get them back when he left the boat. He nodded as if he understood, made two quick deep bows and joined the rest of his group, facing forward. Once or twice, one turned to see what was going on, but snarls from the guards got the message across and they all finally stared straight ahead. When we had about twenty-five prisoners aboard and installed on the bow, I called a halt. There were no swimmers left waiting to climb the net. A few were still in the water some distance away, but they made it clear that they had decided to stay. It was their funeral, with Vella Lavella at least five miles away. It was now close to dark. I went back to the cockpit and came up on the radio for the first time. "Cease exercise," I said cryptically. All boats stopped taking on prisoners, I signaled for them to join up, and we took off for the southwest and the return trip to Rendova.

Standing next to Shearer at the wheel, I leaned on the cockpit and studied our prisoners. Most of them seemed very young and remarkably fit but very tired. They were also afraid of us—I could tell by the set of their backs that they were tense, as if they expected something bad to happen. So be it, I thought, and I realized that they must be very thirsty. I told one of the gunners to take cups of water up. I said, "Leave your weapon and don't get close." He went up on the forecastle deck, got down on his hands and knees because we were now doing twenty-five knots, and slid two cups of water up to the wall of bare backs. Two men turned, took the cups, and passed them around. Each man took a sip. It wasn't much water for twenty-five men, but they made it do. The guard then, on his own, slid forward a lighted cigarette, followed by a full pack. This seemed to be an even better signal than the water that we meant them no harm. One prisoner turned his head to nod his appreciation at the guard and then back at Bob and me in the cockpit. I nodded back but flipped my finger to tell him to turn around. Having accomplished his minimal act of mercy, our guard came back to the cockpit.

Darkness fell in its sudden way. It was time to call the base even though using the radio might attract night-bombers, but our long wakes shining like fluorescent arrows would do that anyway. As I thumbed the mike, a vagrant thought slid through my mind. I was glad I hadn't come up earlier and asked for instructions. The response might have been, "Japs! In the water? Drop depth charges." The only time I'd deliberately disobeyed an order had been when my base commander had ordered me to break off an attack and follow a division leader who'd turned and run—I always did what I was told except that once. I knew the officer who had dropped the depth charges on the floating Japanese in New Guinea. In a group he would have been picked as the least likely to lead such an action. He was a very gentle man.

I decided that brevity was in order on the radio; there was no point in letting the Japanese command know that we had a potfull of their people aboard. Just the suspicion alone would be enough for them to send me a terminal case of Zeros. Anyway, we were usually short-winded on the radio in order to prevent triangulation.

"Oak Base from Oak King. Over."

"This is Oak Base. Over."

"Have prisoners aboard. Returning to base. Over."

We continued heading toward home at cruising speed. While waiting for a reply I checked the positions of the other three boats. They were in a close vee formation. These were all experienced boat crews and captains, staying close with guns pointing up and sternward. I could see them well enough to make out the stern twenty-millimeter gunners, ready to fire at any bomber sneaking up our wakes. I felt secure in their company. The radio receiver was silent for so long that I began to wonder whether my transmission had even been heard. I was about to retransmit when the receiver clicked and issued a terse message.

"Drop cargo at Base Zebra." This was the code name for an advance Army base on Vella Lavella. This order startled me. I'd assumed that I'd be going back to Rendova. The radio voice continued, "After dropping cargo, proceed back and patrol between coordinates five and six."

I was supposed to return to the waters I was now passing through: Wilson Strait, a five-mile-wide passage between Rononnga Island and the southwest coast of Vella Lavella. I deduced that we were to act as a picket line against enemy ships returning after last night's battle. This was bad news indeed. My legs and back were already aching and I just wanted to go home and sack out. Maybe we were too low on fuel. I asked, "Bob, how is our fuel supply?" He had already checked, and said, "We still have two full tanks, enough to get us through."

So that was no good. Dammit, why couldn't Shearer ever lie a little? Why couldn't they send up other boats? They were sitting down there by the dozen playing acey-deucy while poor old Gunga did double duty. It was dumb. After a mission like this, crews weren't up to an all night patrol. (Once, after three nights' duty in a row, I'd leaned down from the cockpit to glance at the radar screen, and there I found a target blip that the sleepy radarman was staring at without seeing.)

I thought, "Oh well, mustn't whine. Not out loud, anyway. Our first task is to drop our cargo and that means finding and entering a harbor at night that I have never seen by day." I was adept at picking my way into harbors at night, if I had a visual imprint in my memory of what the skyline looked like when I was on the right course. Now that we had radar, we could theoretically get into a harbor at night but I did not trust radar. Fortunately I had Bob Shearer. Bob trusted radar and therefore knew how to get around on it.

So I said, "Bob, take us in to Base Zebra," as if asking to be dropped off at the corner of Forty-second and Sixth. I busied myself with the important task of watching our prisoners, who continued to sit stoically, staring forward, riding the pitching bow as if they always rode PT boats like this. Bob turned the wheel over to his exec and swung back and forth between the cockpit and the charthouse, glancing at the screen and then at the coast. Occasionally he'd swing into the charthouse to study the chart briefly, estimating his position mainly by sight, and then led all four boats through the narrow entrance and into the harbor. (If you are not impressed, let me tell you that Harry Crist, a first-class boat captain (later killed in action in the British Channel when he rammed an E-Boat), ran aground twice while getting into this harbor.)

We drifted, waiting for someone to come out. An LCVP manned by two sailors and carrying two soldiers approached out of the dark and pulled alongside after I hailed them. The man in charge took one look at the group sitting on the bow and exclaimed, "No way! We were sent out to get a couple of Japs. No way!"

I should have thought of this. My too-brief message had led my base command to assume that we only had a few prisoners and this is what they had told the Army base. I came out of the cockpit and, leaning over the starboard torpedo tube, I yelled down at them at full volume, "My orders are to drop these prisoners off here. I gotta go back on patrol. Go back and get people to handle this bunch. Now, shove off!" I was working myself into the sort of eye-popping rage that got results from eighteen-year-old seamen. They hurriedly pulled away and headed back to the beach and I settled back against the dayroom canopy. We continued drifting for a while and then a large ramp lighter pulled up alongside. I peered down and saw four soldiers cradling rifles and submachine guns on the stern platform. They were a different sort from the two on the first boat. They had the mean, hard look of those who had been there before; they were probably veterans of the bitter New Georgia campaign. I motioned our prisoners over the side. One older prisoner hesitated and pointed at the pile of clothes. I waved him over impatiently and when they were all off the boat, the clothes went down after them in one sodden bundle. The prisoners were done in. Some fell as they hit the deck of the lighter and had to be helped up by their comrades. I could see by the way they turned toward the bow of the boat that they were in mortal fear of their new, grim-faced guards.

After they were off, I checked to see how the operation was going on the other boats. In the darkness, I could only make out that there were lighters alongside the others. I had just begun to relax when there was a staccato of shots from the boat nearest us, then silence.

"Christ! What's happening there?" I yelled, stiffening with fright. Shearer grabbed the mike and called, "Boat that fired, come in. Over." No reply. He repeated, "Boat that fired, come in. Over." I ran up on the bow and called back, "Let's get over there." We idled over to what I could now identify as the 163. It was silent. Still standing on the bow as we closed to less than a boat length, I couldn't make out any movement. I was frightened clear through. In back of me, the guns of the 104 were all trained on the 163, ready to open fire. I knew that if the prisoners had somehow taken over, then the signal for the 104 to commence firing would be when I went down under an opening blast from the eerily silent 163.

I was feeling very lonely. Then came a calm, "All secure," from the boat captain. Reassured and concluding that a guard had accidentally fired a burst, I returned to the cockpit and began thinking about getting us back on patrol. Shearer didn't ask me what had happened. In our world, we were not curious. Whatever had happened was over. As we headed out of the harbor—an operation just as treacherous as coming in—the 163 came on the radio: "Oak King, we have casualty. Request permission to return to base. Over." "Roger, permission granted," I replied, disheartened by the grim tone of the request and knowing now that the gunshots hadn't been accidental. I wasn't sure how bad things were on the 163, but I decided the boat should have company and called Gene Foncannon on the 106 to escort him.

The casualty was dead. He was Seaman First Class Raymond Albert, who had been a member of Jack Kennedy's crew when the 109 was rammed and sunk. After a week of hiding from the enemy he'd been rescued along with the rest of the crew and had returned to action soon after as a member of the 163. His boat was beginning the transfer of prisoners when one of them asked him for a cup of water. The prisoner drank the water, handed the cup back, and simultaneously pulled Raymond's gun from him. He shot Raymond and started for the other guards, along with a few of the other prisoners who'd leaped to their feet at the sound of the shot. Before the prisoner could get another shot off one of the other guards cut him down, along with a couple of the others standing. It was all so fast that I'd thought I heard only one burst of fire. For a tense and dreadful moment, as the guards saw Raymond lying dead on the deck, all of the prisoners could have been shot. But these were disciplined veteran fighters and they instantly obeyed orders to hold their fire. It seemed ironic to me that a sailor should have survived the sinking of the 109 and then lose his life in this way. Raymond Albert died for showing compassion. Why is it that so often "the good die first?"

Gene Foncannon told me later that when he arrived back at the base at 0100, the Squadron Five CO was anxiously waiting on the dock. Our terse radio exchanges had, of course, been monitored back at the base and he had been left wondering what I had been up to. He stayed up long past his bedtime, waiting to hear the worst. Gene persuaded him that I'd done the right thing in picking up the Japanese even though we'd lost a good man in the process. I was due for a hard enough time without having my own CO on my back.

My two boat patrol for the rest of the night was uneventful, and I returned to Rendova at 0700. Walking off the dock and up to the base command tent I was oddly exhilarated: Raymond Albert had vanished, joining George Cookman, Sid Hix, Phil Hornbrook, and other dead comrades whose ghosts knew better than to add grief to the mixture of deadly fatigue and fear that already burdened their squadron mates. I write this today with a touch of shame at my seeming callousness; but that was the only way for me and, I think, for most of us to survive. We did not mourn the departed or berate ourselves with guilt over how we might have prevented the loss of a comrade. I had a habit of reviewing my last patrol in order to learn what I'd done wrong and how I might do better, but I didn't berate myself. That would have used up the meager, and now dwindling, resolve which served to get me through the next patrol.

Then, I had no touch of shame or regret. I felt that I'd pulled off a coup, bringing in over seventy prisoners—about the same number that Sergeant York captured in World War I. Of course all of mine had been water-soaked but I'm sure that it was the biggest haul in the war up to that point. When I walked into the base command tent I was expecting some sign of approval—maybe not a hurrah, but at least an appreciative grunt. Instead, the atmosphere ranged from cool to unfriendly. There were a dozen officers sitting on benches arranged in an open square: the base command at the head, my four boat captains on one side, and an assortment of officers opposite them. I sat on the bench with my boat captains. A shortish, rosy-cheeked lieutenant opposite me was doing the talking. He was excited and angry.

I asked myself, "who is this guy?" Then I noticed the wings on his shirt and caught the drift of what he was saying, which was that he had dropped smoke pots on American sailors and why hadn't we picked them up? He glared at me, "Why, one of them even stood up in his swamped raft and waved his skivvy shirt at us. Why did you leave them there?" It was like getting hit in the face with a soaked swab. This was the pilot of the PBY that had dropped smoke pots, true—but not on American sailors. Fatigue suddenly overwhelmed me. I couldn't begin to think how to answer. One of my boat captains saw that I was only going to stare dumbly, so he broke in on the pilot's rantings: "Waved a skivvy shirt, did you say?"

"Right, a Navy-issue, skivvy shirt."

"White, was it?"

"Right!" said the pilot, looking away from me and toward the boat captain, glad that he had someone to talk to other than this dull-eyed, dirty-looking chap.

"Well," drawled the boat captain, "I wondered about that skivvy shirt myself because it sure looked like one of ours, but the guy waving it was a Jap and so were his buddies, in some kind of swamped raft, just like you said."

The pilot looked silently around. If he hadn't mentioned the skivvy shirt and the swamped raft, we might have been in a yes-you-did-no-we-didn't bout, but it was plain that he'd mistaken those heads in the water for Americans. The boat captain, in the same quiet and conversational tone, attacked with, "You left us, after dropping those smoke pots, right? Didn't care to stick around, right?" I wondered if this boat captain had been a lawyer in his other life. I still can't remember who he was. I wish I could because he sure saved my ass—for the moment, that is.

The base command lost interest and the pilot decided he had nothing further to contribute and left the tent. Oddly enough, I felt that I should say something nice to him. He'd taken a big risk, flying in a sector so close to enemy airfields; and his search had been a good one even if he'd found the wrong people. His unexpected attack on me and the unfriendly looks I was still getting from some on the head bench had confused me. I decided to keep my mouth shut until I got a better fix on the problem. I could sense there was another problem, and the base operations officer stated it.

"You left a lot of the enemy alive, swimming around. They'll swim ashore and kill American boys." That last sentence is an exact quote. I remember it because it sounded like something in the *Saturday Evening Post*. He irritated me just enough that my fatigue vanished and my cunning and guile came into play. So, the problem was that I hadn't disposed of the people in the water. They were at least five miles from shore, but arguing that they could not make it to the beach would not fly. How could I wiggle out of this one? I had arrived late at the briefing. Did they already know that I'd stopped the crewman who'd opened fire? I did not think so. These boat captains weren't second-guessers. I felt that they also believed as I did.

Which was what? I was a PT boat captain. This had been my trade for a year and a half. The time wasn't measured in days, weeks, or months; it was measured in content—and the last year and a half measured as a life. I seldom thought about my other life, before the war, and even less about my life, if any, after the war. I was a professional PT boat officer. I knew my profession, and that was destroying enemy ships and men, but no one had taught me to shoot men floating in the sea with just their heads sticking out of the water. When the opportunity had arisen, I'd declined and there had been no one around to tell me otherwise.

The issue (I suppose at times I thought like a lawyer) was not whether terminating those in the water was a right or wrong decision. This officer was attacking a decision I'd made when I was over eighty miles from the command dugout. This wasn't a question of cowardice in the face of the enemy. I had just decided one way instead of the other way. If this officer did not approve, then let him go out. Come to think of it, when was the last time he had gone out? I couldn't say any of this, of course, because it would have come across as sheer arrogance—and maybe it was. This guy also seemed to have the approbation of the base command. Even Bob Kelly, sitting on the head bench, was looking at me mournfully.

The difference between Kelly and some of the others in the base command was that he rode on patrols. He was a genuine PT boat man. I think Kelly liked me as much as I liked him, but right then he was having trouble. Then it came to me why he looked like he had eaten some rancid Spam. Kelly had always wanted to bring in some prisoners. He had done everything else, so why not that?

He had been on patrol one night when his wish had nearly come true. They'd come upon two Japanese paddling along in a dugout canoe. Kelly saw his chance and ordered the boat captain to bring the PT alongside the canoe. This was far from easy, requiring much backing and turning, and many ahead and astern signals to the engine room by the poor boat captain, who was catching hell from Kelly. Finally the boat drew alongside the canoe and Kelly draped himself over a torpedo tube, grabbed one of the Japanese by the scruff of the neck, and started pulling him aboard—while the other man in the canoe was whacking Kelly over the head with a paddle. At that very moment, the engine room watch changed. The young fireman who'd been handling the rush of engine room signals came on deck, wondering what was up. He saw his Squadron Commander being hauled off the boat by attacking Japanese! Therefore, he drew his forty-five, leaned over the tube beside his Squadron Commander and shot both of the attackers dead. As I recall this story today, I think it is tragic; not so then. We all found it hilarious. The boat captain told and retold the story, imitating the astonished rage on Kelly's face as he turned to glare at the hapless fireman.

I construed the current look on Kelly's face as one of chagrin that it had been I, not he, who had finally brought in some prisoners. He too, however, wanted to know why I'd left men alive in the water. An acceptable answer then came to me.

I said, "My boats had over seventy prisoners aboard. I felt these men could provide valuable intelligence. If I'd opened fire on the men remaining in the water, we might have been attacked by the prisoners on the boats. They were already scared of us, of what we intended to do with them. I had to make a choice and I figured the information we could obtain was worth it."

At that moment I got outside help that reinforced my position. Three reporters from Munda arrived, eager for a story about the capture of seventy Japanese. Instantly it became unclear who had set a record for prisoner taking and the meeting adjourned so everyone could get their names spelled right.

A few days later an officer who had visited Vella Lavella said to me, "Gunga, you know those Japs you picked up and dropped off at the Army base on Vella Lavella?" "What about them?" I asked. "They were all shot. There was an air raid and the prisoners all jumped up and started running for the bush so Army gunners did them in." He leered at me, "All that work for nothing." I remembered the death of Raymond Albert at the hands of a man to whom he gave a drink. I remembered those mean looking guards—could be that all they needed was an excuse. I shrugged: maybe so, maybe no. It was behind me.

November 22, 1990. It's a four-hour drive from Washington, D.C., to my home, so I had plenty of time to think about what the stranger at the breakfast table had said. Something about it had sent me into a stew of irritation and anxiety, but I could not for a time settle on what the problem was. I knew those men I had picked up were sailors, not troops, and besides, who cared? I finally realized what was bothering me: did the men we had picked up survive? or, as that boat captain claimed, had it all been for nothing?

I remembered a letter from the Department of the Navy sometime in the 1960s, which stated that some Japanese sailors were inquiring into the whereabouts of the U.S. Navy men who had saved their lives when their ship had been sunk in the battle of Vella Lavella; they said that an American warship had dropped them a whaleboat and they had been able to make their way back to their base. I knew nothing about it, but later I discovered that the whaleboat in question had been dropped off in case there were any *Chevalier* survivors still in the water, and the Japanese had made good use of it. Since the Navy had asked me a question, I asked them one back: What had happened to the people we had picked up? I did not get an answer. I thought of following up, drafted a letter, and in the process told my secretary what had happened, including my concern that all of the Japanese might have been shot at the Vella Lavella Army base. After I finished my story, the two of us sat in silence for a while. Then she said, "Maybe you had better think about this some more." I did not send the letter.

But now, driving north on the New Jersey Turnpike, I knew I had to find the answer, even if it was the wrong one, even if I risked uncovering something best forgotten. I had a new source of information open to me: My son Jim was a captain in the Navy. I was sure that he could find the answer—and he did. Six months later I opened an envelope from Mr. Minoru Takahashi of Tokyo, Japan. The letter began, "You are the most precious person to me because you saved my life." The air seemed to sparkle around those words. They had indeed survived! The story about their having been slain during a bombing raid was hokum! There had indeed been such a raid, but no harm had come to them.

Minoru Takahashi had been a school teacher before he entered the Japanese Navy, returned to teaching after the war and eventually became a superintendent of schools in Tokyo. We had no language in common, but his daughter was fluent in English and had written that splendid letter. By extraordinary luck (in our monolithic American world, where learning a language other than our own is not high on the priority list) a good friend of mine, Barney Martin, was equally fluent in Japanese, learning it in the Navy and then maintaining his fluency over the years as a hobby. At first all he had to do was translate inscriptions on presents from the Japanese survivors (and marvelous presents they were), but his talents came into full play when we received some recollections written by the survivors—in Japanese, of course.

What had it been like, to be a Japanese sailor rescued by American PT boats? Minoru Takahashi never expressed to me directly how he felt about the fact that he, along with most of his fellow crew members floating helplessly in the water, had chosen to surrender rather than join the few who swam away from us to certain death. I gained some perception of the agonizing difficulty of that decision from one incident he described from his life as a prisoner: he had been a school teacher before the war and, while he was in prison camp in the United States, the prison commander told him that he should set up his own school to further the education of the Japanese prisoners. He refused at first, feeling that because he had surrendered, he'd lost all right to continue in the teaching profession. The prison commander eventually persuaded him to set up the school by pointing out that most of the prisoners were young men who would return to Japan behind in their education—unless he helped them catch up.

Years after the war, when the healing of time had taken effect, I believe that he and the other survivors became reconciled. Members of the Association of the *Yugumo* have visited the Yasukini shrine to the war dead many times on the anniversary of the sinking of the *Yugumo* to honor the memory of their lost comrades. At the same time, they left no doubt about their deep gratitude to the American sailors who rescued them. I think in the case of Minoru Takahashi the healing was certainly aided by his wife and daughter.

Another of the survivors, Masayoshi Saito, who remained in the navy after the war, sent me a marvelous piece of scrimshaw carved out of a piece of teak wood from the deck of the flagship *Mihasa* (commanded by Admiral Togo in the battle of the Sea of Japan in 1905, when the Japanese Navy decisively defeated the Russian fleet). He had carved it himself into a representation of the Rising Sun. This beautiful tablet had to be Saito's most precious possession from his life in the navy, and his giving it to me says all that could be said about his gratitude.

Saito had also written down his recollections of his thoughts as he tried to stay alive after the *Yugumo* was torpedoed and sunk. As they floated through the hours of darkness, one of the officers tried to keep their spirits up by leading them in song but, after a while, the voices got weaker and finally there was silence. Saito's recollections of the next day are cast in a stream of consciousness:

"The direct rays of intense sun—eyes terribly painful, affected by the heavy oil, cannot open them. Enemy island base can be seen dimly on the horizon. A splitting headache, stomach empty. Fortunately a squall comes up and cools the surface of the water. A plane, a flying boat, about seventy or eighty meters high—what's it doing? Dropping something, small black objects, one, two, twelve, thirteen; they land near us but no explosion is heard. Strange, what are they? Oh, white smoke rises, they are smoke bombs. What's going on? 'Oh, there's a ship,' someone shouts. When we look, we see small craft approaching from the enemy shore. 'This looks like trouble. Separate! Form small groups.'

"A large enemy torpedo boat arrives. A man who appears to be the captain says something in a loud voice from the bridge." (Author's note: I always spoke louder when someone didn't understand me; it clarified my meaning.)

"There is no noise from the machine guns, only the sound of the torpedo boat's engines. One of the boats stops right in front of us. Shit! You're getting aboard! Goddam fool!" A long boathook is extended down from the deck. The white hairy hand of an enemy reaches down. Hands and feet so tired I cannot move. Just like a child I am pulled up on the deck, so hungry and weary I cannot stand up.

"Two enemy sailors come over with a cup. It is water or poison? They laugh. They drink themselves. One of the survivors says, 'See, it's not poison. Don't worry.' OK, after all, it's not poison. Let's all drink it. Are we accepting the mercy of the enemy? What confused, mixed up feelings! If we go that way, only death will come. One of the enemy comes over with a cigarette and a lighter. 'Have a smoke,' he says, laughing. Oh well, we have already died, why not have a smoke?

"I pull myself together, look around at the sea, and watch the torpedo boats kicking up their wakes, carrying my comrades. Where to? To what island? Then what awaits? Death? Death."

When we were picking up the men, it did not occur to me that they thought they would eventually be executed. I saw exhaustion, not

The author with Minoru Takahashi at a U.S. Naval Institute symposium in San Antonio in 1990. (author's collection)

fear—although my ludicrous dance with the man who wanted to give me his money should have been a clue. It was only when we delivered them to those Army guards that their fear became apparent. But even then I thought it was only because they were leaving the care of sailors like themselves. The refrain of the Navy Hymn, "Oh hear us as we cry to thee for those in peril on the sea," makes no distinction among men.

At any rate, having at last satisfied myself that they had survived the war, I was content. But the story did not end there. One morning in January 1993 Mrs. Helen McDonald, director of the Admiral Nimitz Museum in San Antonio, Texas, telephoned me. With the years (a half century of them!) I have mellowed—regrettably only on the surface. Beneath the patina of a kind, tolerant old man there remains the arrogance that flashes out now and again, piqued by, say, telephone calls from real estate ladies desiring to sell our eight-bedroom, five-bath (or six?) house, too big for what is now only the two of us, me and that peach I met in Orange, New Jersey, who almost caused a naval disaster in the Hudson river. Anyway, I mistook Helen McDonald for a real estate lady. She kept shouting, "Don't hang up sir, don't hang up! I'm not trying to sell your house, I'm calling from San Antonio, sir, can you hear me? The Admiral Nimitz Museum? Sir, we're inviting you to be our guest in San Antonio, the one in Texas?"

Now she had my attention. The museum and the Naval Institute were sponsoring a symposium in San Antonio on the naval battles of the Pacific in 1943—and they were inviting Mr. Takahashi and me to come down and meet each other. It was a large gathering, an audience of at least a thousand listening to accounts of the Pacific battles. I knew that Takahashi and I were invited only to add color—the year before a Marine fighter pilot met the Zero pilot he had shot down. I was not quite sure what I'd say after I said hello, so Barney Martin helped me memorize a two-sentence speech in Japanese. I did not anticipate what would happen, nor did anyone else.

I was standing on the stage in the hall where the symposium was scheduled for the next morning, listening to instructions from Mrs. McDonald on where to stand and so forth. Mr. Takahashi walked in, having just arrived from Japan. He stood on the opposite side of the stage, looking around uncertainly at the several dozen people there. He was a good-looking man, distinguished in bearing. A Japanese, a former World War II pilot (bombed Pearl Harbor!), saw him, knew who I was, and went over to him and pointed me out. Mr. Takahashi started across the stage, smiling. I walked through the crowd toward him, as if we were two friends who had spotted one another across the room at a crowded cocktail party. As he got closer, his face crumpled in tears. We quickly moved toward each other and embraced. The noisy stage turned dead quiet. No one moved or looked directly at us, giving two old men their chance, after fifty years, to relive a moment in their lives.

ABOUT THE
AUTHOR

Dick Keresey was born in 1916 and grew up in Montclair, New Jersey.
He graduated from Dartmouth College in 1938 and Columbia Law
School in 1941. He practiced law in New York for more than fifty years.
In college he developed an interest in writing, mainly short stories for
the newspaper and literary magazine. After gradually retiring from his
law practice in the late 1980s, he returned to writing. *PT 105* is the result.

He and his wife, Barbara, have four children and nine grandchil-
dren. He remains active in the Columbia Law School, serving on its
board of visitors. He and Barbara play a lot of golf—both in Montclair,
where they still live, and in Florida during the winter. Dick is also a
serious trout fisherman. In addition, he is attempting to write another
book.